World War II: A Pronouncing Dictionary

David B. Chamberlin

CreateSpace

ISBN-13: 978-1523358953
ISBN-10: 1523358955

Introduction

For the last 25 years of my college teaching career I was a film specialist, which brought me into frequent contact with the Second World War, both as a subject and a setting. My curiosity about what really did (or didn't) happen during the war led me to classic studies like Shirer's *Rise and Fall of the Third Reich* and Churchill's six-volume *History of the Second World War*. By the time I retired, I had built a library of 500 books, and World War II had become my chief research interest. I had also discovered in talking to other students of the war that they shared my frustration at the absence of any guide to pronouncing the thousands of important names of people, places, and things in more than fifty major languages. Immediately after retiring, I started working on a book to address that need.

As the book progressed, I added audio materials to my library, including audiobooks, film and video documentaries, and radio broadcasts. My listing of these materials at the end of the book is the only summary of pronunciation sources for World War II, just as the dictionary itself is the only comprehensive guide to pronunciation, and the only one to include a pronunciation key. As a glance at the key shows, my system avoids all artificial letters and symbols. Almost all pronunciations (including all the vowels) are expressed as sounds that exist in English.

The book contains about 2,500 entries, each consisting of one or more pronunciations and five to fifty words of description. The names have been chosen primarily on the basis of importance, as determined by the frequency of reference in the dictionaries, encyclopedias, and histories mentioned at the end. Most European countries and other major participants in the war (e.g. Japan, China) present no pronunciation problem and do not have separate entries. They are more appropriate for the lengthier treatment of an encyclopedia. The same could be said for the major military and political leaders of the war, but they present more pronunciation problems, so all individuals have separate entries. Also listed are lesser-known countries, republics of the Soviet Union, and colonies of the Western nations. Most major

1

Western capitals do not have separate entries. The use of boldface type for a name within an entry indicates that it has its own entry; in other words, it is a cross-reference. Alternate names and spellings may follow the name in an entry or be listed separately with a cross-reference.

Specific dates are given whenever possible, in the form month/day/year (9/1/39 for the German invasion of Poland, 6/6/44 for D-Day). Night battles (usually naval) and bombing raids are shown as two consecutive dates (e.g. the 3/9-10/45 firebombing of Tokyo). It should be kept in mind that the International Date Line (corresponding roughly to 180° longitude) passes just west of Midway Island in the central Pacific, so the Pearl Harbor attack at 8:00 A.M. 12/7/41 occurred at 3:00 A.M. on 12/8 in Tokyo and 1:00 P.M. on 12/7 in Washington. Most books, including this one, use local time for all events.

Any book that deals with WWII as a whole must consider the question of what time period is involved. The official end of the war is marked by the signing of the surrender documents – 5/8/45 in the European Theater and 9/2/45 in the Pacific Theater. Any history that goes beyond those dates usually does so in the form of an epilogue. If the defining fact of the war was the attempt by the leaders of Germany, Italy, and Japan to conquer regions beyond their borders, and the efforts of other countries (the Allies) to prevent them, then the war clearly ended with the surrenders of Germany and Japan. The next global conflict, known as the Cold War, began immediately when the Soviet Union asserted control over the countries in Eastern Europe that its armies occupied at the end of WWII. In March of 1946, in a famous speech in Fulton, Missouri, Winston Churchill introduced the term Iron Curtain to describe the de facto separation of Eastern and Western Europe that lasted until about 1990. This book contains little that occurred after the Japanese surrender. The main exception is the historically unprecedented war crimes trials, especially those held in Nuremberg, which can only be viewed as part of the resolution of WWII.

Where to begin the story of the war is less clear than where to end it. One approach, best illustrated by Martin Gilbert's *The Second World War* (1989), is to start with Germany's invasion of

Poland on 9/1/39, which triggered declarations of war by Britain and France, and marks the official beginning of the war. The opposite extreme, expressed most strongly in A. J. P. Taylor's *Origins of the Second World War* (1963), is to view the war as a continuation of World War I, with the period 1914-1945 forming a modern Thirty Years War. This view is shared by Winston Churchill, who held high offices in both wars. He quotes Marshal Foch's prophetic comment on the Treaty of Versailles: "This is not Peace. It is an Armistice for twenty years." Mark Arnold-Forster, in *The World at War* (1973), calls the treaty "neither sensible nor enforceable."

Most historians, while recognizing the Treaty of Versailles as a root cause of World War II, also note what Gerhard Weinberg calls "the special character" of the second war. In the first, a group of hereditary monarchs whose intelligence, if not actual sanity, was suspect, drew the world by a complex network of alliances into a kind of war no one envisioned, pursuing only the vaguest of goals. The second, however, followed the historical pattern of a demagogue bent on world conquest, like Alexander the Great, Genghis Khan, and especially Napoleon, who like Hitler drove to Moscow in a failed attempt to conquer Russia. Adolf Hitler's goals were clearly stated in *Mein Kampf* (1925), and his power to accomplish them was enhanced by a century of rapid technological advancement. After completing the A-Z listing in this book, I was not surprised to find that Hitler's name appears in more entries (113) than the next three world leaders combined – Churchill (28), Roosevelt (25), and Stalin (20).

If Hitler had been killed in World War I, there would probably have been no World War II. Mussolini would still have gone adventuring in North Africa and the Adriatic. Franco would still have seized power in Spain. The Japanese would still have conquered territory in China and the Western Pacific, and perhaps even provoked the United States into a Pacific War. But the World War, and especially the German invasion of the Soviet Union, which caused an estimated 20 million of the war's 50 million deaths, was Hitler's doing. His generals didn't want it, his people didn't want it, and Stalin went to extraordinary lengths to avoid it. Also directly attributable to Hitler was the

Holocaust, which, along with the slave labor program and the systematic starvation of prisoners of war, accounted for another 10 million of the war's death toll.

If World War II is defined by the expansionist policies of Hitler, Mussolini, and the Japanese military, another starting point suggests itself – 9/18/31, the date of the so-called Mukden Incident in Manchuria, which is the accepted beginning of Japan's aggression against China. Like the chronological tables of events in *The Simon and Schuster Encyclopedia of World War II* and *The Oxford Companion to World War II*, I have used this date. Thus the earliest entries in this book include Mukden, Manchuria (or Manchukuo), the Kwantung Army, the League of Nations, and Henry Puyi (the "last emperor" of China). Entries for Italy begin with its invasion of Abyssinia in 1935, and for Germany with its reoccupation of the Rhineland in 1936. Stalin was content to consolidate his control within the Soviet Union until 1939, while the United States roused itself slowly during 1940-41. There are entries for the Spanish Civil War (1936-39), such as the Condor Legion, the Falange, and Guernica, since Germany and Italy played an active role, even though Franco disappointed Hitler by keeping Spain neutral during World War II.

I have included a few figures whose role in the war was small, but of interest, I felt, because of their later importance, such as Presidents Kennedy, Ford, and Bush, Sr. Anne Frank died unknown in a concentration camp at age 15, but her diary has made her one of the most famous names to emerge from the war. With regard to places, entries always use the most common form and spelling of the name during the war, but usually also give the present status, name, and pronunciation. Many former colonies have become independent, such as the Dutch East Indies (now Indonesia). Some countries have changed their name, such as Burma (now Myanmar). Some cities began the war in one country and ended it in another. The German city of Breslau became the Polish city of Wroclaw, while the Polish city of Brest-Litovsk became part of Belorussia in the Soviet Union, now the independent country of Belarus.

Certain conventions used in the A-Z listings can be mentioned briefly:

1) All entries are proper nouns and should be capitalized, with a few exceptions like sonar, plutonium, and kamikaze.

2) The A-Z listings are strictly alphabetical, without regard to spacing or punctuation, so the first six entries in letter E are Eagle Day; Eagle, HMS; Eagle's Nest; Eaker, Lt Gen Ira C.; Eastern Solomons, Battle of the; and East Prussia. Names beginning Mac or Mc are not treated separately, so the first page of letter M contains the following sequence: Machinato Line; MacIntyre, Captain Donald; Mackensen, Col Gen Eberhard von.

3) I have used capitals liberally to call attention to job titles (Ambassador, Commander, Director, Governor, Vice-President, Assistant Secretary).

4) Letters N, S, E, W, and C (central) indicate directions or general areas, but are written out when part of place names (North Sea, South Dakota).

5) Ranks given are normally the highest attained by the person before the end of the war (5/45 in the West, 8/45 in the East).

6) Code names of major operations like Overlord, Torch, Anvil/Dragoon and Barbarossa have their own entries, but since code names deliberately have little or no relation to the specific nature of the operation, I usually use place names (like Normandy, NW Africa, S France, and the Soviet Union for the code names given above) when referring to the operations in other entries.

7) Battles are listed in the form "Coral Sea, Battle of the." For that reason, battles mentioned in other entries use boldface only for the identifying place name (e.g. Battle of the **Coral Sea**). This is also true for geographical features, such as Bay of **Biscay**, Strait of **Gibraltar**, and Sea of **Azov**.

8) When the pronunciation of an English-language name is obvious, usually because it matches a commonly used word, a dash is used and no pronunciation given (Atlantic Wall, Black Sea, Commander Ernest E. Evans, Joseph C. Grew, Oboe). Since I wanted to err on the side of caution about what is obvious, there are relatively few such entries.

9) In many entries, both the U.S. and foreign pronunciations are given, especially when the foreign name is easy to pronounce in English. The first pronunciation given can be considered preferred. Some entries, like Tunisia, include both U.S. (too•nee•zhuh) and British (too•nis•ee•uh) pronunciations.

10) The reader will occasionally find "sic" after pronunciations outrageous enough to sound like mistakes, such as kir•uh•bas for Kiribati or ming•is for Menzies.

11) Unlike most languages, including English, Japanese places the family name before the given name (Tojo Hideki rather than Hideki Tojo). This book uses the English order, so Tojo's listing is Tojo, General Hideki.

12) I use Holland instead of the more official the Netherlands, which is awkward to fit into entries.

13) Sicily is part of Italy, but is often treated separately because it was a separate campaign.

Regarding pronunciation, it should be emphasized that being fluent in a language, like English, does not guarantee that one will pronounce names in that language correctly. Neville Chamberlain's last name should either be pronounced "layn" at the end or spelled logically like mine. And his first name would be difficult for someone who hadn't previously encountered it, especially if they *had* encountered the American singing brothers named Neville, whose name is pronounced differently. Similarly, the island nation of Antigua in the Caribbean ought to be pronounced an•tee•gwuh, as the Spaniards who named it intended, but the current inhabitants choose to say an•tee•guh, and since they speak English, that is the only correct pronunciation for an English-language dictionary. In cases like Paris and Berlin, there is an accepted English pronunciation that differs from the one used by their French and German inhabitants. In general, the more a foreign name is used in English, the more it tends to acquire a separate pronunciation.

Since this book consists almost entirely of proper (capitalized) nouns, which don't follow normal pronunciation rules as consistently as common (non-capitalized) nouns, I have avoided giving any pronunciation not supported elsewhere, either in another dictionary or an audio source. My lengthy list of audio sources would be twice as long if I had included feature (fiction) films, as well as documentary (non-fiction) films, but fiction films don't provide enough help with pronunciation to justify a lengthy listing. The most valuable sources, I have found, are audio books. I wish there were more, especially if I could choose the titles.

In describing the pronunciation of a word, there are three qualities to consider: the accents (primary and secondary), the syllable divisions, and the sounds (chiefly vowel sounds). Accents are easy to represent, and there are several ways to do it. For a single accent, I use **boldface** type. When a word has a primary and secondary accent, I use **boldface** for both and add an accent mark (') for the primary (**boo'•kuh•rest** for Bucharest). Some Far Eastern languages, notably Chinese and Japanese, are considered unaccented in the Western sense of loud and soft syllables. This principle is often followed, here and elsewhere, in English rendering of Chinese names, but Japanese names in English usually follow the following patterns: soft-loud-soft (as in Yamato) for three-syllable words and loud-soft-loud'-soft (as in Yamamoto) for four-syllable words. Once Japanese is trans-literated from pictorial characters to the English alphabet, it is relatively easy to pronounce. The same cannot be said, unfor-tunately, for some other transliterated languages, like Polish.

Division of syllables produces many differences of opinion, even among college dictionaries. A good example is Churchill, which we all know how to pronounce – or do we? Is it church•hill, deriving from a church on a hill? Or church•ill, perhaps deriving from a church but not a hill? Or chur•chill, having nothing to do with either? The pronunciations are too similar to cause a serious problem, but they do show how syllable divisions occasionally raise interesting questions.

Over several years, I arrived at a system of representing vowel sounds that contains only normal English letters – no artificial letters or letter combinations, no special (diacritical) markings. All vowel sounds given in the book exist in English, which means that they don't always match the foreign sound. A good example is the German umlaut (ä, ö, ü), which has no

English equivalent. The o in Göring (or oe in Goering) is somewhere between air and ur, and is shown here, as in most other sources, as ur. I use u for the short oo sound (as in "book") in college dictionaries, while using uh for the short u (as in "but"). One advantage of this is that the Microsoft Word software program, which I use, does not include any markings that span two letters, like the horizontal line above the long oo (as in "boot") or the elongated u above the short one. I also use uh in unaccented syllables like around, easel, merrily, wagon, and sinus. This usage is called the schwa, and is represented in college dictionaries by the symbol ə. The schwa is usually pronounced uh, but it can vary in the direction of a short i, as in America (uh•mair•ih/uh•kuh).

I use ah to represent both pot and par (as paht and pahr), which would be pot (or pŏt) and pär in most college dictionaries. I use aw to represent both fall and for (as fawl and fawr), which would be fŏl and fŏr in most college dictionaries. My final step in eliminating diacritical markings was to replace the long vowel symbol (ā, ē, ī, ō, ū) with ay, ee, y, oh, yoo. The y for long i is the least obvious in this group, but is usually clear when attached to consonants, as in Faïd (fy•eed), Seyss (sys), Shanghai (shang•hy), and Zyklon (zy•klahn). When used alone, the y looks like a consonant, so in those rare instances I have used eye, as in Iceland (eye•sluhnd), Ijssel (eye•suhl), Eicke (eye•kuh), and Eisenhower (eye•zuhn•how•uhr). One advantage of eliminating the diacritical markings is that they can be difficult to see for those of us over 60. Distinguishing the long mark (ā) from the double dot (ä) can be particularly challenging in some college dictionaries.

Anyone whose eyes have glazed over during the last two paragraphs is encouraged to proceed directly to the rest of the book, referring back to the Pronunciation Key when necessary, which shouldn't be very often.

Pronunciation Key

<u>Vowels</u>   (*Random House Webster's College Dictionary*)

A   <u>ay</u> as in <u>day</u>   ā (long <u>a</u>)

    <u>a</u> as in <u>sat</u>   a (short <u>a</u>)

    <u>ah</u> as in <u>car</u>   ä

    <u>air</u> as in <u>care</u>   â

    <u>aw</u> as in <u>fall</u>   ô

E   <u>ee</u> as in eat   ē (long <u>e</u>)

    <u>e</u> or <u>eh</u> as in <u>pet</u>   e (short <u>e</u>)

I   <u>y</u> or <u>eye</u> as in <u>kite</u>   ī (long <u>i</u>)

    <u>i</u> or <u>ih</u> as in <u>wit</u>   i (short <u>i</u>)

O   <u>oh</u> as in <u>toe</u>   ō (long <u>o</u>)

    <u>ah</u> as in <u>fox</u>   o (short <u>o</u>)

    <u>aw</u> as in <u>for</u>   ô

    <u>ow</u> as in <u>mouse</u>   ou

    <u>oy</u> as in <u>boy</u>   oi

    <u>oo</u> as in <u>root</u>   oo (long <u>oo</u>) (horizontal line above <u>oo</u>)

U   <u>yoo</u> as in <u>cute</u>   yoo ("long" <u>u</u>) (horizontal line above <u>oo</u>)

    <u>uh</u> as in <u>cup</u>   u (short <u>u</u>)

    <u>u</u> as in <u>look</u>   oo (short <u>oo</u>) (elongated <u>u</u> above <u>oo</u>)

    <u>uhr</u> as in <u>fur</u>   ûr

<u>Consonants</u>

<u>gh</u> as in <u>game</u>, <u>log</u>   g (hard <u>g</u>)

<u>kh</u> a variety of soft <u>k</u> sounds, especially in German. In English a normal <u>k</u> sound is acceptable

(<u>n</u>) as in bonjour (boh(n) **zhoor**) and many French names. Just hint at the <u>n</u>.

<u>r</u>   Almost every language has its own pronunciation of this letter. Unless you know the other language, treat the <u>r</u> as in English.

<u>zh</u> as in <u>pleasure</u>   zh

<u>Accents</u>

Words with one accented syllable show the accent with **boldface**.

Words with a primary and secondary accent show the primary accent with **boldface′** plus an accent mark, and the secondary accent with **boldface**.

Abbreviations used in the A-Z entries

1) Geographical locations

N	northern or north
N-most	northernmost
S, E, W	(as above)
C	central
NE	northeast, northeastern
NW, SE, SW	(as above)
NC	north-central
SC, EC, WC	(as above)

2) Military ranks

Brig Gen	Brigadier General
Maj Gen	Major General
Lt Gen	Lieutenant General
Col Gen	Colonel General
FM	Field Marshal
CoS	Chief of Staff
CiC	Commander in Chief
SAC	Supreme Allied Commander

3) Languages (accompanying some pronunciations)

US	American English
Brit, Fr, Ger, Nor, Rus, etc.	other languages

4) Others

HQ	headquarters
PM	prime minister
POW	prisoner of war

A

Aachen (**ah•**kuhn) German city near the border with Holland and Belgium, the first one captured by the **Allies** (US 1st Army, 10/44). Its French name is **Aix-la-Chapelle** (**eks•**lah•shah•**pel, ayks-** , -shuh-)

Aarhus (or **Árhus**) (**awr•**hoos) city in Denmark whose **Gestapo** HQ was destroyed in a British low-level bombing raid 10/31/44

Aaron Ward, USS -- destroyer sunk near **Guadalcanal** by Japanese planes from **Rabaul** 4/7/43

Abadan (**ah•**buh•**dahn′**, **ab•**uh•**dan′**) port city and island in SW Iran, site of oilfields and a refinery, captured by British forces 8/25/41 as part of the Anglo-Soviet occupation of Iran

Abbeville (US **ab′•**ee•**vil**, Fr **ab•veel**) town in N France on the **Somme** river, captured by German **Panzer** forces under **Guderian** 5/20/40

ABDA (**ab•**duh) American-British-Dutch-Australian combined command for operations in SE Asian waters, established 1/15/42, lasted only six weeks before the Japanese overran the area

Abe, Vice-Admiral Hiroaki (**ah•**bay, **hee•**roh•**ah•**kee) led the Japanese attack on **Wake Island** 12/41, a group of battleships and cruisers at **Midway** 6/42, and a task force to destroy **Henderson Field** on **Guadalcanal** 11/42 whose failure led to his removal from command 12/21/42

Abe, Nobuyuki (**ah•**bay, **noh•**bu•**yu•**kee) PM of Japan 8/39-1/40

Abemama -- see **Apamama**

"Aberdeen" (**ab**•uhr•**deen′**) British landing site behind Japanese lines in Burma 3/44

Abetz, Otto (**ah**•bets, **ah**•toh) German ambassador to occupied France 6/40-8/44

Abrams, Lt Col Creighton W. (**ay**•bruhmz, **crayt**'n) broke through the German siege of **Bastogne** 12/26/44, commander of US forces in Vietnam 1968-72, US Army CoS at the time of his death in 1974

Abrial, Admiral Jean (ab•ree•al, **zhah(n)**) French Governor General of **Algeria** 7/40-7/41, head of the French Navy from 11/18/42 to 3/26/43

Abwehr (**ahb**•vair) intelligence branch of the German High Command (**OKW**)

Abyssinia (**ab**•uh•**sin′**•ee•uh) traditional name for **Ethiopia**

Acasta, HMS (uh•**kas**•tuh) British destroyer sunk during the evacuation of **Narvik** 6/40

Acheson, Dean (**ach**•uh•suhn) pro-British US Assistant Secretary of State 2/41-8/45, Secretary of State 1949-53

Achilles, HMS (uh•**kil**•eez) New Zealand cruiser which helped destroy the **Admiral Graf Spee** 12/39

Adachi, Lt Gen Hatazo (ah•**dah**•chee, uh- , hah•**tah**•zoh) Commander of the Japanese 18th Army in **New Guinea** from 11/42 to the end of the war

Adak Island (**ay**•dak) American airbase in the **Aleutian** chain

Adana (**ah′**•dah•**nah**, **ah**•duh•nuh) city in S **Turkey** where **Churchill** unsuccessfully urged government leaders to join the **Allies** 1/30/43

Addis Ababa (**ad**•is **ab**•uh•buh, **ah**•dis **ah′**•buh•**bah**) capital of **Ethiopia**, held by Italian forces 1936-41, liberated by British forces 4/6/41

Addu (ah•**doo**) an atoll at the S end of the **Maldive Islands,** about 600 miles SW of **Ceylon**, site of a British naval base

Aden (ahd'n, **ayd**'n) British protectorate on the SW tip of the Arabian peninsula, on the **Gulf of Aden**, now part of Yemen (**yem**•uhn, **yay**•muhn)

Adenauer, Konrad (**ad**•'n•ow•'r, **kahn**•rad) Mayor of **Cologne** 1917-33, arrested following the **July Bomb Plot** 6/44, Chancellor of West Germany 1949-63

Adige (**ah′**•dih•**jay**, **ad′**•ih-) river in NE Italy, site of a German defense line crossed easily by US forces 4/45

Adlertag (Eagle Day) (**ahd′**•luhr•**tahg**) maximum **Luftwaffe** attack on British air defenses, 8/13/40

Admin Box, Battle of the (**ad**•min **box**) first notable victory of British and Indian troops over the Japanese in Burma, 2/44

Admiral Graf Spee (grahf **shpay**) German pocket battleship scuttled in **Montevideo** harbor (Uruguay) to avoid capture by British cruisers 12/17/39

Admiral Hipper (**hip**•puhr) name ship of a class of German heavy cruisers, saw action in the German invasion of Norway and operated against Allied Arctic convoys to the Soviet Union until beached by **Hitler** at the end of 1942

Admiral Scheer (**shair**) German pocket battleship, sister ship to the **Admiral Graf Spee**, best known for a successful commerce raiding expedition in the Atlantic and **Indian** Oceans 11/40-4/41

Admiralty Islands (**ad**•muhr•uhl•tee) Pacific island group 200 miles N of E **New Guinea**, the largest of which are **Manus** and **Los Negros**, taken by US forces 3-4/44

Adriatic Sea (ay•dree•**at**•ick) a part of the **Mediterranean** between Italy and Yugoslavia

Aegean Sea (ih•**jee**•uhn) a part of the **Mediterranean** between Greece and **Turkey**

Afrika Korps (Africa Corps) two German tank divisions in N Africa first commanded by **Rommel**

Agaña (ah•**gah**•nyah, uh•**gahn**•yuh) the capital of **Guam**

Agedabia (n/s **Ajdabiya**) (ahj•**dah**•bee•uh, -**dab**•yuh) town in **Libya** S of **Benghazi**, key defensive position

Agra (**ah**•gruh) a city in NC India, home of the Taj Mahal, HQ of British Commanding General **Wavell** from 1942

Agrigento (**ahg**•rih•**jen**′toh, **ag**-) small city in SW **Sicily**, taken by **Patton** 7/15/43 to begin his independent drive to **Messina**

Ainsworth, Rear Admiral Walden Lee (**aynz**•wuhrth) commanded numerous battles in the Pacific, notably in the **Solomon Islands**

Airedale, HMS (**air**•dail) British destroyer sunk in the **Mediterranean** 6/42

Aisne (US **ayn**, Fr **en**) river in N France, together with the **Somme** a key French defense line overrun by German forces in early June 1940

Aitape (eye•**tap**•ee) town on the N coast of **New Guinea**, taken by Allied forces 4/22/44 in an amphibious landing

Aix-la-Chapelle -- see **Aachen**

Ajax, HMS (**ay**•jaks) British cruiser which helped destroy the **Admiral Graf Spee** 12/39

Akagi (ah•**kah**•ghee) Japanese aircraft carrier in action at **Pearl Harbor**, sunk during the Battle of **Midway** 6/42

Akyab (**ak**•yab, ak•**yab**) port city and island off the **Arakan** coast of Burma, now called **Sittwe** (**sit**•way, -wee), taken by the Japanese 3/31/42, retaken by British forces 1/3/45

Alam Halfa (al•**ahm** hal•**fah**) ridge near **El Alamein (Eygpt)**, the limit of **Rommel**'s advance, 8/31/42

Alamogordo (**al**•uh•muh•**gawr**'•doh) town in New Mexico about 50 miles SE of the first atomic bomb test 7/16/45

Alaska (also **Alcan**) **Highway** (uh•**las**•kuh, **al**•kan) constructed during 1942 to connect Alaska with the US and facilitate aid to the Soviet Union

Alban Hills (**awl**•buhn, **ahl**•bin) inland from **Anzio**, controlled by the Germans until the Allied breakout 6/43

Albania (al•**bay**•nee•uh) annexed by Italy 4/39, inspiring a resistance movement that produced a communist state after the war

Albert Canal (**al**•buhrt) defense barrier in N Belgium, overrun by the German invasion 5/40

Alderney (**awl**•duhr•nee) one of the smaller **Channel Islands**

Alençon (ah•lah(n) **saw(n),** al•ah(n)-) key crossroads town in **Normandy**, taken by Allied forces 8/12/44

Ålesund (or **Aalesund**) **(ohl•uh•sund)** coastal town in C Norway

Aleutian Islands (uh•loo•shuhn) chain extending 1,200 miles W from the Alaska Peninsula

Alexander, Earl Albert V. -- First Lord of the British Admiralty throughout the war

Alexander, FM Sir Harold -- commanded the British 1ˢᵗ division in France 1939-40, where he was the last British soldier to leave **Dunkirk**, British CiC in **Burma** (1942), Middle Eastern Command (including N Africa) (1942-43), and Italy (1943-44), SAC **Mediterranean** from 12/44 to the end of the war

Alexandria (al•ig•zan'•dree•uh) port city in **Eygpt**, base of the British **Mediterranean** fleet

Algeria (al•jeer•ee•uh) French colony in N Africa, gained independence in 1962

Algiers (al•jeerz) capital city of **Algeria**, **Mediterranean** port, E-most landing site for the US invasion of NW Africa, **Eisenhower**'s HQ from 11/23/42

Aliakmon Line (ahl•yahk•mawn) Allied defensive position along that river in N Greece, overrun by German forces 4/41

Allies, the (al•lyz, uh•lyz) also **Allied** nations, forces, etc. (uh•lyd, al•lyd) Great Britain, the United States, the Soviet Union, China, and countries fighting with them, notably members of the British Empire -- Canada, **South Africa**, India, Australia, and **New Zealand**

Alsace-Lorraine (US **al•**sas lawr•**rain,** Fr al•**sas** law•**ren**) region in NE France on the German border, annexed by Germany in 1940, returned 1945

Alor Star (al•awr **stahr**) or **Alor Setar** (al•awr see•**tahr**) town and British airbase in N **Malaya**, captured by Japanese forces 12/41

Alsos (**ahl**•sohs, -saws) (Greek for "grove") a US intelligence unit created late in 1943 to determine the progress of German atomic research and, as the war ended, capture German technology and scientists ahead of the Soviet Union

Altenfjord (**ahl**•tuhn fyawrd) German naval base in N Norway 1942-44

Altmark (**ahlt**•mahrk) German supply ship boarded by the British destroyer **Cossack** in Norwegian waters 2/16-17/40, rescuing 299 British seamen

Alvarez, Luis (al'•vuh•**rez**, US **loo**•is, Sp loo•**ees**) Nobel Prize-winning (1968) US experimental physicist who participated in the **Manhattan Project** and observed the atomic bomb exposions in New Mexico and over **Hiroshima** from B-29s

Alytus (ah•**lee**•toos) small city in **Lithuania** SW of **Kovno**, site of a key bridge captured by German forces on the first day of the invasion of the Soviet Union

Amagi (ah•**mah**•ghee) Japanese aircraft carrier sunk at the naval base at **Kure** 7/45

Ambérieu (**ah(n)**•bair•**yu'**) railroad center in E France sabotaged by the French Resistance 5/44

Amboina Island (am•**boy**•nuh) now known as **Ambon** (ahm•**bawn**) naval base in the **Dutch East Indies**, taken by Japanese forces 2/4/42 and held until the end of the war

Ambrosio, General Vittorio (am•**broh**•zhyoh, veet•**tohr**•yoh) became CoS of the Italian Army 1942, worked to get Italy out of the war

Amchitka (am•**chit**•kuh) **Aleutian** island E of **Kiska**, occupied by US forces 1/12/43

American-British Conversations (ABC) -- contingency planning for an American entrance into the war, held in Washington 1-3/41

Amerika -- **Hitler**'s personal train

Amery, Leopold (**ay**•muhr•ee) member of the British Parliament who quoted Cromwell in telling **Neville Chamberlain**, "In the name of God, go!"

Amiens (ahm•**yen**) city in N France

Amsterdam (**am′**•stuhr•**dam**) largest city in Holland, under German occupation from 5/40 to 4/45

Anami, **General Korechika** (ah•**nah**•mee, uh- , **kawr**•ee•**chee**′kuh) Japanese Minister of War 4-8/45, argued against surrender, then committed suicide 8/15/45

Åndalsnes (**ahn**•duhls•nes) Norwegian port, occupied by the **Allies** 4/40 and the Germans from 5/40 to the end of the war

Andaman Islands (**an**•duh•muhn) Indian territory S of Burma between the **Bay of Bengal** and the **Andaman Sea**, held by the Japanese from 3/42 to 12/44

Anders, **General Wladyslav** (**ahn**•duhrz, an- , **vlahd**•is•**lahv**) leader of the Polish 2nd Corps, which fought with the **Allies** in Italy, notably at **Monte Cassino**

Angaur Island (sic) (**ang**•wahr, eng•**wahr**) S-most of the **Palau Islands,** about 2 miles long and a few miles from **Peleliu**, taken by US forces 9/44

Angers (ah(n)•**zhay**) city in W France, taken by the US 5th Division via **Normandy**, 8/11/44

Ankara (**ang**•kuhr•uh, **ahng-**) replaced Istanbul as the capital of **Turkey** in 1923

Anschluss ("Annexation") (**ahn**•shlus) the policy of incorporating ethnic Germans in neighboring countries into the Reich, applied primarily to the annexation of Austria, 3/13/38

Antonescu, Marshal Ion (ahn•taw•**nes**•koo, **yawn**) pro-German dictator of Romania 9/40-8/44, formally joined the **Axis** 11/23/40 and sent most of the 33 divisions of the Romanian Army to support the German invasion of the Soviet Union, with casualties later estimated at over 600,000. Executed for war crimes 6/1/46

Antonov, General Alex(s)ei I. (an•**tohn**•awf, uh•**lek**•say) high-ranking Soviet staff officer, Soviet CoS from 2/45

Antwerp (**an**•twerp) principal port of Belgium, taken by the British 2nd Army 9/4/44 but not open to shipping until 11/29/44 because the Germans held the **Scheldt** estuary

Anvil, Operation -- Allied invasion of S France beginning 8/15/44, also called **Dragoon**

Anzio (US **an**•zee•oh, It -tsoh) Allied landing point in Italy S of Rome 1/22/44, where the mostly US forces were held in the beachhead until 5/44

Aosta, Amadeo, Duke of (ah•**aw**•stuh, **ahm**•ah•**day**′oh) Italian Viceroy of **Abyssinia** from 1937, surrendered to British forces 5/17/41

Apamama (or **Abemama**) (ap•**ah**•mah•mah) atoll about 100 miles SE of **Tarawa**, taken by US forces 11/22/43

Aparri (uh•**pahr**•ee) Japanese landing point on the N tip of **Luzon** 12/10/41, site of a garrison in the small city and airfields nearby for the rest of the war

Apeldoorn (**ah**•puhl•dawrn, dohrn) city in Holland, residence of Kaiser Wilhelm from 1919 until his natural death in 1941

Apennines (**ap′**•uh•**nynz**) mountain range extending the entire length of the Italian peninsula, rising to almost 10,000 feet

Aqaba, **Gulf of** (**ah**•kuh•buh, **ak**•uh-) a 100-mile branch of the **Red Sea** between Egypt and Arabia, also a Jordanian town at the N end

Arakan (**ahr′**•uh•**kahn, ar′**•uh•**kan**) coastal region of W Burma, on the Bay of **Bengal**

Arawe Peninsula (**ahr**•uh•way, **ar**-) W end of **New Britain**, site of an American landing 12/15/43

Arcadia Conference (ahr•**kay**•dee•uh) meeting of British and American leaders in Washington, 12/22/41-1/14/42

Archambault, Jean-Paul (**ahr**•shahm•**boh′**, **zhah(n) pawl**) British **SOE** agent from Canada who aided resistance activity in France and Burma, where he died 5/45

Archangel (**ahrk**•ayn•juhl) N Russian port city on the **White Sea** used by Allied Arctic convoys, which were diverted to **Murmansk** when Archangel became icebound in winter

Ardennes (ahr•**den**) forested plateau in NE France and SE Belgium and Luxemburg, site of German attacks in 1940 and 1944

Ardent, HMS (**ahr**•dnt) British destroyer, sunk during the evacuation of **Narvik** 6/8/40

Arendal (ahr'•uhn•dahl, -en-) port in S Norway

Arezzo (uh•**ret**•soh, ah-) small city SE of **Florence**, a center of Italian partisan activity

Argentan (ahr•zhahn•tah(n)) town in N France, S boundary of the **Falaise Gap** 8/44

Argentia (ahr•jen•shuh) British naval base in **Newfoundland**, ceded to the US for 99 years as part of a bases-for-destroyers agreement concluded 9/2/40

Argentina (ahr•juhn•**tee**•nuh, -jen-) declared war on Germany and Japan 3/27/45, but contained many German sympathizers and provided refuge for Nazis after the war

Argonne (ahr•**gahn**) 1) forest in NE France 2) base force flagship in **Pearl Harbor**

Argus, HMS (ahr•guhs) British aircraft carrier dating from WWI, which saw limited service in WWII, mostly in the **Mediterranean**

Arizona, USS -- battleship sunk in **Pearl Harbor**, now a memorial

Ark Royal, HMS -- British aircraft carrier, sunk by a **U-boat** off **Gibraltar** 11/13-14/41 with the loss of only one man

Armavir (ahr•muh•veer') city in the **Caucasus** mountains, occupied by German forces 8/42-1/43

Armenia (ahr•mee•nee•uh) republic in the S USSR, beyond the limit of the German S advance in 1942

Arnhem (ahrn•hem, -uhm) city in Holland, site of a failed attempt by British paratroopers to seize and hold a bridge across the lower **Rhine** 9/44, subject of a 1974 book and a 1977 film, both titled *A Bridge Too Far*

Arnim, Col Gen Jurgen (Curt) von (ahr•nim, yur•ghen) took over command of German forces in **Tunisia** from **Rommel** 3/43, surrendered 5/12/43, ending the N African campaign

Arno River (ahr•noh) runs W through **Florence** and Pisa in Italy, crossed by American forces 8-9/44

Arnold, General Henry ("Hap") -- Chief of US Army Air Forces 1941-46 and a member of the Joint Chiefs of Staff

Arras (US ar•uhs, -as, Fr ah•rahs) small city in N France, site of a British counterattack against the advancing Germans 5/21/40

Arromanches (ah•roh•mah(n)sh) site of a vital "**Mulberry**" harbor off the **Normandy** beachhead

Arrow Cross, The -- pro-German fascist military organization in Hungary, whose leader, Major Ferenc Szálasi (**fehr•**en(t)s tsah•lahsh(ih)), took power 10/16/44 after the Germans removed **Horthy** and occupied **Budapest**

Artois (ahr•twah) former province and small city in NW France

Aruba (uh•roo•buh) Dutch island off Venezuela, targeted by German **U-boats** for its oil shipping

Aryan (ar•ee•uhn, air-) in **Nazi** doctrine, a non-Jewish Caucasian, especially Nordic

Arzew, Gulf of (ahr•zoo, ahr•zoo) E of **Oran** in N Africa, US landing area in Operation **Torch**

Asaka, Lt Gen Prince Yasuhiko (ah•**sah**•kah, **yah**•su•**hee**•koh) an uncle of **Hirohito**, nominal commander of the Japanese troops that committed the Rape of **Nanking**

Ascension Island (uh•**sen**•shuhn) British colony and US base in the S Atlantic, with an area of 34 square miles

Aschersleben (**ah′**•shuhrz•**lay**•ben) city in C Germany, site of an aircraft factory, bombed by the **Allies** 1-2/44

asdic (**az**•dik, **as**-) A(nti-) S(ubmarine) D(etection) I(nvestigation) C(ommittee), the British name for **sonar**

Askaris -- see **Southern Rhodesia**

 Aslito (as•**lee**•toh) airfield on the S end of **Saipan**, renamed **Isely Field** after US capture

Asmara (ahs•**mahr**•uh, az-) capital of **Eritrea**

Assam (a•**sam**, ah•**sahm**) NE Indian state bordering Burma and a British railroad running through it

Astoria, USS (as•**tawr**•ee•uh, uhs-) heavy cruiser, sunk 8/8-9/42 in the Battle of **Savo Island** near **Guadalcanal**

Astrakhan (as•truh•kuhn, -**kahn**, -**kan**) Russian city at the mouth of the **Volga River** on the **Caspian Sea**, part of an Allied supply route through Iran, remained beyond the German S advance in 1942

Atabrine (**at**•uh•brin, -breen) anti-malarial drug used by US forces in the Pacific from 1/43

Atago (ah•**tah**•goh, uh-) Japanese heavy cruiser, **Kurita**'s flagship in the Battle of **Leyte Gulf** until sunk 10/23/44 by the US submarine **Darter**

Athenia (uh•**thee**•nee•uh) British passenger liner torpedoed and sunk by a German submarine 9/3-4/39, the first ship to be sunk in the European war

Atlanta, USS (at•**lan**•tuh) US light cruiser and class, sunk off **Guadalcanal** 11/42

Atlantic Charter -- commitment to post-war freedom issued by **Roosevelt** and **Churchill** following their first summit conference off **Newfoundland** (the Atlantic Conference) 8/9-12/41

Atlantic Wall -- German coastal defenses against the Allied invasion of W Europe

Atlantis (at•**lan**•tis) the most successful German commerce raider of the war, sunk in the S Atlantic 11/22/41 by the British cruiser HMS **Devonshire**

Atsugi (at•**soo**•ghee) airport near **Yokohama** where the first Allied occupation forces landed 8/28/45 and General **MacArthur** arrived 8/30

Attlee, **Clement R.** (**at**•lee, **clem**•ent) Labour party leader and deputy PM in the coalition war cabinet 1940-45, succeeded **Churchill** as PM during the **Potsdam Conference** 7/45

Attu (**at**•too) W-most island of the **Aleutians,** occupied by the Japanese 6/7/42, retaken by US forces 5/43

Aube (**ohb**) river in N France

Auchinleck, General Sir Claude (awk'•en•lek, ow'-) British CiC Middle Eastern Command (including N Africa) 7/41-8/42 and India 1943-47

Augsburg (US **awgz**•buhrg, Ger **owks**•burk) city in S Germany, site of an aircraft factory bombed several times by the **Allies** starting 4/42

Augusta, USS (aw•**guhs**•tuh, uh-) heavy cruiser active throughout the war in Europe: carried **Roosevelt** to **Placentia Bay** (1941), flagship of the **Torch** landing near **Casablanca** 11/42, General **Bradley**'s ship on **D-Day**, supported the 8/44 landings in S France, and took **Truman** to Europe for the **Potsdam Conference** (1945)

Aung San, General U (**owng sahn, oo**) Burmese nationalist leader who switched his support from the Japanese to the British early in 1945, assassinated 7/47

Aurora, HMS (uh•**rawr**•uh) light cruiser which participated in the Norwegian campaign and then the **Mediterranean**, notably at **Malta**, until the end of the war

Auschwitz (US **owsh**•witz, Ger -vitz) the largest and best known German concentration camp, in S Poland, where an estimated two to three million people, mostly Jews, were killed

Auvergne (oh•**vairn**, -**vuhrn**) region and former province in SC France

Avignon (av•een•**yaw(n)**, ah•veen-) small city on the **Rhone** river in S France

Avranches (av•**rahnsh**, ahv-) key town in SW **Normandy**, taken by Allied forces 7/30/44 and held against a German counter-attack while **Patton**'s 3rd Army broke out from Normandy

Axis, the -- countries allied with Germany, originally the Rome-Berlin alliance

"Axis Sally" (**Mildred Gillars**) -- a US citizen living in Germany who broadcast largely ineffectual **Nazi** propaganda to Allied troops, served a 12-year prison term for treason and died in Columbus, Ohio, at age 88

Azerbaijan (**az**•uhr•by•**jahn′, -jan′**) S-most of the Soviet republics, on the **Caspian Sea**, beyond the limit of the German S advance in 1942

Azores, the (**ay**•zawrz, uh•**zawrz**) islands in the mid-Atlantic belonging to neutral Portugal, whose use by the **Allies** was permitted from 10/43

Azov, Sea of (**az**•awf, **ay**•zawf) N extension of the **Black Sea**

B

Babi (or **Baba**) **Yar** (**bah**•bee **yahr**) site of a German massacre of 33,000 Jews, POWs, and partisans in a ravine outside of **Kiev** 9/41

Bach-Zelewski, General Erich von dem (**bahk** zuh•**loo**•skee, zeh•**lev-** , **ay**•rikh vahn dem) highest ranking officer of the **Waffen-SS**, in charge of all anti-partisan and anti-guerrilla operations from 10/42, commanded the troops which suppressed the **Warsaw Uprising** 8/1/44-10/2/44

Backe, Herbert (**bah**•kuh, **hehr**•behrt) German Food Minister 1944-45

Backebo (**bahk**•eh•boh) town in Sweden where an errant experimental **V-2** rocket was recovered and sent to England for study 6/44

Baden (**bahd′n, bad′n**) region in SW Germany

Bader, Wing Commander Douglas (**bay**•duhr) British pilot who lost both legs in 1931, returned to the RAF with artificial legs in 1939, led five squadrons in the Battle of **Britain**

Badeyev (bah•**deh**•yev) four-acre food warehouse in **Leningrad**, bombed by the Germans 9/41

Badoglio, Marshal Pietro (bah•**doh**•lyoh, **pyeh**•troh) became PM of Italy 7/25/43 after the arrest of **Mussolini**

Baedecker raids (**bay**•dih•kuhr) German bombing of English cultural centers 4-6/42, named after a German travel guide

Bagac (bah•**gahk**) port on the **Bataan** peninsula, W end of the major US/Philippine defense line

Baghdad (**bag**•dad) capital of Iraq, site of fighting 4-5/40 when British-led forces overthrew the pro-**Axis Rashid Ali**

Bagration, Operation (US bah•**grah**•tee•ahn, -awn, Rus **buh•gruh**•tih•**yawn′**, ba•gra•**tyuhn**) main Soviet summer offensive of 1944, directed against German Army Group Center, destroyed 25 German divisions with 350,000 troops, named after a general killed in 1812 during Napoleon's invasion

Bahrain (bah•**rain**) oil-rich island off Arabia in the **Persian Gulf**, a British protectorate from 1861 to 1971, independent since 8/15/71

Baka (**bah**•kuh, -kah) manned suicide bomb launched from a bomber, first used by the Japanese against ships off **Okinawa** 4/45

Baku (buh•**koo**, ba-) capital of **Azerbaijan**, Soviet port city and oil center on the **Caspian Sea**, never reached by the German drive S in 1942

Balanga (bah•**lahn**•gah) town on the E coast of the **Bataan** peninsula, starting point of the Bataan death march

Balaton, Lake (**bal′**•uh•**tahn**) in Hungary, the largest lake in C Europe, site of the last major German offensive 3/45

Balbo, Marshal Italo (**bahl**•boh, **bal-** , **ee**•tah•loh, ta-) Italian Fascist and airman who led **Mussolini**'s march on Rome in 1922 and helped build the Italian Air Force between the wars, Governor of **Libya** from 1935, shot down and killed by Italian anti-aircraft fire over **Tobruk** 6/40, probably by accident, possibly on **Mussolini**'s orders

Balck, Lt Gen Hermann (**bahlk**, **hair**•mahn) German tank commander on various fronts throughout the war

Balearic Islands (bal•ee•ar′•ik) a province of Spain in the W **Mediterranean**, including **Majorca**, Minorca, and Ibiza

Bali (bah•lee, bal•ee) small island in the **Dutch East Indies**, E of **Java**, occupied by the Japanese 2/19/42 and held until 1945

Balikpapan (bah•lik•pah′•pahn) city and oil terminal on the E coast of **Borneo**, occupied by the Japanese from 1/42 to 7/45

Balkans (bawl•kuhnz) the SE peninsula of Europe, including Yugoslavia, **Albania**, Greece, Bulgaria, Romania, and European **Turkey**

Baltic Sea (bawl•tik) the major waterway of N Europe

Baltic States (bawl•tik) **Lithuania**, **Latvia**, and **Estonia**, annexed by the Soviet Union 7/21/40

Baltimore, USS (bawl′•tuh•mawr, -mohr) name ship of a class of 14 heavy cruisers completed 1943-45

Ba Maw, Dr. U (bah maw, oo) first PM of Burma 1937-39, imprisoned by the British 8/40-1/42, reinstated by the Japanese 1943-45

Bangkok (bang•kahk, bang•kahk) capital of **Thailand**, occupied by Japanese troops 12/9/41

Banjarmasin (or **Band-**) (bahn•juhr•mah′•sin, ban-) port city in S **Borneo**, occupied by the Japanese 2/42

Banmauk (bahn•mowk) town in NW Burma, retaken from the Japanese by British forces 12/44

Banzai (bahn•zy, bahn•zy) shout used by Japanese soldiers in final, often suicidal, charges, roughly translated as "may the Emperor live 10,000 years"

Bao Dai -- see **Viet Minh**

Bär (or **Baer**), **Col Heinrich ("Heinz")** (**bair**, **hyn**•rikh)
German pilot with 220 kills from 1940, the top jet fighter ace of
the war with 16 kills

Baranowicze (now **Baranovichi**) (buh•**rah**'•nuh•**vich**•ee)
small city in E Poland, key Soviet defense center, overrun by
German forces 6/41, now in Belarus

Barbara Line (bahr•**bar**•uh) German defense line S of **Cassino**

Barbarossa, Operation (**bahr**•buh•**rahs**'•uh) German invasion
of the Soviet Union, 6/22/41. Named for a 12th-century Holy
Roman Emperor (Frederick "Red Beard") who launched a
crusade to the Holy Land

Barbey, Vice-Admiral Daniel E. (**bahr**•bee) Amphibious
Force Commander under **MacArthur** in the SW Pacific 1943-45

Barbie, Klaus (**bahr**•bee, **klows**) **Gestapo** chief in **Lyons**,
11/42-9/44. In spite of his nickname, "the butcher of Lyons,"
and his myriad war crimes, he was not imprisoned until 1987,
dying in 1991

Bardia (**bahr**•dee•uh) fortified Libyan port near the Egyptian
border

Barents Sea (**bar**•uhnts, **bahr**-) N of **Archangel**, part of the
Arctic convoy route, scene of a major battle 12/30-31/42

Barham, HMS (**bahr**•uhm) British battleship, sunk by a
U-boat off **Crete** 11/25/41

Bari (**bahr**•ee, **bar**-) **Adriatic** port in S Italy

Barratt, Air Marshal Sir Arthur S. (**bar**•at) Commander of
British Air Forces in France during the German invasion 5-6/40

Barré, General Georges (bar•ay, zhawrzh) **Vichy** French Army Commander in **Tunisia** 11/42, joined the invading **Allies**

Baruch, Bernard M. (buh•rook) economic advisor to **Roosevelt** from 1934 and also, during the war, to **James F. Byrnes**.

Basra (bahs•ruh, -rah, **bahz**-) port city in SE Iraq

Bassein (buh•sayn) city on the **Irrawaddy** river in SW Burma

Bastico, Marshal Ettore (bas•tih•koh, eh•tawr•ay) Commander of Italian forces in N Africa, 7/41-2/43

Bastin, Jules (bas•teh(n), zhool) CiC Belgian underground military forces from 12/30/42, died in German captivity 12/1/44

Bastogne (US bas•tohn, Fr bah•stohn•yuh, bas•tohn-) Belgian town in the **Ardennes**, an important road and rail junction, where American forces successfully resisted a German siege during the Battle of the **Bulge** 12/44-1/45

Basutos (buh•soo•tohz, bah-) Black African volunteers from Basutoland (now Lesotho) who fought with the British

Bataan Peninsula (buh•tan, -tahn) W of **Manila** Bay, it was the last American-**Filipino** stronghold on the Philippine mainland. Its fall to the Japanese 4/42 was followed by the infamous Bataan Death March.

Batavia (buh•tay•vee•uh) port city in **Java**, HQ of **ABDA** 1/15/42-2/25/42, fell to the Japanese 3/42. Former name of Jakarta (juh•kahr•tuh), the present capital of Indonesia

Bath (bath) -- see **Baedeker raids**

Batum (bah•toom, buh-) Soviet city on the **Black Sea** near **Turkey**, now called Batumi (buh•too•mee, bah-)

Baudouin, Paul (boh•**dweh(n)**) Foreign Minister of the **Vichy** government 6/40-1/41

Bavaria (buh•**vair**•ee•uh) state in SE Germany whose capital is Munich

Bayerlein, Lt Gen Fritz (**by′**•uhr•**lyn**) German staff officer and **Panzer** commander who served on several fronts during the war

Bayonne (US bay•**ohn**, Fr bah•**yaw(n)**) small city on the SW coast of France, near which almost 200,000 French and Polish troops were evacuated 6/19/40

B-Dienst (**bay**•**deenst**) ("Observation Service," B = Beobachtung) cryptoanalytical department of the German Navy, helping **U-boats** to locate Atlantic convoys

Bear Island -- small island in the Arctic Ocean, about 400 miles N of Norway

Beaufighter (**boh′**•**fyt**•uhr) versatile British night fighter/bomber in use from 7/40. About 6,000 were built by the end of the war.

Beaverbrook, Lord Maxwell -- Minister of Aircraft Production during the Battle of **Britain**, British head of the Anglo-American military mission to **Moscow** 8-9/41

Beck, Jozef (**bek**, **yoo**•zef) Foreign Minister of Poland 1932-39. His hostility toward France and the Soviet Union prevented him from realizing the full menace of **Nazi** Germany.

Beck, General Ludwig (**bek**, US **luhd**•wig, Ger **loot**•vikh) German CoS 5/35-8/38. After his forced retirement he became the most prestigious opponent of **Hitler**'s policies, the probable head of state if a coup succeeded. He committed suicide under duress after the failure of the **July Bomb Plot** 7/20/44.

Beda Fomm (bay•duh, -dah, fuhm) (now spelled Bayda Fumm) site of a major Italian surrender to the British in NE **Libya**, 2/7/41, leading to the arrival of **Rommel** in **Tripoli** on 2/12/41

Bedouin, HMS (bed•oo•in, -uh•wuhn, beh•dwin) British destroyer, sunk in the E **Mediterranean** 6/42

Beirut (bay•root) present-day capital of **Lebanon**, taken by the **Allies** (7th Australian Division) 7/41 in a campaign against the **Vichy** French forces in **Syria**

Beja (or Béja) (bay•zhah, bay•zhah) key road center 60 miles W of **Tunis,** scene of fighting from 11/42 to 2/43

Belfast (bel•fast) 1) capital of Northern Ireland 2) **HMS** -- British cruiser, saw action from late 1942 in Arctic convoys, the sinking of the **Scharnhorst,** and the **Normandy** landings

Belfort (bel•fawr) fortress city and mountain pass in E France

Belgorod (bel'•guh•rahd) city and important rail junction in SW Russia on the **Donets** River, 50 miles N of **Kharkov**, which changed hands four times during 1941-43

Belgrade (bel•grade, bel•grade) capital of Yugoslavia, captured by the Germans 4/41 after heavy punitive bombing, liberated by Soviet and Yugoslav forces 10/44

Belorussia (bel•uh•rush'•uh) a republic of the W Soviet Union adjacent to the **Baltic States**, **East Prussia**, and Poland, recaptured from the Germans during Operation **Bagration** (1944), now the independent republic of Belarus (**bel•uh•roos'**)

Belsen (or Bergen-Belsen) (buhr•guhn, bair•ghen, bel•zuhn) first German concentration camp to be liberated by the W **Allies**, 4/13/45

Belzec (US **bel•**zhets, Pol bzhoo•**zhets**, byoo-) German extermination camp in Poland, opened 3/42, razed in late 1943, estimated death toll 600,000

Benes, Eduard (**ben•**esh, **ed•**u•ahrt) president of Czechoslovakia 1935-38, 1946-48, headed the Czech government-in-exile in London during the war

Bengal (ben•**gawl**, -**gahl,** beng-) province in NE India, now divided between India and Bangladesh

Bengal, Bay of (see above) a part of the **Indian Ocean** between India and Burma

Benghazi (ben•**gah•**zee, beng-) port city in **Libya** which changed hands several times during the N African campaign

Ben-Gurion, David (ben•**gur•**ee•uhn) born in Poland, led Israel to independence and became its first PM in 1948

Bennett, Air Vice-Marshal Donald (**ben•**uht) Australian-born **RAF** pilot who directed several projects during the war, notably the Pathfinder Force to guide strategic bombers over Germany

Benouville (beh•noo•**veel**) village near the **Normandy** coast, site of the first landing, by glider, of the Normandy invasion

Berbera (**bur•**buh•ruh) capital of **British Somaliland**

Berchtesgaden (**bairk′•**tuhs•**gahd′**n, **berkh′-**) town in SE **Bavaria**, site of **Hitler's** fortified mountain chalet

Berdichev (behr•**dee•**chev) city in **Ukraine**, where **Hitler** visited the HQ of Army Group South 8/6/41, retaken by Soviet forces 1/5/44

Berdyansk (buhr•**dyahnsk, dyansk**) Soviet city on the Sea of **Azov**, captured by the Germans 10/6/41 with more than 100,000 prisoners

Berezina (or **Beresina**) (bih•reh•zuh•nuh) river in **Belorussia** whose marshy terrain provided effective defense utilized by the Soviets in 1941 but not by the Germans in 1944

Bergamini, Admiral Carlo (bair•guh•mee'•nee) killed while leading Italian naval forces to Allied ports after the surrender in 9/43

Bergen (**buhr**•guhn, **bair**•ghen) Atlantic port city in S Norway captured by the Germans 4/9/40

Berger, SS General Gottlob (bair•guhr, gawt•lohp) crushed a **Slovak** uprising preceding the arrival of Soviet troops, 9-10/44

Berggrav, Eivind (bair•grahv, eye•vind) Norwegian theologian and resistance leader

Berghof (**bairg**•hohf) ("mountain court") **Hitler's** self-designed house at **Berchtesgaden**

Bergonzoli, General Annibale (bair•guhn•zoh'•lee, ahn•nee•bahl'•lay) Italian Commander in N Africa, defeated at **Bardia**, captured in the Battle of **Beda Fomm** 2/7/41

Beria, Lavrenti P. (behr•ee•uh, bair- , luhv•ren'•tee, lahv-) chief of the Soviet secret police (**NKVD**) from 1938 to 1953, executed for conspiracy shortly after **Stalin**'s death in that year

Bering Strait (bair•ing, bir-) separates Alaska and Siberia at the N end of the Bering Sea

Berlin, Battle of (US buhr•lin, Ger bair•leen) heavy bombing raids by the RAF 11/43-3/44. US air attacks began 3/4/44.

Bern (or **Berne**) (**buhrn, bairn**) The capital of Switzerland, used for unofficial diplomatic negotiations during the war, especially in the last year

Bernadotte, Count Folke (**buhr•nuh•daht, bair-**) Swedish Red Cross official and nephew of the king, respected mediator, approached by **Himmler** to negotiate with the **Allies**, who rejected negotiation 2-4/45

Bernhard, Prince (**bairn•**hahrt) German-born son-in-law of **Queen Wilhelmina** of Holland, fought with the Dutch and British throughout the war

Bernhard Line (**bairn•**hahrt) German defensive line in Italy a little S of the more important **Gustav Line**

Bessarabia (**bes•uh•ray'•bee•uh**) province in NE Romania, annexed by the Soviet Union 6/40, returned 1941, annexed again by the end of the war, now part of **Ukraine**

Béthouart, Emile (bay•**too'ahr**, -**twahr**, ay•**meel**) French general who commanded forces in Norway (1940), N Africa (1940-44), France (1944-45) and Germany (1945)

Betio (**bay•**chyoh, **bet-**) chief island of the **Tarawa** atoll, taken from 5,000 Japanese defenders by US forces in fierce fighting 11/21-23/43

Bevan, Colonel John (**bev•**uhn, **bee•**ven) in charge of British deception to conceal the destination (N Africa) of Operation **Torch**

Bevin, Ernest (**bev•**in) directed British mobilization of manpower for war as Minister of Labour and National Service 1940-45, became Foreign Secretary under **Clement Attlee,** whom he joined at **Potsdam**

Biak (bee•**yahk**) large island (950 square miles) off the NW coast of **New Guinea**, occupied by the Japanese 4/42, taken by US forces from 10,000 Japanese defenders 5/27/44-6/22/44

Bialystok (bee•ahl′ee•**stawk**, **byah**•lih•stawk, **bya**′- , -wih-) city in Soviet-occupied Poland, part of a salient where the Soviets suffered huge losses 7/41

Bidault, Georges (bih•**doh**, **zhawrzh**) succeeded **Jean Moulin** as President of the French National Council of Resistance 6/43, became Minister of Foreign Affairs in **DeGaulle**'s provisional government 9/44

Bigot (**big**•uht) code name for the secret plans for the **Normandy** Invasion (**D-Day**), carried the highest Allied security designation

Big Week -- 2/20-26/44, heavy Anglo-American bombing of German aircraft and ball bearing factories

Bihać (bee•hahch) partisan base in Yugoslavia

Bilibid (**bil**′•uh•**bid**) prison in **Manila**

Billotte, General Gaston H. (bee•**yut**, gah•**staw(n)**, ga-) French commander of 1st Army Group 1940, died in a road accident during the German invasion 5/40

Billotte, Colonel Pierre (bee•**yut**, pee•**air**) son of **General Billotte**, **DeGaulle**'s CoS in London and **Algiers**, led the first Allied forces (French) into Paris 8/25/44

Bir Hakeim (or **Hacheim**) (**beer** hah•**kaym**′, ah-) key military objective in the Libyan desert near the Egyptian border, S end of the **Gazala Line**

Birkenau (**beer**•ken•ow, **bir-**) concentration camp attached to **Auschwitz**, primarily occupied by slave laborers for nearby munitions factories

Biscari (bis•**kahr**•ee) town and airfield in **Sicily**, 6-8 miles from the S coast, captured by US forces 7/13-14/43

Biscay, Bay of (bis•kay) portion of the Atlantic bordered by SW France and N Spain

Bismarck (biz•mahrk) with **Tirpitz**, one of the two largest German battleships, sunk in action against British ships 5/27/41

Bismarck Archipelago (biz•mahrk ahr•kuh•**pel**•uh•goh) island group NE of **New Guinea**, which includes the **Admiralty Islands**, **New Britain**, and New Ireland

Bismarck Sea (biz•mahrk) bounded by the **Bismarck Archipelago** and **New Guinea**, site of a major naval defeat for Japan 3/2/43. Also the name of a US escort carrier, sunk off **Iwo Jima** by a **kamikaze** attack 2/21/45

Bison (bee•zoh(n)) French destroyer sunk off **Namsos** 5/40

Bizerte (or **Bizerta**) (bih•**zuhrt**•uh, bih•**zairt**, -uh) port city in N **Tunisia**, captured by Allied forces 5/7/43

Bjerkvik (**byirk**•veek) Norwegian village 30 miles NE of **Narvik**, taken by French forces 5/40

Black, Captain G. D. -- British commando who blew up a key hydro-electric power station in Norway 9/42, captured by the Germans and shot by the **Gestapo**

Black Sea -- bounded by **Turkey**, Bulgaria, Romania, and the Soviet Union

Blackett, Patrick M. (**black•**it, -uht) British physicist, director of operations research in the Admiralty 1942-45, awarded the Nobel Prize 1948

Blakeslee, Colonel Donald -- US fighter ace, fought with Canadian and British as well as US air forces

Blamey, Lt Gen Sir Thomas A. -- the highest ranking Australian general in the war, Deputy CiC Middle East 1941, CiC Allied land forces under **MacArthur** 1942-45

Blaskowitz, Col Gen Johannes von (**blas•**kuh•wits, yoh•**hahn•**uhs) German CiC East 10/39-5/40, commanded 1st Army 10/40-5/44 and Army Group G in France 5-9/44, commander of Army Group A in Holland 1-5/45, committed suicide in **Nuremberg** prison while awaiting trial 2/5/48

Blechhammer (**blekh•**hahm•muhr) site of a German synthetic oil plant in **Silesia**, opened 4/44, employed some 4,000 Jewish prisoners from **Auschwitz**

Bleicher, Hugo (**bly•**khuhr) German secret agent who operated successfully against the French underground networks, including the capture of Peter Churchill (no relation to Winston) and Odette Sansom 4/16/43

Blenheim (**blen•**uhm, -im) British bomber and night-fighter

Bletchley Park (**blech•**lee) country house about 50 miles NW of London, the center of British decoding activities

Blida (**blee•**dah, -duh) city in N **Algeria**, site of an airport

Blitz, the (**blits**) German night bombing of London and other British cities, primarily 9/40-5/41

Blitzkrieg (blits•kreeg) "lightning war," rapid coordinated attack by tactical air and mobilized land forces, conceived and used with great success by Germany 1939-41

Blockbuster -- British 4,000-pound bomb capable of destroying a city block (hence the name). First used 4/1/41 in an attack on Emden. The term is also applied to even larger British and US bombs.

Blomberg, FM Werner von (blahm•bairg, vair•nuhr) Defense Minister (1/33-3/35) and War Minister (3/35-1/38) of Germany, dismissed after a scandalous marriage, died in **Nuremberg** prison 3/14/46

Blücher (blu•khuhr, -shuhr) German heavy cruiser, sister ship of **Admiral Hipper**, sunk by Norwegian shore batteries off **Oslo** on her first mission 4/9/40

Blum, Léon (bloom, lay•ah(n)) Socialist PM of France 1936-37, 38, 46-47, liberated from **Flossenburg** concentration camp 5/4/45

Blumentritt, General Günther (bloom'•en•tritt, gun•tuhr) German staff officer and infantry commander, active throughout the war

Bobruisk (now spelled **Babruysk**) **(buh•broo•isk)** city on the **Beresina River** in W Russia, in German hands 6/41-6/44, now part of S Belarus

bocage (boh•kahzh) the dominant terrain of **Normandy**, consisting of small farms surrounded by three to four foot high "hedgerows" – earth and stone banks covered with thick shrubbery – which favored the German defenders and slowed the Allied advance after **D-Day**

Boche (or **boche**) **(US, Fr bahsh, Ger bawsh)** disparaging term for German soldiers dating from World War I

Bock, FM Fedor von (bahk, fay•dawr) commanded German armies in Poland, France, and the Soviet Union, permanently relieved of command by **Hitler** 7/42

Bock's Car -- B-29 bomber that dropped the second atomic bomb on **Nagasaki** 8/9/45, named for its usual pilot but flown on this occasion by **Major Charles W. Sweeney**

Bofors Gun (boh•fawrz, furs) Swedish designed anti-aircraft gun used by the US, Britain, and other participants in the war

Bogdanov, General Semyon I. (buhg•dahn•awf, syim•yawn) Soviet tank commander throughout the war

Bogor (boh•gawr) city in W **Java**

Bogue, USS -- escort aircraft carrier, name ship of a class, helped drive **U-boats** out of the N Atlantic 5/43

Bohemia-Moravia (boh•hee•mee•uh mawr•ay•vee•uh, muh•ray-) W part of Czechoslovakia, German protectorate 1939-45

Bohol (boh•hawl) island and strait in the C **Philippines**

Bohr, Niels (bawr, bohr, neelz) atomic physicist who won the Nobel Prize 1922, escaped to Sweden with nearly all of Denmark's other 7,000 Jews 9-10/43, worked on the US atomic bomb from 1943

Bolivia (buh•liv•ee•uh, boh-) despite a large German community and **Nazi** agitation for a coup, remained aligned with the US and declared war on the **Axis** powers 4/7/43

Bologna (buh•lohn•yuh) city in N Italy, held by German forces from the Italian surrender until 4/45

Bolshevism (**bohl′•**shuh•**viz•**uhm, **bawl′-** , **bahl′-**) negative term for Soviet Communism

Bone (or **Bône**) (**bohn**) Algerian port city near the Tunisian border, occupied by the British 11/12/42 as part of Operation **Torch**. Now named Annaba (an·**nah**·buh)

Bong, Major Richard I. -- the leading US fighter ace of the war, shot down 40 Japanese planes

Bonhoeffer (or -**höf-**), **Dietrich** (**bahn•**hur•fuhr, **dee•**trikh) German Protestant theologian, an outspoken opponent of Nazism, arrested 4/43, executed along with **Canaris** and **Oster** 4/9/45. His older brother Klaus, a leading conspirator against **Hitler**, was executed 4/23/45 in Berlin.

Bonin Islands (**boh•**nin) a chain of volcanic islands N of **Iwo Jima**, not invaded by the US, not surrendered until 12/13/45

Bonn (**bahn**) city on the **Rhine**, seat of the government of West Germany after the war

Bonomi, Ivanoe (boh•**noh•**mee, ee•**vah•**noh•ay, ee•vah•**noy**(ee)) served briefly as Italian Premier in 1921, exiled from the government by **Mussolini**, succeeded **Badoglio** as Premier 6/44 after the **Allies** took Rome

Bordeaux (bawr•**doh**) port city in SW France, last seat of the French government before the surrender in 6/40

Borghese, Prince Junio Valerio (bawr•**gay•**zee, -zay, **yoo•**nee•oh, vah•**lair•**ee•oh) Italian naval commander known as the "Black Prince," who led a series of successful underwater raids on British ships in **Mediterranean** harbors, notably **Gibraltar** (9/20-21/41) and **Alexandria** (12/18-19/41)

Boris III, King of Bulgaria -- joined the **Axis** powers under duress 3/41, declaring war on the US and Britain but not the

Soviet Union, supported the Bulgarian parliament's successful refusal to deport Jews 3/43, killed 8/28/43 by a pro-Soviet assassin

Borisov (bawr•ee•sahv, - sahf) small city on the **Berezina** river in W Russia, visited by **Hitler** 8/41

Bor-Komorowski, Lt Gen Tadeusz (**bawr kahm•awr•ahv'•skee, tah•deh•oosh**) commander of the underground Polish Home Army during the German occupation, led the **Warsaw Uprising** 8/1/44-10/2/44

Bormann, Martin (US **bawr•muhn**, Ger **bawr'•mahn**) **Nazi** leader, **Hitler**'s personal secretary and gatekeeper, killed trying to escape from Hitler's bunker 5/1-2/45

Borneo (**bawr•nee•oh**) the largest island in the **Dutch East Indies,** third largest in the world, under Japanese occupation 1/42-9/45

Bornholm (**bawrn•hoh(l)m**) Danish island in the **Baltic Sea**, between Sweden and Germany

Borodino (**bawr•uh•dee'•noh**) town 70 miles W of **Moscow**, which saw the first Soviet use of Far Eastern (Siberian) troops against the Germans 10/41

Bose (also **Bhose), Subhas Chandra** (**bohs, bohz, sub•hahsh,** shub- , **chawn•draw**) recruited Indian nationalists, mostly from German and Japanese POWs, to fight against the British, died in a plane crash in 1945

Bosporus (also **Bosphorus**) (**bahs•puhr•uhs, -fuhr•uhs**) a strait in **Turkey** connecting the **Black Sea** to the **Mediterranean** via the Sea of Marmara (**mahr•muhr•uh**)

Bothnia, Gulf of (**bahth•nee•uh**) the part of the **Baltic Sea** between Sweden and **Finland**

Bottomley, Sir Norman H. -- British Deputy Chief of Air Staff 1943-45, succeeded **Harris** as CiC Bomber Command in 1945

Bougainville (boo′•ghin•vil, boo•ghin•veel′) largest of the **Solomon Islands**, at the NW end, an important Japanese stronghold 3/42-12/43

Bougie (boo•zhee) (now called **Béjaia** (bay•jy•eh)) Algerian port about 100 miles E of **Algiers**, taken by British forces 11/11/42 as part of the **Torch** landings

Boulogne (US boo•lohn, Fr boo•lawn•yuh) port city in N France

Bourguebus Ridge (boor•guh•bus) SE of **Caen**, site of a major tank battle 7/18/44 in which German defenders repulsed British forces under **Montgomery**

Boyington, Major Gregory (boy•ing•tuhn) US Marine Corps ace and squadron leader who shot down 28 Japanese planes, was himself shot down over **Rabaul** 1/3/44, and spent the rest of the war as a POW

Brack, Dr. Victor (brahk) directed the German euthanasia program 1939-41 and helped launch mass murder by gassing 1941. Tried at **Nuremberg** and hanged 6/2/48

Bracken, Brendan R. -- British Minister of Information from 7/41 to the end of the war

Bradley, General Omar N. (brad•lee, oh•mahr) West Point classmate (1915) and close friend of **Eisenhower**, protégé of **George C. Marshall**, commander of 2nd Corps in **Tunisia** and **Sicily**, head of 1st Army in **Normandy,** and from 8/44 12th Army Group in France and Germany

Brandenburg (bran′•duhn•buhrg) 1) German city 40 miles W of Berlin 2) a famous monumental gate in Berlin

Brandenburgers (bran′•duhn•buhrg•uhrz) German Army Commando units

Brandt, Dr. Karl (US brant, Ger **brahnt)** a personal physician to **Hitler**, co-director of the euthanasia program 1939-41, later head of Germany's medical services, including experiments in concentration camps. Tried at **Nuremberg** and hanged 6/2/48

Bratislava (braht•uh•slah′•vuh, brat-) capital of **Slovakia**

Brauchitsch, FM Walther von (brow•khich, vahl•tuhr) CiC of the German Army 2/4/38-12/41, relieved of command after his failure to capture **Moscow** and replaced as CiC by **Hitler** himself

Braun, Eva (brown, ay•vuh) Hitler's mistress from 1932, married him 4/29/45, one day before their joint suicide

Braun, Wernher von (Ger brown, vair•nuhr, US brawn) German rocket scientist who designed the **V-2**, worked in the US after the war

Brazil (bruh•zil) declared war on Germany and Italy 8/22/42, the first South American country to do so, sent a force of 25,000 to fight in Italy 7/44

Brazzaville Declaration (US braz′•uh•vil, brahz′- , Fr **brah•zuh•veel′) DeGaulle's** announcement from **French Equatorial Africa** on 10/27/40 of the **Free French** Movement's Empire Defense Council, which he viewed as replacing the illegitimate **Vichy** regime as the government of France

Breendonk (brain•dahnk) village in Belgium, site of a German concentration camp near **Antwerp**

Bremen (US brem•uhn, Ger bray•muhn, -mehn) German port city on the **Weser** river near the **North Sea**, heavily bombed during the war

Bren Gun (brehnc) British light machine gun of Czech design, in use from 1936 until well after the war

Brenner Pass (brehn•uhr) mountain pass in the Alps on the border between Austria and Italy, site of meetings between **Hitler** and **Mussolini**, notably on 10/4/40

Brereton, Lt Gen Lewis H. (brair•eh•tuhn) US Air Force commander who played a major role in a remarkable number of operations worldwide, including the **Philippines** (11-12/41), **ABDA** (1-2/42), **El Alamein**, **Sicily**, the **Ploesti** raid of 8/1/43, **Salerno**, **D-Day**, and **Market-Garden**

Breskens Pocket (bres•kuhnz) area of Holland S of the **Scheldt** estuary, held by the Germans until 11/44, delaying Allied use of **Antwerp**

Breslau (bres•low, brez-) principal city of SE Germany (**Silesia**), now in SW Poland and renamed **Wroclaw** (**vrawts•lahf**)

Brest (brest) W-most port city in France, an important German submarine base, too damaged by fighting and German demolition to be used after the US capture 9/44

Brest-Litovsk (brest-lih•tahfsk) city on the **Bug** river in E Poland, now called simply **Brest** and located in SW Belarus

Bretagne (bruh•tahn•yuh) French battleship named for a province in NW France (see **Brittany**), sunk by the British at **Mers-el-Kébir** 7/3/40

Bretton Woods (bret′n) New Hampshire site of the final conference to establish the International Monetary Fund (IMF) and the World Bank, 7/44

Brezhnev, Maj Gen Leonid I. (US **brezh•**nef, Rus -nyuhf, **lay•**uh•nid, **lee-**) political administrator during the war, General Secretary of the Soviet Communist Party 1966-82

Briare (bree•**ahr**) French town on the **Loire** river 100 miles S of Paris, refuge of the French government leaders before the fall of France 6/40, where they were visited by **Churchill**

Brighton (bryt′n) resort city on the S English coast

Brindisi (brin′•duh•zee, breen′-) Italian port city on the S **Adriatic**, site of the Italian government after the overthrow of **Mussolini** and surrender to the **Allies** 9/8/43

Bristol (brist′l) port city in SW England 100 miles W of London, heavily bombed 1940-41

Britain, Battle of -- unsuccessful German attempt to attain air superiority over England in preparation for an invasion, summer 1940

British East Africa -- former name of Tanzania, Uganda, and Kenya, which saw no fighting but provided troops to the **Allies**

British Expeditionary Force (BEF) -- British forces serving in France 9/39-6/40

British Somaliland (soh•**mah′•**lee•**land**, suh-) N section of present-day Somalia

Brittany (brit′n•ee) (Fr **Bretagne**) peninsula between the **English Channel** and the Bay of **Biscay**, the W-most part of France, site of a campaign led by US **Maj Gen Troy H. Middleton** that began 8/1/44 and ended with the capture of the major port city of **Brest** 9/18

Brno (buhr•noh) city in C Czechoslovakia, taken from occupying German forces by advancing Soviet forces 4/26/45

Broadway -- Allied air landing point behind Japanese lines in Burma 3-5/44

Bromley, Major William (**brahm**•lee) American assigned to send German rocket equipment from **Nordhausen**, in C Germany, to the US via **Antwerp** before the Russians occupied the area on 6/1/45

Brooke, General Sir Alan (later **FM Viscount Alanbrooke**) -- British Chief of the Imperial General Staff (CIGS) 12/41-1/46

Broome (**broom**) NW Australian port and flying boat base, bombed by the Japanese 3/3/42

Brossolette, Pierre (broh•soh•**let**, pee•**air**) French resistance leader allied with the **Free French** 1942-44, killed himself 3/22/44 while a prisoner of the **Gestapo** in Paris

Browning, Captain Miles -- **Spruance**'s CoS at **Midway**, who calculated the optimal time to attack the Japanese carriers, **Halsey**'s CoS before and after Midway

Broz, Josip -- see **Tito**

Brûly-de-Pesche (broo•lee•duh•**pesh**) Belgian village near the French border, **Hitler**'s HQ from about 6/4 to 6/18/40

Brunei (broo•**ny**) British protectorate on the NW coast of **Borneo**, under Japanese control throughout the war, an independent sultanate since 1984

Bruneval (broo•n'**vahl**) site of a German-built radar station near **Le Havre**, successfully raided by British paratroopers 2/27-28/42

Brunswick (**bruhnz**•wik) manufacturing center in NC Germany, heavily bombed by the **Allies** throughout the war

Brussels (bruhs•uhlz) capital of Belgium, taken by German forces 5/17/40, liberated by Allied forces 9/3/44

Bryansk (bree•**ahnsk**) Russian city 200 miles SW of **Moscow**, a center of partisan activity during the German occupation

Buariki (bwah•**ree**•kee) island at the N end of the **Tarawa** atoll

Bucharest (boo'•kuh•**rest)** capital of Romania

Buchenwald (US **boo'•**kuhn•**wawld**, Ger -khuhn•**vawlt**) **Nazi** concentration camp near **Weimar** from 1933 to 4/45, site of medical experiments on prisoners

Buckner, Lt Gen Simon Bolivar, Jr. (buk•nuhr, **sy•**muhn **bohl'•**ih•**vahr)** served in Alaska and the **Aleutians** 7/40-1943, commander of US forces (10th Army) on **Okinawa**, where he was killed in action 6/18/45

Budapest (boo'•duh•**pest, -pesht)** capital of Hungary, site of a 52-day siege of German forces by Soviet armies 12/44-2/45

Budënny (or **Budyenny), Marshal Semyon M.** (boo•**dyeh**•nee, syim•**yawn**) Soviet Commander of the SW Front in 1941, denied permission to withdraw from **Kiev** and dismissed by **Stalin** 9/41, fought in the defense of **Moscow** (1941) and the N **Caucasus** (1942), but played little part in the war after that

Bug (boog) river in Poland

Buin (boo•**een**) major Japanese base at the S end of **Bougainville**

Buka (boo•kah) W-most of the **Solomon Islands**, occupied by the Japanese 3/10/42, now part of **Papua New Guinea**

Bukovina (or **Buc-**) **(boo•**kuh•**vee'•**nuh) district in N Romania, the N part of which was annexed by the Soviet Union 6/40

Bulganin, Nikolai A. (US bul•**gan**•in, -**gahn**•uhn, Rus bul•**gahn**•yeen) Deputy Soviet Commissar of Defense from 1944, later (1955-58) Premier of the Soviet Union

Bulgaria -- see **Boris III**

Bulge, Battle of the (aka **Ardennes** Offensive) -- last major German offensive on the W front, in Belgium and Luxemburg, 12/44-1/45

Buna (boo•nuh, -nah) N coastal port on the E peninsula of **New Guinea**, taken by the Japanese 7/42, retaken by Australian forces 11-12/42

Bunche, Ralph J. (buhnch) US diplomat, won the Nobel Peace Prize in 1950

Bungo Suido (**Bungo Strait**) (buhn•goh **swee**•doh) Japanese channel between **Kyushu** and **Shikoku**

Bunker Hill, USS -- aircraft carrier which lost 396 men to a **kamikaze** attack off **Okinawa** 5/11/45

Burgers, Jean (boor•zhay, zhahn) Belgian engineer who led sabotage activity against the occupying Germans, notably the "great cut-off" of electric power 1/15/44. Hanged at **Buchenwald** 9/6/44

Burke, Admiral Arleigh A. (buhrk, ahr•lee) commanded a destroyer flotilla known as the Little Beavers against Japan

Burma Road (buhr•muh) -- the only land supply route from the W **Allies** to the Chinese Army, running 700 miles from **Lashio** in Burma to **Kunming** in China, closed by Japanese forces in Burma from 4/42 to 1/45

Busch, FM Ernst von (bush, airnst) a **Hitler** loyalist who served on several fronts with little distinction

Bush, George H. W.-- fighter pilot in the Pacific 1944, age 20. Later 41st US president, 1989-1993

Bush, Vannevar (**vuh•nee′•vahr**) conceived and directed (from 6/41) the Office of Scientific Research and Development (OSRD), which began US development of the atomic bomb

Bushido (**boo′•shee•doh**, boo•**shee**•doh) Japanese warrior code

Butaritari (boo•**tahr•ee•tahr•**ee) chief island in the **Makin** atoll

Bydgoszcz (**bid•gawshch**) small city in NW Poland, site of a massacre of about a thousand German civilians, who allegedly fired on Polish troops, on 9/3/39 ("Bloody Sunday")

Byrnes, James F. (**buhrnz**) US Director of War Mobilization 1942-45, Secretary of State 4/45-1/47

C

Cabanatuan (kah•vah•nah•**twahn′**) city in C **Luzon**, site of a Japanese prison camp where a dramatic rescue of over 500 Americans occurred 1/30/45

Cabcaben (kahb•kah•bin) mountain town near the S end of the **Bataan** peninsula

Cadogan, Sir Alexander (ka•**duhg**•uhn, kuh-) British Under-Secretary of State and close associate of **Churchill** throughout the war

Caen (US **kahn,** Fr **kah(n)**) French city near the **Normandy** beaches, captured by British forces 7/9/44 after heavy German resistance

Caesar Line (see•zuhr) German defensive line 15 miles S of Rome, broken by the US 5th Army 5/30/44

Cairo (ky•roh) largest city and capital of **Egypt**, British HQ for the Middle East

Cairo Conference -- meeting of **Roosevelt, Churchill,** and **Chiang Kai-shek** 11/22-26/43 in preparation for the meeting of the first two with **Stalin** at **Tehran**

Calabria (kuh•**lay**•bree•uh, -**lah**- , -**la**- , kah-) province in the toe of Italy which gives its name to a naval skirmish between British and Italian forces 4/9/40

Calais (US ka•**lay,** Fr **kal**•ay) French port on the **English Channel**, taken by German forces 5/26/40, retaken by Allied forces 9/30/44. Since this area of France is the closest to England, an elaborate hoax persuaded **Hitler** that the main Allied invasion of France would occur there rather than **Normandy**.

Calcutta (kal•**kuht**•uh) 1) port city in NE India 2) **HMS** --
light cruiser sunk 5/31/41 during the evacuation of **Crete**

Callaghan, Rear Admiral Daniel J. -- killed in action off
Savo island near **Guadalcanal** 11/12-13/42 while commanding a
group of 5 cruisers and 10 destroyers

Cambrai (kahm•**bray**) small city in N France, reached by
Rommel 5/18/40, visited by **Hitler** 5/29/40

Cameroons (**kam**•uh•**roonz**′) French colony in WC Africa that
broke with **Vichy** to support **DeGaulle's Free French**
movement

Campoleone (kam•**poh**•lee•**oh**•nee) Italian town 15 miles N of
Anzio, not taken by Allied forces until 6/44

Cam Rahn Bay (**kam**•rahn bay, **kahm**) naval base in **French
Indo-China** (now Vietnam), occupied by the Japanese from 7/41

Canaris, Admiral Wilhelm (kuh•**nahr**•is) Head of German
Military Intelligence (the **Abwehr**) from 1/1/35 to 2/18/44.
Always skeptical of **Hitler**, he was arrested after the **July Bomb
Plot** in 1944 and executed 4/9/45.

Canary Islands (kuh•**nair**•ee) Spanish islands off NW Africa
which remained uninvolved during the war as Spain remained
officially neutral

Canberra (Aus **kan**•buh•ruh, -beh- , US **kan**′•**bair**•uh)
Australian heavy cruiser, named for the country's capital city,
sunk during the initial landings on **Guadalcanal** 8/42

Cannes (US **kan**, Fr **kahn**) coastal city in S France, E
boundary of Allied landings (Operation **Dragoon**) on 8/15/44

Cap (Cape) Bon (cahp **boh(n)**, ca(p)-) NE tip of **Tunisia**, part of the Germans' last refuge in N Africa before their surrender 5/43

Cape Engaño (en•**gahn**•yoh) site of a naval engagement 10/25/44, part of the Battle of **Leyte Gulf**

Cape Esperance (es•puhr•**ahnts′**, -pehr- , **-ents**) on the NW coast of **Guadalcanal**, chief Japanese landing point for troops and supplies, site of a US-Japanese night naval battle 10/11-12/42

Cape Gloucester (**glahs**•tuhr, **glaws-**) W end of **New Britain**, site of an American landing 12/26/43

Cape of Good Hope -- S tip of Africa, the primary supply route for British forces in **Egypt** until the Germans were driven out of N Africa 5/43

Cape Matapan (**mat′**•uh•**pan**) S-most point of Greece, site of a British naval victory over Italy 3/28/41

Cape Passero (pah•**sair**•oh) British landing site on the S tip of **Sicily** 9/10/43

Cape Spartivento (spahr•tih•**ven′**•toh) S-most point of the toe of Italy, site of a naval encounter between British and Italian ships 11/27/40

Cape St. George -- part of New Ireland, site of a US naval victory over Japan 11/25/43

Cape Verde Islands (**vuhrd**) Portuguese colony off the W coast of Africa which remained largely uninvolved during the war as Portugal remained neutral, independent since 1975

Capra, Frank (**kap•**ruh) Hollywood director, producer of the **Why We Fight** series of seven US documentary/propaganda films released during the war

Carentan (US **kar•en•tahn′**, **kair-** , Fr kar•ah(n)•**tah(n)**) key French town near the **Normandy** beachhead, captured by US paratroopers 6/12/44 after five days of fighting

Caribbean Sea (kar•uh•**bee′•**uhn, kuh•**rib•**ee•uhn) a part of the Atlantic Ocean E of Central America

Carlson, Colonel Evans F. -- applied guerrilla methods learned from **Mao Tse-tung** in China to Marine actions in the Pacific with his "**Carlson's Raiders**," including **Makin** atoll and **Guadalcanal**, 8-12/42

Carol II, King of Romania -- see **Michael, King of Romania**

Caroline Islands (**kar′•**uh•**lyn**) large archipelago N of **New Guinea**, controlled by the Japanese throughout the war, though US bombing beginning 2/17/44 neutralized the major base at **Truk**

Carpathians (kahr•**pay•**thee•uhnz) mountain range in E Europe, German stronghold near the end of the war

Carton de Wiart, Lt Gen Adrian (kahr•**toh(n)** du wee•**ahr**) head of the British mission to Poland 7-9/39, commander of the C Norwegian Expeditionary Force 4-5/40, POW in Italy 4/41-8/43, **Churchill**'s personal representative to **Chiang Kai-shek** 10/43-1946

Casablanca (kas•uh•**blang′•**kuh) Atlantic port city in **French Morocco**, Allied landing site for Operation **Torch** 11/42, site of a British-American summit meeting 1/43, title of a famous Hollywood film 1943

Caserta (kuh•**zair**•tuh, -**sair**-) Italian town 15 miles NE of **Naples**, Allied General HQ in Italy 1944-45, site of the surrender of all German troops in Italy 4/29/45

Casey, William J. (**kay**•see) aide to the chief of the **OSS** in London and chief of Secret Intelligence in Europe 1943-45, Director of the CIA 1981-87

Caspian Sea (**kas**•pee•uhn) a salt-water lake in the S Soviet Union, E of the **Caucasus** mountains, the largest inland body of water in the world. Threatened but never reached by the German army.

Cassibile (kuh•**see**•buh•lay, ka-) **Alexander**'s HQ on the SE coast of **Sicily**, where the armistice was signed 9/3/43 between the **Allies** and Italy

Cassino (kuh•**see**•noh, kah- , ka-) a town in Italy, 50 miles NW of **Naples**, at the base of **Monte Cassino** (**mahn**•tay, -tee) and its monastery, anchor of the German **Gustav Defense Line** 12/43-5/44

Castellano, General Giuseppe (kas•tel•**ah**•noh, joo•**zep**•pay, jyoo-) negotiated the Italian surrender 8/43 and signed the armistice document at **Cassibile** 9/3/43

Catania (kuh•**tahn**•yuh) city on the E coast of **Sicily**, occupied by the British 8th Army 8/7/43

Caucasus (**kaw**•kuh•suhs) mountain range in the S Soviet Union between the **Black** and **Caspian** seas, scene of heavy German-Soviet fighting 6-12/42

Cavallero, Marshal Ugo (kah•vahl•**lair'**•oh, **oo**•goh) Italian CiC E Africa 1937-40, successor to **Badoglio** as Chief of General Staff, 11/40-1/43

Cavite (kuh•**vee**•tay, kah- , -tee) port city and US navy yard on **Manila** Bay, largely destroyed by Japanese bombing 12/10/41

Cebu (or **Cebú**) (say•**boo**, seh- , suh-) **Philippine** island and city recaptured 4/45 by US forces after lengthy resistance by about 15,000 Japanese defenders

Celebes (**sel'**•uh•**beez**, suh•**lee**•beez) large island in the **Dutch East Indies**, taken by the Japanese 1-2/42 and held to the end of the war. Now called Sulawesi (**soo**•lah•**way'**•see) and part of Indonesia

Cephalonia (**sef**•uh•**loh'**•nee•uh, -**lohn'**•yuh) W Greek island, site of a mass murder of Italian troops by Germans 9/43

Ceylon (sih•**lahn**, say-) S island of India, attacked by Japanese aircraft carriers 4/42. Now the independent country of Sri Lanka (sree **lahn**•kuh, **lang**-)

Chad (**chad**) French colony in C Africa which broke with **Vichy** to support **DeGaulle**'s **Free French** movement 8/40

Chamberlain, Neville (**chaym**•buhr•lin, -luhn, **nev**•uhl, -il) British PM 5/37-5/40, who followed a policy of appeasement toward **Hitler** and **Mussolini**

Chamorro(s) (chuh•**mawr**•ohz, chah-) language and people of **Guam** and **Saipan**

Changi (**jahng**•ghee, **chang**•ee) peninsula on the NE end of the island of **Singapore** containing an airfield, and barracks which the Japanese converted into a POW camp

Channel Islands -- British islands off the NW coast of France, principally **Guernsey** and **Jersey**, occupied by Germany 7/40-5/45

Chatfield, Alfred Lord -- British Naval CoS 1933-38 and Minister of Defense under **Chamberlain** 2/39-3/40

Chelmno (**khelm•**noh) town in W Poland, site of the first German extermination camp, from early 1942 to 1944

Chennault, Maj Gen Claire L. (shen•**awlt**, shuh•**nawlt**, **klair**) US airman, founder and commander of the **Flying Tigers** in China from 12/41 to 7/42, continued to lead air forces in China until the end of the war

Cherbourg (US **shair•**boorg, Fr shair•**boor**) coastal city in NW France at the tip of the **Cotentin Peninsula**, occupied by Germany 6/40-6/44

Cherwell, Lord (**Frederick A. Lindemann**) (**chahr•**wuhl, -well, **chair-**) Oxford physics professor, scientific advisor to **Churchill**, and influential member of the House of Lords from 1941

Cheshire, Group Captain Leonard (**chesh•**uhr) British bomber pilot whose numerous heroic exploits during the war earned him the **Victoria Cross** (1944) and led to his selection as British representative on the camera plane at **Nagasaki**

Chetniks (**chet•**neekz, niks) Serbian nationalist resistance movement in Yugoslavia, unsuccessful rivals of **Tito**'s communist partisans

Chiang Kai-shek (**chang•**ky•**shek**) leader of Nationalist China from the death of Sun Yat-sen in 1925 until his own death on **Taiwan** in 1975

Chicago, University of -- site of important atomic bomb research, including the first self-sustaining nuclear chain reaction in a converted squash court 12/2/42

Chikuma (chee•koo•muh) Japanese cruiser, damaged by planes from the US carrier **Hornet** in the Battle of the **Santa Cruz Islands** (10/26-27/42), sunk by escort carrier planes off **Samar** 10/25/44 during the Battle of **Leyte Gulf**

Chindits (**chin•**dits) British, Indian, and Burmese forces led by **Orde Wingate** that carried out successful sabotage operations from 2/43 behind Japanese lines in Burma

Chindwin (**chin•dwin**) river in NW Burma

Chinen (**chee•**nen) peninsula on the SE end of **Okinawa**

Chittagong (**chit′•**uh•**gahng, -gawng**) port city in NE India (now SE Bangladesh)

Choiseul (shwah•**zul**) one of the **Solomon Islands**, site of an invasion 10/27-28/43 by a US parachute battalion to divert Japanese attention from the much larger invasion of **Bougainville** 11/1/43

Chokai (choh•ky, chuh-) Japanese cruiser, **Vice-Admiral Mikawa**'s flagship in the Battle of **Savo Island** (8/9/42), sunk by escort carrier planes off **Samar** 10/25/44 during the Battle of **Leyte Gulf**

Choltitz, General Dietrich von (**khohl•**tits, **dee•**trikh) ordered the bombing of **Rotterdam** 5/40, fought at **Sevastopol** and **Normandy**, as German commander of Paris surrendered the city to the **Allies** 8/24/44 after disobeying **Hitler**'s order to destroy it

Chou (or **Zhou**) **En-lai** (**joh en•ly**) second to **Mao Tse-tung** in the Chinese Communist hierarchy, chief negotiator to **Chiang Kai-shek**'s Nationalists, became Premier in 1949

Christian X (US **kris•**chuhn, Dan -tyahn) King of Denmark, who ordered his army to surrender to the invading Germans without resistance 4/9/40

Christmas Island -- Australian territory S of **Java**, S-most area invaded by the Japanese, 3/31/42, abandoned four days later and occupied by the US

Chuikov (or **Chuykov**), **General Vasily I.** (US **choo**•ee•kahf, **vah**•suh•lee, Rus choo(ee)•**kahf**, vah•**see**•lee) commanded the Soviet 8th Guards Army from **Stalingrad** to Berlin

Chungking (**chung•king**) or **Chongqing** (**chawng•ching**) Chinese Nationalist capital and HQ of **Chiang Kai-shek** 1938-45

Churchill, Sir Winston Leonard Spencer (**chuhr**•chil, -chuhl, **chuhrch**•hil) British PM and Minister for Defense 5/40-7/45, won the Nobel Prize for Literature in 1953 upon completion of his six-volume history of the war

Ciano, Count Galeazzo (chee•**ah**•noh, gah•lee•**aht**•zoh) son-in-law of **Mussolini**, Italian Foreign Minister 6/36-2/43, voted to remove Mussolini from office 7/43, executed 1/11/44 in Mussolini's German-backed **Salo Republic**

Cisterna (US sis•**tuhr**•nuh, It chis•**tair**•nuh) town near **Anzio** held by the Germans until 5/25/44

Citadel (Ger **Zitadelle**), **Operation** -- code name for the German offensive against the **Kursk** salient 7/5/43

Clark Field -- US airbase N of **Manila**, attacked by the Japanese 12/8/41

Clark, General Mark Wayne -- **Eisenhower**'s deputy in Operation **Torch**, Commander of the US 5th Army in Italy, later CiC of UN forces in the Korean War, 1952-53

Colditz (**kohl**•dits) town in E Germany, site of a castle used as a maximum-security POW camp

Colleville-sur-Mer (cohl•veel•sur•mair, cuhl-) town near the **Normandy** coast where British troops from **Gold Beach** reached American troops from **Omaha Beach**

Collins, Lt Gen Joseph ("Lightning Joe") L. -- completed the US capture of **Guadalcanal**, assaulted **Utah Beach** as commander of 7th Corps, took **Cherbourg**, helped close the **Falaise Gap**, and drove through Germany, eventually meeting the Soviet Army at the **Elbe** River 4/45

Colmar Pocket (US **kohl'•mahr**, Fr kohl•**mahr**) city and region in NE France where US and French forces took 22,000 German prisoners 2/45

Cologne (kuh•**lohn**) W German industrial city on the **Rhine** river, heavily bombed by the **Allies**, notably in the British "thousand-bomber raid" of 5/30/42

Colombo (kuh•**luhm**•boh) capital of **Ceylon** (now Sri Lanka), its harbor was bombed by the Japanese 4/5/42 sinking four British ships

Combined Chiefs of Staff -- British-American joint command, established in Washington 12/41

Comintern (**kahm'•**in•**tuhrn**) "Communist International" movement, founded by Lenin 1919, dissolved by **Stalin** 5/15/43

Commissar Decree (**kahm**•uh•sahr, -ih-) directive for the invasion of the Soviet Union issued by **Hitler** 3/41, which called specifically for the execution of all commissars (Communist officials) and more generally for unprecedented brutality

Como (**koh**•moh) lake in N Italy

Comoro Islands (**kahm'•**uh•roh, kuh•**mawr**•oh) strategically important group located between N **Madagascar** and E Africa

Compiègne (koh(n)•**pyen**) forest in N France, site of the German surrender in WWI and the French surrender in WWII (6/22/40), both in the same railway car

Conant, James B. (**koh**•nuhnt) chemist and President of Harvard (1933-53). As chairman of the National Defense Resources Committee 1941-46, he played a major role in the development of the atomic bomb.

Condor Legion -- German air group fighting in support of **Franco** in the **Spanish Civil War**, 1936-39

Coningham, Air Vice-Marshal Sir Arthur (**cuhn**•ing•hem) commanded British air forces in tactical support of ground troops in N Africa, S Italy, and **Normandy**

Conolly, Rear Admiral Richard L. (**kahn**•uh•lee) directed amphibious landing operations in **Sicily** and Italy (7-9/43) and the S Pacific (10/43-1/45), notably **Guam** (4-7/44)

Conti, Dr. Leonardo (**kahn**•tee, **lay**•oh•**nahr'**•doh, **lee**•uh-) Chief Medical Officer of the German Reich, helped plan the **Euthanasia Program**, conducted medical experiments in concentration camps, committed suicide awaiting trial at **Nuremberg** 10/6/45

Convoy PQ17 -- Allied convoy to **Murmansk** which lost 22 of 33 ships to German attacks in 7/42, known as "the doomed convoy"

Cooper, Alfred Duff -- political ally of **Churchill**, served in various positions during the war, notably as British ambassador to the **DeGaulle** government 1/44-12/46

Copenhagen (**koh'**•puhn•**hay**•guhn, -**hah**-) capital of Denmark, occupied by German troops 4/9/40 and held until **V-E Day**, 5/8/45

Coral Sea, Battle of the -- occurred the night of 5/7-8/42, NE of Australia. It was the first naval battle fought entirely by air, with US and Japanese ships making no contact.

Cori (kawr•ee) Italian town, part of the German outer defense perimeter around **Anzio**

Corregidor (kuh•**reg'•ih•dawr**) heavily fortified **Philippine** island off the tip of the **Bataan Peninsula** in the entrance to **Manila** Bay, taken by the Japanese 5/6/42, retaken by US forces 2/16-26/45

Corsica (kawr•sih•kuh) large French island 80 miles off the NW Italian coast, evacuated by the Germans 9/43 after the Italian surrender to the **Allies**

Cossack, HMS -- see **Vian**

Cotentin (US coh•**ten**'n, Fr coh•tah(n)•**teh(n)**) French peninsula, W boundary of the **Normandy** landings

Courageous, HMS -- British aircraft carrier sunk off SW Ireland by torpedoes from German submarine U-29, 9/17/39, the first British naval disaster of the war

Courland (kur•luhnd) W part of **Latvia**, jutting into the **Baltic Sea**, held by Germany until the end of the war

Coventry (kuhv•uhn•tree, kahv-) city in C England which suffered a massive fire-bombing attack 11/14-15/40

Crace, Rear Admiral Sir John (crays) British admiral who effectively led a squadron of cruisers in the Battle of the **Coral Sea**

Cracow (or **Krakow**) (US **krak•ow, krah•kow**) city in SW Poland on the **Vistula** river

Crerar, General Henry (kree•rahr, kreer•uhr) Canadian Chief of General Staff 7/40-11/40, commanded the 1st Canadian Army in France and Germany from 7/44 to the end of the war

Crete (**kreet**) E **Mediterranean** island about halfway between Greece and **Egypt**. Taken by the Germans, who began with a costly but successful airborne assault against about 40,000 British, Commonwealth, and Greek defenders on 5/20/41 and controlled the island within ten days

Crimea (kry•mee•uh) Soviet peninsula in the **Black Sea**, invaded by the Germans 10/41, regained by Soviet forces 5/44 (see also **Sevastopol**)

Cripps, Sir Stafford -- served **Churchill**'s coalition government as Ambassador to **Moscow** (1940-42), emissary to the Indian Nationalists (1942), and Minister of Aircraft Production (11/42-1945)

Croatia (kroh•ay•shuh, -shee•uh) part of N Yugoslavia, declared a separate state after its capture by the Germans 4/41, reunited with Yugoslavia after the war, independent since 1991

Croix de guerre ("cross of war") (**krwah•duh•ghair′**) French medal for bravery in combat

Crutchley, Rear Admiral Victor -- Captain of **HMS Warspite** during the Norwegian campaign (5/40), succeeded **Crace** in 5/42 as commander of an Australian cruiser squadron serving with US forces under **MacArthur** in the SW Pacific

Cunningham, Lt Gen Sir Alan G. -- younger brother of **Andrew**, led British forces to victory over the Italians in **Abyssinia** 1940-41, then commanded the 8th Army in **Egypt** and **Libya** from 8/41 until relieved of command 11/41 by **Auchinleck**

Cunningham, Admiral Sir Andrew -- highly regarded CiC of the British **Mediterranean** Fleet 1939-43, succeeded **Pound** as First Sea Lord 10/43-6/46

Cunningham, Admiral Sir John -- CiC of the British **Mediterranean** Fleet 1943-46, First Sea Lord 1946-48

Cunningham, Group Captain John -- RAF pilot whose night-fighting exploits during 1940 earned him the nickname "cat's eyes"

Curtin, John (**kuhrt**'n) Australian Labor Party leader from 1935, PM from 1941 to 1945, when he died in office

Curzon Line (**kuhr**•zuhn) a border between Poland and the Soviet Union proposed at **Versailles** after World War I, implemented with minor modifications after World War II

Cyprus (**sy**•pruhs) British island in the E **Mediterranean**, garrisoned by British forces 5/41, saw no fighting during the war, independent since 1960

Cyrenaica (**sir**•uh•**nay**'•ih•kuh) province of **Libya** bordering **Egypt**

D

Dace, USS -- submarine which sank the Japanese heavy cruiser **Maya** in the **Palawan** Passage 10/23/44 at the start of the Battle of **Leyte Gulf**

Dachau (**dah•**khow, **da-**) the first German concentration camp, 12 miles NW of **Munich**, in operation from 1933 to 1945

Dahlerus, Birger (**dah•**leh•rus, **beer•**guhr) Swedish businessman who acted as an emissary for peace negotiations between Germany and Britain during 1939

Dahlquist, Maj Gen John E. (**dahl•**qwist) led the US 36ᵗʰ Army Division N after the landings in S France 8/44

Dakar (dah•**kahr**, dak•**ahr**) **Vichy**-controlled Atlantic coastal city in **French West Africa** (now Senegal) where the French battleship **Richelieu** was stationed and helped prevent British and **Free French** forces from occupying the port 9/23-25/40

Daladier, Édouard (US duh•**lah'•**dee•ay, dah- , Fr duh•lah•**dyay**, ay•**dwahr**) French Socialist PM 4/38-3/40, signed the **Munich Agreement** 9/28/38, declared war on Germany 9/3/39

Dallas, USS -- destroyer which went up the mouth of the **Sebou** river 11/10/42, neutralized the **Kasbah** fortress, and landed a raiding party which took control of the airfield at **Port Lyautey**

Dalmatia (dal•**may•**shuh) region of Yugoslavia on the **Adriatic Sea**, lined with numerous islands

Daluege, Kurt (dah•**lu•**guh) SS General who succeeded **Heydrich** as Governor of **Bohemia and Moravia**, executed in **Prague** for war crimes 10/24/46

Damascus (duh•**mas**•kuhs) capital of Syria, taken from **Vichy** defenders by British and **Free French** forces 6/21/41

Dannecker, Theodor (**dahn**•eh•kuhr, **tay′**•oh•dohr) **Nazi** official in charge of the deportation of Jews from France and Greece. Committed suicide in a US prison camp 12/10/45

Danube (**dan**•yoob) the major river of E Europe, flowing from SW Germany past Vienna, **Budapest**, and **Belgrade** into the **Black Sea**

Danzig (US **dant**•sig, Ger **dahnt**•sikh) German **Baltic** port city awarded to Poland in 1919, retaken by Germany 9/39, returned to Poland after WWII (now **Gdansk** (guh•**dahntsk, -dantsk**))

Darby, Col William O. (**dahr**•bee) formed the 1st US Ranger Battalion 6/42, then led Ranger units in N Africa, **Sicily**, and Italy, where he was killed in action 4/30/45

Dardanelles (**dahrd′n**•elz) narrow strait in **Turkey** joining the **Aegean** Sea and the Sea of **Marmara**, divides Europe and Asia, formerly Hellespont (**hel′**•uh•**spahnt**)

Darlan, Admiral Jean (dahr•**lah(n)**, **zhah(n)**) CiC French Navy 1939, Minister of the Navy and then Vice-Premier under **Pétain**, supported the Allied landing in **Algiers** 11/8/42, then was recognized as French head of state by the US but not Britain, murdered by a young French anarchist and supporter of **DeGaulle** 12/24/42

Darmstadt (US **dahrm**•stat, Ger -shtaht) city in W Germany where 12,000 people were killed by British firebombing 9/11/44. Its jet airfields were captured by Allied forces 3/25/45, site of a war crimes trial 7/45

Darnand, Joseph (dahr•**nah(n)**, zhoh•**zef**) retired French admiral and right-wing politician, pro-German head of the

French Security Police (the **Milice**) during the **Vichy** regime, executed in France 10/3/45

Darter, USS -- submarine which began the Battle of **Leyte Gulf** on 10/23/44 by sinking one Japanese heavy cruiser (**Kurita**'s flagship **Atago**) and disabling another (**Takao**) in the **Palawan** Passage

Darwin (dahr•win, -wuhn) city and naval base in N Australia, heavily bombed by the Japanese 2/19/42

Davao (dah•vow, dah•vow,) city on the SE coast of **Mindanao** in the **Philippines**, taken by the Japanese 10/20/41, retaken by the US 7/4/45

Davis, Brig Gen Benjamin O. -- highest ranking black officer in the US Army, special adviser to **Eisenhower** for the deployment of black troops in NW Europe 1944-45

Davis, Elmer H. -- US radio journalist, Director of the Office of War Information (OWI) 6/13/42-8/31/45

Dayan, Moshe (dah•yahn, moh•shuh) lost an eye fighting against **Vichy** forces in **Lebanon** and Syria 6/41, later became a military leader in Israel, directing the victorious Six-Day War in 1967

D-Day (or **D-day**) (dee'•day) the start of any Allied military operation (the D stands for day), but it normally refers to the **Normandy** landings 6/6/44

Death's Head Division -- elite German **SS** force, known for exceptional ruthlessness and brutality

Debrecen (deb'•ruh•tsen, -reh-) city in E Hungary

DeGaulle, General Charles (US dih•**gawl**, Fr du•**gohl**, **shahrl**) leader of the **Free French** forces 1940-44, President of France 1958-69

DeGrelle, Leon (duh•**grel**, lay•**oh(n)**) Flemish fascist leader, commander of the **Walloon Legion** of Belgian **SS** volunteers, personally decorated by **Hitler** 8/27/44

DeGuingand, General Sir Francis ("Freddie") (duh•ga(n)•**gah(n)**) British general, **Montgomery**'s CoS from N Africa to the end of the war. In 1947 he published an account titled *Operation Victory*.

Dempsey, General Sir Miles C. -- assumed command of the 13th Corps in **Montgomery**'s 8th Army 12/42 in N Africa and led it into **Sicily** and Italy. Led the 2nd Army from **D-Day** to the German surrender, then became CiC Allied Land Forces in SE Asia until the Japanese surrender.

Demyansk (dem•**yahnsk**) Soviet town S of **Lake Ilmen**, 230 miles NW of **Moscow**. Site of the first major airlift of the war, from 1/42, when the 16th German Army was isolated by a Soviet attack, until 5/42, when they were reached by a German counterattack

Dentz, General Henri (**dahnz**, ah(n)•**ree**) pro-**Vichy** High Commissioner and CiC of Armed Forces in Syria, who fought invading British and **Free French** forces from 6/8/41 until surrendering 7/11/41

Deptford (**dep**•fuhrd) borough in SE London where a **V-2** rocket hit a Woolworth's department store at lunchtime killing 160 people, 11/25/44

De Ruyter (duh•**roy**•tuhr) Dutch light cruiser, the flagship of **Admiral Doorman** in the Battle of the **Java Sea** (2/42), sunk by the Japanese with the admiral aboard

Desna (duh•snah, deh-) river in the W Soviet Union, which joins the **Dnieper** near **Kiev**

DeValera, Eamon (dev•uh•lair'uh, -leer'- , ay•muhn) PM of the Republic of Eire (**air•**uh, **eye•** ruh, **air•**ee, **eye•**ree) (now Ireland) 1937-48. His policy of strict neutrality throughout the war, including a refusal to let Britain use its S bases, angered **Churchill**. President of Ireland 1959-73

Devers, General Jacob L. (dee•vuhrz) US commander of landings in S France 8/15/44, led the 6th Army Group from 9/44 and accepted the surrender of the forces in S Germany 5/5/45

Devonshire, HMS (dev'•uhn•sheer, -shuhr) British cruiser which carried **King Haakon** of Norway to England 6/40 and sunk the German commerce raider **Atlantis** 11/22/41

Dewey, Thomas E. (doo•ee, dyoo-) US Republican candidate for president in 1944 and 1948

Diego Garcia (dyay•goh gahr•see•uh) small island in the **Indian Ocean**, about halfway between **Madagascar** and **Ceylon**

Diego Suarez (dyay•goh swahr•es) port city on the N tip of **Madagascar**, taken from the **Vichy** French by British amphibious landings 5/5/42, now called Antsiranana

Dieppe (US dee•ep, Fr **dyep**) French port on the **English Channel**, site of a disastrous landing attempt 8/19/42 by 6,000 mostly Canadian forces, planned by **Lord Mountbatten**

Dietl, Maj Gen Eduard (deet'l, ay•doo•ahrt) German commander of the 3rd Mountain Division in N Norway 1940, commander of Army Group North in Operation **Barbarossa**, commander of German troops in Lapland 1942-44, died in an airplane crash 6/23/44

Dietrich, Otto (dee•trikh) press chief of the Reich 1933-45, controlled the presentation of war news to the German public, though officially subordinate to **Goebbels**

Dietrich, SS Col Gen Sepp (dee•trikh) led **Hitler**'s personal bodyguard until 1933, played a major role in the "Night of the Long Knives" 1934, organized and led **Waffen SS** units in Poland (1939), France (1940), Greece (1941), and Russia. Led the 6th **Panzer** Army in the Battle of the **Bulge** and received a life prison sentence (reduced to 25 and then 10 years) for the massacre of US prisoners at **Malmédy**.

Dijon (dee•zhoh(n), zhah(n), zhaw(n)) city in C France

Dill, FM Sir John -- Chief of the Imperial General Staff (CIGS) 5/40-12/41, then headed the British Joint Staff Mission in Washington with great success until his death in 11/44

Dimitrov, Georgi M. (dih•mee•trahf, -trawf, gay•awr•ghee) Bulgarian Communist acquitted of charges in the **Reichstag** Fire Trial (1933), appointed General Secretary of the **Comintern** in **Moscow** 1935, Soviet-backed leader of the Bulgarian Communists from 1944, ruler of Bulgaria from 11/46 until his death in 7/49

Dirlewanger, Oskar (duhr•luh•wahn•guhr, ahs•kuhr) led the most savage and undisciplined of SS commando groups, killing partisans and civilians primarily in **Belorussia** and **Warsaw**

Djebel Lessouda (jeb'l les•oo•dah′) key hill in C **Tunisia**

Djedeïda (jed•eh•dah) town and airfield 25 miles W of **Tunis**

Dnepropetrovsk (nep•roh•pih•trawfsk′, nee•proh-) industrial city in the **Ukraine** on the river **Dnieper**

Dnieper (or **Dniepr**, or **Dnepr**) (nee•puhr, **d'nee-**) river in the
W Soviet Union, flowing S past **Smolensk** and **Kiev** into the
Black Sea. An important German defense line in late 1943

Dniester (**nee•**stuhr) or **Dnestr** (d'nes•truh) river flowing SE
through **Ukraine** into the **Black Sea** W of **Odessa**

Dobbie, General Sir William -- British Governor of **Malta**
6/40-5/42

Doctors' Trial -- **Nuremberg** trial of 23 **SS** doctors and
scientists 12/46-8/47

Dodecanese (doh•dek•uh•neez, -nees) an Italian-owned group
of islands off **Turkey** in the **Aegean Sea**, the largest of which is
Rhodes, invaded by British (9/43) and then German (10/43)
forces, now part of Greece

Dohnanyi, Hans von (dahk•nahn•yee) Deputy CoS of the
Abwehr, involved in attempts to assassinate **Hitler**, executed at
Sachsenhausen 4/8/45

Dolomites (doh'•luh•myts, dahl'•uh-) the portion of the Alps
in N Italy

Don (**dahn**) river starting about 150 miles S of **Moscow** and
flowing S about 1,200 miles into the Sea of **Azov** at **Rostov-on-
Don**

Donets (or **Donetz**) (US duh•nets, Rus **-nyets**) river between
the **Dnieper** and the **Don**, which it flows into, about 650 miles
long

Donetsk (US duh•netsk, dah- , Rus **-nyetsk**) a city in the
Donets basin, now in E **Ukraine**

Dönitz (or **Doenitz**), **Admiral Karl** (**du(r)•**nits) head of
Germany's **U-boat** force 1939-43, CiC German Navy from

1/30/43, appointed by **Hitler** to succeed him as **Führer** 4/30/45, sentenced to 10 years imprisonment at **Nuremberg**

Donovan, Maj Gen William J. ("Wild Bill") -- founding Director (1942-45) of the Office of Strategic Services (**OSS**), the US wartime intelligence agency

Doolittle, Lt Gen James H. -- led a famous bombing raid on Tokyo 4/18/42, commanded the 12th and 15th Air Forces in N Africa 1942-43 and the 8th Air Force against Germany and Japan from 1/44

Doorman, Admiral Karel (**dawr•**muhn, **kahr•**uhl) Dutch admiral who led a multi-national Allied (**ABDA**) naval force against the Japanese in the Battle of the **Java Sea**, 2/27-28/42. Doorman went down with his flagship, the light cruiser **De Ruyter**, in the course of an overwhelming defeat.

Dornberger, Maj Gen Walter (**dawrn•**buhr•guhr, **vahl•**tuhr) head of German rocket development 1930-45, based at **Peenemünde** from 1936, responsible for development of the **V-2**, worked in the US after the war

Douglas, Air Marshal Sir William Sholto (**shawl•**toh) succeeded **Dowding** as Chief of RAF Fighter Command 11/40, served under **Tedder** in the Middle East and N Africa 1943, led Coastal Command in the 1944 preparations for **D-Day**

Dover (**doh•**vuhr) closest British city to France, across the Strait of Dover from **Calais**

Dowding, Air Chief Marshal Sir Hugh (**dow•**ding) led RAF Fighter Command from 7/36 through the Battle of **Britain** until 11/25/40

Dragoon, Operation -- see **Anvil**

Dresden (**drez•**duhn) city in E Germany, destroyed by the worst firestorm of the European war following British and American bombing raids 2/13-15/45, with an estimated death toll of at least 60,000

Drina (**dree•**nuh, -nah) river in Yugoslavia

Drohobicz (droh•**hoh•**bich) town S of **Lvov** in SE Poland, site of oilfields, annexed by the Soviet Union 9/39, now Drogobych in W **Ukraine**

Drvar (**duhr•**vahr) town in W Yugoslavia, **Tito**'s HQ 1-5/44

Dubrovnik (du•**brawv•**nik) small coastal city in Yugoslavia, liberated from the Germans by **Tito**'s partisans 10/20/44, now part of **Croatia**

Duilio (doo•**ee•**lee•oh, **dwee-**) Italian battleship, sunk in **Taranto** harbor by British torpedo bombers 11/11/40

Duke of York, HMS -- British battleship which helped sink the German battlecruiser **Scharnhorst** in the Battle of North Cape, N of Norway 12/25-26/43

DUKW ("Duck") -- US amphibious truck in use from 1943

Dulles, Allen W. (**duhl•**is, -uhs) Chief of the US Office of Strategic Services (**OSS**) in Europe from 11/42. Based in **Bern**, Switzerland, he negotiated the surrender of all German troops in Italy with **SS General Karl Wolff** from 2/25 to 4/29/45, effective 5/2/45. Head of the CIA 1953-61, younger brother of John Foster

Dumbarton Oaks (**duhm•**bahrt'n) estate in Washington, site of the first planning session for the formation of the United Nations 8/21/44-10/7/44

Dunkerque (duh(n)•**kuhrk, kairk**) French modern battle cruiser, damaged by British ships at **Mers-el-Kébir** 7/3/40, scuttled at **Toulon** 11/27/42 by the French to keep it from falling into German hands when the Germans occupied all of France following the Allied invasion of N Africa (Operation **Torch**)

Dunkirk (US **duhn**•kirk, Brit duhn•**kirk**) French port on the Strait of **Dover**, site of an evacuation of over 330,000 British and French troops to England 5/26/40-6/3/40

Düsseldorf (or **Due-**) (**dus'•uhl•dawrf**) W German industrial city on the **Rhine** river, heavily bombed by the British, including an early use of two-ton "**blockbusters**" (9/8/42) and the first use of a radar targeting system called **Oboe** (12/31/42)

Dutch East Indies -- large oil-rich group of islands between SE Asia and NW Australia, occupied by the Japanese 1-3/42 and held until 5-8/45. The Dutch regained control 9/45, but were finally driven out by Indonesian nationalists 9/49.

Dutch Harbor -- US base in the E **Aleutian Islands**, bombed by Japanese carrier planes 6/3-4/42 as part of a diversion from the attack on **Midway**

Dutch Volunteer Legion -- about 1,000 Dutchmen who fought with the Germans against **Leningrad** 1941-42

Dvina (**dvee**•nuh) river in N Russia flowing to the **Baltic Sea** at **Riga** (**Latvia**), crossed by German troops 6/26/41

E

Eagle Day -- see **Adlertag**

Eagle, HMS -- British aircraft carrier active in the **Mediterranean**, sunk 8/11/42 by a German submarine while escorting a convoy to **Malta**

Eagle's Nest -- **Hitler**'s mountaintop retreat near **Berchtesgaden**

Eaker, Lt Gen Ira C. (ay•kuhr) US Commander of the 8th Air Force 12/1/42-1/1/44, CiC **Mediterranean** Allied Air Forces (MAAF) from 1/44 to the end of the war, best known for directing daylight precision bombing operations

Eastern Solomons, Battle of the -- naval action 8/23-25/42 in which US forces prevented a Japanese fleet from landing troops at **Guadalcanal**

East Prussia -- region of Germany on the **Baltic Sea**, separated from the rest of Germany by the **Polish Corridor**, divided after the war between Poland and Russia

Eben-Emael (US eb•en eh•mahl) Belgian fort at the junction of the **Albert Canal** and the **Meuse** river, captured 5/11/40 by the Germans with the help of an elite force of 85 glider pilots who landed on the roof 5/10

Eboli (eb•oh•lee) Italian town SE of **Salerno**

Eboué, Félix (ay•boo•ay′, eb•oo- , fay•liks) French Guianan Governor General of **French Equatorial Africa** 1940-44, supported **DeGaulle**'s **Free French**

Ecuador (ek′•wuh•**dawr**) severed diplomatic relations with the **Axis** powers 1/42 and allowed US bases on the Galapagos (guh•**lah**•puh•guhs, -gohs, -**lap**•uh-) islands

Eden, Anthony -- British Foreign Secretary 12/35-2/38, 12/40-7/45, PM 4/55-1/57

Eder Dam (**ay**•duhr) located on the **Weser** river in Germany, breached by "bouncing bombs" from RAF **Lancasters** the night of 5/16-17/43

Edson, Maj Gen Merritt ("Red Mike") A. -- led the 1st US Marine Raider Battalion in actions throughout the Pacific 1942-44, namesake for **Edson's Ridge** on **Guadalcanal**, CoS of the Fleet Marine Force, Pacific, from 8/44

Egypt (**ee**•jipt, -juhpt) became a British protectorate in 1914 and remained largely under British control throughout the war, despite being nominally independent since 1922 (see also **Farouk**)

Eichelberger, Lt Gen Robert L. (eye′•kuhl•**buhr**•guhr) led US and Australian forces to victory over the Japanese on the **Buna-Gona** front in E **New Guinea (Papua)** 12/42-1/43, commanded the US 1st Corps in subsequent New Guinea campaigns 2/43-5/44, then led the 8th Army from 9/44, including the liberation of the **Philippines**

Eichmann, Adolf (US ike•muhn, **ay**•dahlf, Ger -mahn, ad•awlf) **Gestapo** official in charge of the Jewish extermination program, termed the **Final Solution** at the **Wannsee Conference** 1/20/42. Tried and convicted in Israel 4-8/61, executed 5/31/62

Eicke, SS General Theodor (eye•kuh, **tay**′•oh•**dohr**) Chief Inspector (Head) of Concentration Camps 1934-11/39, commander of the first Death's Head Division from 11/39, decorated by **Hitler** in 1942, killed on the E Front 2/26/43

Eindhoven (**ynt'•hoh•**vuhn, -ven) Dutch city liberated by Allied forces 9/44 as part of Operation **Market-Garden**

Einsatzgruppen ("Special Employment Units") (**ine•**zahts**•grup•**puhn) four **SS** groups which followed the German Army into the Soviet Union and from 1941 to 1944 killed about two million Jews, Communists, and other "Anti-German" groups

Einstein, Albert (**ine•**stine) as a Jew, left Germany in 1933 for the US, where he sent a letter 10/39 (written by another physicist, **Leo Szilard**) to President **Roosevelt** explaining the potential of the atomic bomb, which helped launch the **Manhattan Project**

Eisenhower, General Dwight D. (**eye'•**zuhn**•how•**uhr) commanded the Allied campaigns in NW Africa (from 11/42) and **Sicily** (from 7/43), SAC in Europe from 1943, US President 1953-61

Eisenhower, Milton (**eye'•**zuhn**•how•**uhr) brother of Dwight, Director of the War Relocation Agency (WRA), which interned 120,000 West Coast Japanese-Americans following **Pearl Harbor**

El Agheila (**el** uh**•gay'•**luh, ah-) Libyan coastal town S of **Benghazi**, which changed hands several times during the N African campaign

El Alamein (el **al•**uh**•mayn'**, ah•luh-) N Egyptian town 60 miles W of **Alexandria**, site of two decisive battles in 1942. In July, the British 8th Army under **Auchinleck** stopped **Rommel**'s advance; in October-November, the same army, now under **Montgomery**, forced a German retreat that finally ended with the expulsion of all German forces from N Africa 5/43

Elba (el•buh) small island off the NW Italian coast, site of Napoleon's first exile 1814-15, liberated from German control by **Free French** forces 6/17/44

Elbe (Ger el•buh, US **elb**) river flowing NW from the Czech Republic through **Dresden** and into the sea at **Hamburg**. Russian and American troops first linked up on the Elbe about 80 miles S of **Berlin**

Elbrus (or **Elbruz**) (el•**broos**, -**brooz**) mountain in the **Caucasus**, the highest peak in Europe (18,500 feet), reached and climbed by German forces 8/42

El Guettar (el gih•**tahr**) town in C **Tunisia**, held by German forces 12/42-3/43, recaptured by **Darby**'s Rangers 3/18/43

El Hamma (el **hah**•mah) town in **Tunisia**, German defensive position 50 miles behind the **Mareth Line**

Elista (eh•**lees**•tah) Soviet town 200 miles S of **Stalingrad**, near the limit of the German advance toward the **Caspian Sea**, held 8-12/42

Ellice Islands (el•is, -uhs) a group of 9 islands in the SC Pacific totaling about 10 square miles in area and extending about 360 miles in length, SW of the **Gilberts**, a British colony until 1978, now the independent country of Tuvalu (**too′•vuh•loo**, too•**vah**•loo)

Elser, Johann Georg (el•suhr, **yoh**•hahn gay•awrg) a German communist who tried to assassinate **Hitler** in **Munich** 11/8/39, executed at **Dachau** 4/9/45

Embry, Air Vice-Marshal Sir Basil (em•bree, baz•uhl, bay•zuhl) Commander of RAF Bomber Group #2 from 1943, personally led attacks on **Gestapo** HQ in **Aarhus**, **Copenhagen**, and **Odense** in Denmark

Empire Defense Council -- established by **DeGaulle**, on behalf of the **Free French** movement, in the **Brazzaville Declaration**, 10/27/40

Empress Augusta Bay -- on the W coast of **Bougainville** in the **Solomon Islands**, site of a landing by the US 3rd Marine Division 11/1/43, followed on 11/2 by an American naval victory over the Japanese known as the Battle of Empress Augusta Bay

Enfidaville (en•fee•duh•veel, ahn-) Tunisian town about 50 miles S of **Tunis**, the E end of a final German defense line that resisted the British 8th Army in late April 1943 while Allied forces from the W overran **Axis** positions

Engebi (en•geb•ee) island in the **Eniwetok** atoll, taken by US forces 2/18/44

Engel, Captain Gerhard (eng•guhl, gair•hahrt) **Hitler**'s army adjutant, whose diary is an important historical record

English Channel -- a strait that separates SE England and NW France, crossed for the **D-Day** landings

Enigma -- the major German encoding machine throughout the war. Allied success in breaking its codes played an important role in their victory in the N Atlantic.

Eniwetok (or **Enewetak**) (en•uh•wee′•tahk, eh•nee′•wuh•tahk) atoll and island in the **Marshalls**, taken by US forces from the Japanese 2/17-20/44, site of the first hydrogen bomb explosion 1952

Enna (en•uh) crossroads town in C **Sicily**

Enola Gay (en•oh•luh gay) the specially equipped B-29 bomber, named for the mother of its pilot, **Colonel Paul W. Tibbets**, which dropped the atomic bomb on **Hiroshima** 8/6/45

Enterprise, USS -- the most decorated US aircraft carrier, out of port during the bombing of **Pearl Harbor** 12/7/41, accompanied **Hornet** on the **Doolittle Raid** 4/42, in action at **Midway** 6/42, **Guadalcanal** 8/42, and on to **Okinawa** 5/45

Epp, Franz von -- **Nazi** Governor of **Bavaria** 1933-45

Eritrea (air•uh•tree′•uh, ehr•ih- , -tray′-) Italian colony on the S end of the **Red Sea**, conquered by the British 4/41, part of **Ethiopia** 1952-93, independent since then

Espiritu Santo (ez•peer′•ih•too sahn•toh) island in **New Hebrides**, site of a US naval and air base which supported operations in **Guadalcanal**

Essen (es•uhn, es'n) city in the **Ruhr** industrial area of WC Germany, site of **Krupp** armament factories, bombed heavily throughout the war

Essex (es•iks) name ship for a class of US aircraft carriers of which 16 were in service 1943-45

Estéva, Admiral Jean-Pierre (es•tay•vah, zhahn-pee•air) **Vichy** Resident-General of **Tunisia** who allowed the Germans to establish a stronghold there after the Allied **Torch** landings 11/42, sentenced to life imprisonment by a French court 3/15/45, died 1/11/51

Estonia (eh•stoh•nee•uh, -nyuh) small **Baltic** state, annexed by the Soviet Union 8/6/40, regained full independence in 1991

Etajima (et•uh•jee•muh, -ah- , -mah) the Japanese Naval Academy

Ethiopia (ee•thee•oh′•pee•uh) formerly **Abyssinia**, a large country in the E horn of Africa, conquered by Italy 1935-36, liberated by the British 4/41

Etna (or **Aetna**), **Mount** (et•nuh) volcano in E **Sicily** blocking **Montgomery**'s invasion route north to **Messina**

Euthanasia Decree (yoo•thuh•nay'•zhuh) issued by **Hitler** 10/39, began his program of killing the "mentally defective" in Germany

Evacuation Council -- established in **Moscow** immediately after the German invasion of the Soviet Union 6/22/41 to supervise the transporting of armament and industrial factories to regions E of the **Urals**

Evans, Commander Ernest E. -- Captain of the destroyer **USS Johnston**, sunk 10/25/44 attacking **Kurita**'s battleship force during the Battle of **Leyte Gulf**

Exeter (ek•sih•tuhr) 1) city in SW England, bombed 4/23-25/42 2) British cruiser which helped destroy the **Admiral Graf Spee** (12/39) and was sunk during the Battle of the **Java Sea** 2/27/42

F

Faeroe (or Faroe) Islands (fair•oh) a group of 21 islands belonging to Denmark, between **Iceland** and the Shetland Islands, occupied by Britain 4/12/40 following the German takeover of Denmark

Faïd Pass (fy•eed, fah-) key position in C **Tunisia**, starting point for the German **Kasserine** tank offensive

Falaise (fal•ez) town in **Normandy** which gives its name to the **Falaise Pocket**, where about 80,000 German troops were trapped after a misguided offensive ordered by **Hitler**, and the **Falaise Gap**, where about 20,000 of them escaped before it was belatedly closed by Allied forces 8/20/44

Falange, The (US fay•lanj) **Franco**'s Spanish Fascist party, whose name is similar in meaning to "phalanx" (fay•langks) and comes from the same Greek root

Falkenhausen, General Alexander Freiherr von (fahl•ken•how•zen, ahl•ek•sahn′duhr fry•hair) German Military Governor of Belgium and N France 1940-44, imprisoned by **Hitler** 7/44 for leniency and sympathizing with conspirators, but survived the war

Falkenhorst, Col Gen Nikolaus von (fahl′•ken•hawrst) planned and led the German invasion of Denmark and Norway 4/40, CiC German troops in Norway 1940-44

Falkland Islands (fawk•luhnd) British colony in the S Atlantic, garrisoned by 2,000 British troops from 1939 to prevent a possible seizure by **Argentina**

Fanshaw Bay, USS (fan•shaw) escort carrier serving as flagship for the Taffy 3 force during the Battle of **Leyte Gulf** (10/44)

Farouk (or **Faruk**) **I** (fuh•**rook**) King of **Egypt** 1936-52, pro-**Axis** with a pro-**Nazi** cabinet, but bound by treaty to Britain. Declared war on Germany and Japan 2/45 so that Egypt could join the United Nations

Fedala (or **Fedhala**) (fay•dah•**lah**) town and cape NE of **Casablanca**, landing point for the C Group of the W Task Force (US) in Operation **Torch** 11/42

Feodosiya (fee•oh•**doh**•see•yah, -yuh) Ukrainian city on the SE coast of the **Crimea**, site of a large Soviet amphibious landing 12/28-30/41 to relieve German pressure on **Sevastopol**

Fermi, Enrico (**fair**•mee, **fuhr-** , en•**ree**•koh) Italian-born Nobel Prize winner in Physics (1938) working in the US who played a major role in the development of the atomic bomb

Fiji (**fee**•jee) archipelago of over 300 islands in the SW Pacific, a former British colony whose planned invasion by Japan was canceled by the defeat at **Midway**, independent since 1970

Filipino (**fil**•uh•**pee'**•noh) inhabitant of the **Philippines**

Final Solution -- see **Wannsee Conference**

Finland (**fin**•luhnd) invaded by the Soviet Union 11/30/39, surrendered 3/12/40, but inflicted enough damage on the Soviet army to convince **Hitler** that an invasion of the Soviet Union would be successful. The Finns joined Germany in this invasion (6/41) and recovered most of their lost territory, ceded most of it again in an unfavorable armistice with the Soviet Union 9/44, and emerged from the war bruised but still independent.

Finschhafen (**finch**•hah•vuhn) port city in NE **New Guinea**, taken from the Japanese by Australian forces 9-10/43

Fitch, Vice-Admiral Aubrey W. -- Commander of US Task Force 11 in the Battle of the **Coral Sea** 5/42, from late 1942

overall commander of aircraft in the S Pacific, from 1944 Deputy Chief of Naval Operations

Fiume (**fyoo•**may, -meh) Italian **Adriatic** port city on the Yugoslav border, now in **Croatia** and named Rijeka (ree•**yek•**uh)

Flanders (**flan•**duhrz) historical coastal region in W Belgium, including parts of N France and SW Holland

Flensburg (US **flenz•**buhrg, Ger **flens•**boorkh) German town near the Danish border, HQ of Grand Admiral (now **Führer**) **Dönitz** during the last week of the war

Fletcher, Rear Admiral Frank Jack -- US commander of the Battle of the **Coral Sea** (5/42), the first part of the Battle of **Midway** (6/42), and the Battle of the **Eastern Solomons** (8/42)

Florence (**flawr•**uhns, **flahr-**) city in C Italy on the **Arno River**, taken 8/44 by Allied forces, relatively unharmed by the retreating Germans because of its cultural importance

Flossenburg (**flahs'•**en•**burg**) concentration camp in S Germany

Flying Tigers -- group of US volunteer pilots who fought under **Claire Chennault** in China and Burma from 12/41, absorbed into the US 14th Air Force 7/42

Focke-Wulf FW-190 (**foh•**kuh **vuhlf**) considered the best German fighter plane of WWII, used with various modifications from 1941 to 1945

Foggia (**foh•**jyuh, **fawd•**jyah) city in S Italy whose airfields were captured by the **Allies** 9/28/43 and used to bomb targets outside Italy, notably **Ploesti**

Fokker, Anthony (fahk•uhr, foh•kuhr) Dutch aircraft designer and planes that bear his name

Folkestone (fohk•stuhn) English resort on the Strait of **Dover**

Forbes, Admiral Sir Charles M. -- CiC British Home Fleet 1938-1940, CiC Plymouth from 12/40

Ford, Gerald R. -- naval officer aboard the aircraft carrier Monterey in the S Pacific, President of the US 8/74-1/77

Ford Island -- US naval air station in the center of **Pearl Harbor**

Formidable, HMS -- British aircraft carrier which saw action from the Battle of **Cape Matapan** in the **Mediterranean** (3/41) to a **kamikaze** attack in the **Ryukyus** (5/45)

Formosa (now **Taiwan**) (fawr•**moh•**suh) (ty•**wahn**) large island off China, a Japanese possession since 1895, held by the Japanese throughout the war, occupied by **Chiang Kai-shek** and the Nationalist Chinese in 1949 after losing a civil war to **Mao Tse-tung**'s Communists, now the flourishing capitalist Republic of China

Forrestal, James V. -- first US Under-Secretary of the Navy, from 8/40, Secretary from 5/44, and the first Secretary of Defense 9/47-3/49. An unhappy man, he committed suicide two months later.

Forster, Albert (fawr•stuhr, **ahl•**bairt) Appointed German Governor of Greater **Danzig**-W **Prussia** by **Hitler** 10/27/39, with the general directive of removing all Poles and Jews, he was sentenced to death in Danzig (by then **Gdansk**) 4/28/48, and served life imprisonment.

Fort Driant (dree•ah(n)) part of a chain of forts in NE France protecting **Metz** which held out against US forces under **Patton** 9/12/44

Fort-Lamy (fawr lah•mee′) capital of **Chad**, a key stop on the **Takoradi** Allied air supply route accross N Africa. Now called **N'Djamena** (uhn•jah•may•nuh)

Foss, Major Joseph J. -- top-scoring US Marine fighter pilot of the war with at least 26 kills, all Japanese planes at **Guadalcanal**, later Governor of South Dakota

Franco, General Francisco (US **frang**•koh, fran•**sis**•koh, Sp **frahng**•koh, frahn•**sees**•koh, -**thees**-) known as "El Caudillo" (el coh•**dee**•yoh) ("The Leader"), became dictator of Spain (1939-1975) after Germany and Italy helped him win the **Spanish Civil War** (1936-39). Though pro-**Axis**, he kept Spain neutral throughout WWII.

Frank, Anne (**frank, frahnk**) Her diary, written while her family and other Jews were hiding in an attic/warehouse in **Amsterdam** from 7/42 to 8/44, is world famous as a book, play, and film. She died at **Belsen** in 1945 at the age of 15.

Frankfurt (or **Frankfurt-am-Main**) (US **frank**•fuhrt, Ger **frahnk**•furt ahm **myn**) city in W Germany on the Main River

Frank, Hans (**frahnk, hahns**) German Governor of the C area of Poland (the "**General Government**") not annexed by Germany or the Soviet Union, 1939-44. Tried at **Nuremberg** and hanged 10/16/46

Frank, Karl Hermann (**frahnk, kahrl hair**•mahn) a leader of the **Sudeten** German **Nazi** Party who effectively ruled **Bohemia and Moravia** (occupied Czechoslovakia) from 1939 to the end of the war, except for **Heydrich**'s brief tenure as "Protector" 1941-42. Tried and publicly hanged in Prague 5/22/46

Frascati (fruhs•**kaht**•ee) German HQ 20 miles S of Rome, heavily though imprecisely bombed by the **Allies** shortly after the armistice 9/43

Fraser, Admiral Sir Bruce -- CiC British Home Fleet from 5/43, directing the sinking of the **Scharnhorst** 12/26/43, then CiC Eastern Fleet (**Indian Ocean**) from 8/44 and Pacific Fleet from 11/44. Later First Sea Lord and Chief of the Naval Staff (1948-51).

Fredendall, Maj Gen Lloyd (**freed'•n•dawl**) US Commander of the Center Task Force (**Oran**) of the N African landings, replaced by **Patton** after losing the **Kasserine Pass** to the Germans 2/43.

Free French (or **Free France**) -- a movement formed (6/40) and led by **General Charles DeGaulle** which rejected the **Vichy** Government's accommodation with Germany and continued fighting throughout the war

Freeman, Sir Wilfrid R. -- a director of British aircraft production 1938-40, 42-45, Vice-Chief of British Air Staff 1940-42

Freetown (**free**•town) port city in W Africa, capital of **Sierra Leone**, Allied base of the Freetown Escort Force for convoys

Freisler, Roland (**frys**•luhr, **roh**•lahnt) ardent **Nazi** Chief Justice of the People's Court in Berlin 1942-45, killed 2/3/45 in his courthouse during an American bombing raid

Fremantle (**free'•man•**tl) port in SW Australia, one of three US submarine bases for the Pacific during the war

French Equatorial Africa (ek•wuh •**tawr'•**ee•uhl, **ee**•kwuh -) includes **Chad**, Ubangi-Shari (or -Chari) (yoo•**bang**•ghee, oo•**bahng**•ee shahr•ee) (now Central African Republic), the

Middle Congo (now Republic of the Congo), and **Gabon**. All four became independent in 1960.

French Indo-China -- French colony consisting of the present independent countries of Vietnam (vee•et•nahm′), Laos (**lows**), and Cambodia (kam•**boh**•dee•uh, kahm-)

French North Africa -- **Algeria**, **Tunisia**, and S **Morocco**

French West Africa -- Mauritania (mawr•ih•**tay**•nee•uh), French Sudan (soo•**dan**) (now Mali) (**mah**•lee), Niger (**ny**•juhr), Senegal (sen•ih•**gawl**, -**gahl**), French Guinea (now Guinea) (**ghin**•ee), Ivory Coast, Upper Volta (**vahl**•tuh, **vohl**-) (now Burkina Faso) (buhr•**kee**•nuh **fah**•soh), and Dahomey (duh•**hoh**•mee) (now Benin) (beh•**neen**)

Freyberg, General Sir Bernard C. (fry•buhrg, **buhrn**•uhrd) Commander of the 2nd **New Zealand** Division, which fought with distinction from 1940 to 1945 in Greece, **Crete**, N Africa, and Italy

Frick, Wilhelm (frik, vil•helm) **Hitler**'s Minister of the Interior 1933-43, wrote the **Nuremberg** decrees against the Jews 9/35, Reich Protector of **Bohemia-Moravia** 1943-45, tried at **Nuremberg** and executed 10/16/46

Friedeburg, Admiral Hans Georg von (free′•duh•boorg, hahns gay•awrkh) succeeded **Doenitz** as CiC German Navy 5/1-9/45, during which time he signed three surrender documents, then committed suicide 5/23/45

Friedman, Colonel William F. (freed•muhn) Chief cryptanalyst of the US War Department 1921-43, led a team that broke the Japanese code known as Purple 9/25/40

Friedrichshafen (free•driks•hahf•uhn) German city on the Bodensee (**bohd′n•zay**) or Lake of Constance (**kahn**•stuhns), which borders S Germany, N Switzerland, and W Austria, site of steel construction works, bombed by the British 6/20/43 in a raid which also destroyed the **V-2** assembly factory

Friessner, General Johannes (frees•nuhr, yoh•**hahn**•uhs) led hopeless defensive battles against the Soviet Army in the **Baltic States**, Romania, and Hungary, all in 1944

Frisch, Otto, and **Rudolf Peierls** (**frish**, **py**•uhrlz) refugees from **Nazi** Germany working in England, who in 4/40 determined that an atomic bomb could be made with a small enough amount of uranium to be a factor in the war

Frisian Islands (free•zhuhn , **frizh**•uhn) chain along the **North Sea** coast of Holland, Germany, and Denmark

Frisius, Vice-Admiral Friedrich (free•see•us, free•drikh) German commander of the **Dunkirk** fortress, which held out until the end of the war in Europe

Fritsch, General Werner Freiherr von (**frich**, vair•nuhr fry•hair) anti-**Nazi** CiC of the German Armed Forces 5/35-2/38, forced to resign by false charges of homosexuality, killed in action near **Warsaw** 9/22/39

Fritzsche, Hans (frit•chuh, **hahns**) German head of radio propaganda under **Goebbels** from 11/42, broadcasting regularly himself until the end of the war. Acquitted of war crimes at **Nuremberg** 10/1/46

Fromm, General Friedrich (Fritz) (frohm, frahm, free•drikh) German Commander of the Home Replacement Army from 1937 to 7/20/44, executed by the **Gestapo** 3/45 for his tacit support of the **July Bomb Plot**

Fuchida, Commander Mitsuo (foo•**chee**•duh, mit•**soo**•oh) coordinated the Japanese air attack on **Pearl Harbor** and personally led the first wave, argued correctly but unsuccessfully after the second wave for a third wave to destroy fuel tanks and repair facilities

Fuchs, Klaus (fookhs, fyookhs, klows) worked on the atomic bomb project in England and America while serving as a Soviet spy from 1941, tried and imprisoned 1950

Führer (or Fuehrer) (fyur•uhr) German for "leader," **Hitler**'s self-appointed title

Fuji (foo•jee) highest mountain in Japan (12,400 feet), a dormant volcano, and a national emblem

Fukudome, Vice-Admiral Shigeru (foo•koo•doh′may, shih•gair•oo) CoS Japanese Combined Fleet under **Yamamoto** and then **Koga** (until his death 3/44), then CiC 2nd Air Fleet (**Formosa**), then 10th Air Fleet (**Singapore**)

Funk, Walther I. (funk, vahl•tuhr) German Minister of Economics from 2/38, President of the Reichsbank and Director of the War Economy from 1939, sentenced to life imprisonment at **Nuremberg**, released 5/57

Fyfe, Sir David Maxwell (fyf) Chief British Prosecutor at the **Nuremberg Trials**

G

Gabcik, Josef (**gahbt**•shik, **yaw**•sef) one of the Czech assassins of **Reinhard Heydrich**

Gabès (**gah**•bes) 1) coastal town in **Tunisia** behind the **Mareth Line**, captured by Allied forces in late March 1943 2) **Gulf of Gabès** on the E coast of **Tunisia**

Gabon (US ga•**bahn**, Fr ga•**boh(n)**) part of **French Equatorial Africa** on the W coast, independent since 1960

Gafsa (**gahf**•suh, -sah) town in C **Tunisia** on the German invasion route to the **Kasserine Pass**

Galatz (or **Galaţi**) **Gap** (gah•**lahts**, -**laht**•see) named for a Romanian city on the lower **Danube**, site of a Soviet attack on German defensive positions in E Romania, 4-5/44

Gale, Lt Gen Sir Humphrey M. -- **Eisenhower**'s Chief Administrative Officer from the N African landings in 1942 until **V-E Day**

Gale, General Sir Richard -- Commander of the 6th British Airborne Division on **D-Day**, led the parachute force that captured the **Orne** bridges ahead of the main invasion. Later became Chief of the British General Staff

Galen, Clemens von, Archbishop of Münster (**gah**•luhn, **mun**•stuhr) spoke out against the **Nazi** regime from 1933 to 1945, helped end the **Euthanasia Program** in Germany in 1941

Galicia (guh•**liss**•ee•uh, -**lish**•yuh) a region in EC Europe, part of the Austro-Hungarian Empire, in S Poland after WWI, partly in the Soviet Union after WWII

Galland, Lt Gen Adolf (Ger **gahl•**lahnd, **ad•**awlf, US **gal•**luhnd, **ay•**dahlf) a leading German fighter pilot who saw action in Spain, Poland, France, and Britain. Chief of Fighter Operations 11/41-1/45, after which he led a squadron of jet fighters

Gällivare (**gahl•ih•vah•**reh) site of vital iron ore fields in N Sweden which supplied Germany throughout the war

Gambia (**gam•**bee•uh, **gahm-**) British colony in W Africa, independent since 1965

Gambier Bay (**gam•**byeer) American escort carrier, sunk off **Samar** during the Battle of **Leyte Gulf** 10/25/44

Gamelin, General Maurice G. (gahm•**leh(n)**, **la(n)**, gam-) French CiC of Allied Armies in France when the Gemans invaded 5/40, replaced by **Weygand** 5/19/40, confined by the **Vichy** regime until 1943, then imprisoned in Germany until 5/45

Gandhi, M. K. (known as **"Mahatma"** (muh•**haht•**muh, -hat-) – "great soul") (**gahn•**dee, **gan-**) discontinued civil disobedience against British rule in India when WWII broke out, but resumed it 8/42 and was placed under arrest until 5/44. Assassinated 1/30/48, shortly after India became self-governing and Pakistan became a separate Muslim state

Gangi (**ghahn•**jee) mountain town in NC **Sicily**, taken by US forces 7/23/43

Garapan (**gahr•**uh•pan) N end of the Allied landing beaches on SW **Saipan**

"Garbo" (**Juan Pujol Garcia**) -- A Spaniard whom the Germans considered their leading spy in Britain, he was in fact a highly effective British double agent from 4/42.

Garigliano (guh•**reel**•ee•**ah′**•noh, -**ril**-) river in Italy flowing from **Cassino** to the Tyrrhenian Sea, part of the W section of the German **Gustav Line**

Gavin, Maj Gen James M. (**gav**•in, -uhn) US paratroops commander known for his heroism in Allied landings in **Sicily**, **Salerno**, and **Normandy**, succeeded **Ridgway** as commander of the 82nd Airborne Division 8/15/44, at 37 the youngest division commander since the Civil War, and two months later became the youngest Maj Gen in the US Army

Gazala (guh•**zah**•luh, gah-) coastal town and British defense line in **Libya**, site of a British defeat at the hands of **Rommel** 5-6/42

Gdynia (guh•**din**•ee•uh, -**din**•yuh) port city in the **Polish Corridor** near **Danzig**

Geheimschreiber (guh•**hym′**•**shryb**•uhr) German secret teleprinter whose code, comparable to **Enigma** in difficulty and importance, was largely broken by the Anglo-American **Ultra** system

Gehlen, General Reinhard (**gay**•luhn, **ryn**•hahrt) German Intelligence Director for the Eastern Front from 1942 to 1945, worked with the US and West Germany after the war as a Soviet intelligence specialist

Geiger, Maj Gen Roy S. (**gy**•guhr) US Marine Commander of the "Cactus Air Force" on **Guadalcanal**, later led or directed Marine landings on other Pacific islands

Gela (**jay**•lah, -luh) city and gulf on the S coast of **Sicily**, landing point for the US 7th Army 7/10/43

Gelsenkirchen (**ghel**•zuhn•**kir**•khuhn) German city in the **Ruhr**, site of oil installations bombed ineffectively by the British in 1940 and effectively in 1944

Genda, Commander Minoru (ghen•duh, min•oor•oo, mee•**nawr**•oo) Japanese pilot who helped plan the attacks on **Pearl Harbor** and **Midway**, where he led the first wave

General Government -- German controlled administration for the C area of Poland not annexed by Germany or the Soviet Union, established 10/25/39

Genoa (jen•oh•uh) port city in NW Italy, bombarded by the British navy 2/8/41

Gensoul, Admiral Marcel (zhahn•**zool**, -**sool**, mahr•**sel**) French fleet commander at **Mers-el-Kébir** (**Oran**) who made the decision not to accept British terms aimed at keeping the fleet out of German hands 7/3/40

George II, King of Greece -- Forced into exile by the German invasion 4/41, the figurehead king returned following a plebiscite 8/46 supporting the monarchy, died 1947

George VI, King of Great Britain (1936-52) -- official Head of the Commonwealth and Empire throughout the war

Georges, General Alphonse Joseph (**zhawrzh**, ahl•**faw(n)s** zhoh•**zef**) French Commander of the NE Front 9/39-5/40, avoided serving in the **Vichy** government and joined the French Committee of National Liberation (FCNL) in **Algiers** (headed by **DeGaulle** and **Giraud**) 5/43

Georgia (**jawr**•juh) a republic in the SW Soviet Union bordering the E end of the **Black Sea**, beyond the limit of the German advance into the **Caucasus** in 1942

Gerow, Lt Gen Leonard T. (jeh• roh) commanded the US Army 5th Corps from **Normandy** to the **Ardennes**, and from 1/45 the 15th Army

Gestapo (**Geheimestaatspolizei** – Secret State Police) (guh•**stah**•poh) the internal security force of **Nazi** Germany, created in 1933 by **Goering**, who lost control to **Himmler** and **Heydrich** in 1934, increasingly powerful in Germany and German-controlled territory during the war. Known for its routine use of torture, it was declared a criminal organization at the **Nuremberg Trials**.

Ghent (**ghent**) port city in NW Belgium

Ghormley, Vice-Admiral Robert L. (**gawrm**•lee) American Naval Commander, South Pacific, from 4/42, organized the invasion of **Guadalcanal** and **Tulagi** 8/42, replaced by **Halsey** 10/42

Giap, General Vo Nguyen (**jyahp**, **voh noo**•yen, **ngoo**-) military leader of guerrilla forces in Vietnam, fought Japanese rule during the war and French rule after, conquered North Vietnam in 1954 and South Vietnam in 1974

Gibraltar (jih•**brawl**•tuhr, juh-) British seaport and fortress on the S tip of Spain at the narrow W entrance to the **Mediterranean Sea**

Gibson, Wing Commander Guy Penrose -- an outstanding British bomber pilot who won the **Victoria Cross** for leading a raid the night of 5/16-17/43 that destroyed the **Möhne** and **Eder** dams in the **Ruhr**

Gideon Force (**gid**•ee•uhn) a group of about 1,500 guerrilla fighters, primarily Sudanese and Abyssinian, led by **Orde Wingate** against the Italians in **Abyssinia** 1940-41

Gilbert Islands (**ghil**•buhrt) now **Kiribati** (keer•ee•**bah′**•tee, -uh- , keer′•uh•**bas** (sic)) C Pacific archipelago under British mandate, some of whose islands, notably the **Tarawa** and **Makin** atolls, were occupied by the Japanese 12/9-10/41, and retaken by US forces 11/20-25/43

Gillars, Mildred -- see **"Axis Sally"**

Giraud, General Henri (zhee•**roh**, zhih- , ah(n)•**ree**) captured 5/19/40 during the German invasion of France, escaped 4/42, and in 12/42, with US support, became head of French forces in **Morocco** and **Algeria** until pressured into retirement by **DeGaulle** 4/8/44

Gironde (US juh•**rahnd**, Fr zhee•**rohnd**) river and estuary in SW France, site of a British Commando raid 12/42 in which eight ships were damaged or destroyed by limpet mines

Glasgow (**glas**•goh, **glaz**- , -koh) port city in SW Scotland

Gleiwitz (**gly**•vits) now **Gliwice** in SW Poland (glee•**vee**•tsuh), city in S Germany near the Polish border where the **Gestapo** faked a Polish assault on a radio station the evening of 8/31/39 to help justify the German invasion of Poland 9/1/39

Globocnik, SS Maj Gen Odilo (glah•**bahch**•nik, oh•**dee**•loh) a Croatian born in **Trieste**, **SS** Head of the **Lublin** District in E Poland and director of all extermination camps in Poland from 1941 to 11/43, committed suicide after capture by Allied forces in 5/45.

Glorious, HMS -- British aircraft carrier, sunk by the **Gneisenau** and **Scharnhorst** during the evacuation from **Narvik** 6/8/40

Gloucester (**glahs**•tuhr, **glaws**-) port city on the Severn (**sev**•uhrn) River in SW England, site of an aircraft factory

Gluecks, SS General Richard (**gluks**, **rikh**•ahrt) overall director of the German concentration camp system 1940-45

Gneisenau (**ny**•zen•ow) German battlecruiser, participated in the invasion of Norway (5/40) and the sinking of the British carrier **Glorious** (6/40), left the **North Sea** 1/41 with her sister ship **Scharnhorst**, and together they sank numerous merchant ships in the N Atlantic, damaged by mines in the "Channel Dash" of 2/11/42

Godfrey, Vice-Admiral John H. (**gahd•**free) Director of the British Naval Intelligence Department (NID) 2/39-11/42, Commander of the Royal Indian Navy (RIN) 3/43-3/46

Godfroy, Vice-Admiral René Emile (gohd•**frwah**) Commander of a French cruiser division which he allowed to be demobilized in **Alexandria** harbor by the British following the French surrender to Germany 6/40

Goebbels, Dr. Joseph (**gur•**buhlz, **gair-**) **Nazi** Minister of Propaganda 1933-45, committed suicide in the Fuehrerbunker with his family the day after **Hitler**

Goerdelier (or **Gör-**), **Carl F**. (**gur•duh•luhr**) Mayor of **Leipzig** 1930-37, the leading non-military opponent of **Hitler** from 1933, hanged 2/2/45 for his involvement in the **July Bomb Plot** of 6/44

Goering (or **Göring**), **Hermann W**. (**gur•**ing, **gair•**ing, **hair•**mahn) Reichsmarschall of Germany 1939-45, second in command to **Hitler** and his designated successor. As head of the Air Force (**Luftwaffe**), he made a series of damaging overestimates of its capability, including **Dunkirk**, the Battle of **Britain**, and **Stalingrad**. Sentenced to death at **Nuremberg**, he committed suicide 10/15/46 with a cyanide capsule two hours before his scheduled execution.

Goeth, Amnon (**gurth**, **ahm•**nohn, US **am•**nahn) Commandant of the concentration camp at Plaszow in Poland, portrayed in the book and movie *Schindler's List*

Gold -- one of the five landing beaches in the **Normandy** Invasion, taken by British forces

Golikov, Col Gen Filip I. (gah•lee•kahv, -lih-) Head of Soviet Military Intelligence 7/40 to 6/41, the first Soviet envoy to England and America after the German invasion 7-9/41, commanded armies at **Moscow**, the **Bryansk** Front, **Stalingrad**, and the **Voronezh** Front 1941-43, Deputy People's Commissar of Defense 1943-50

Golovanov, Air Chief Marshal Alexander (gah•luh•vah•nuhv) Commander of the Soviet Long Range (bomber) Air Force from 4/42

Gona (goh•nah) town near **Buna** on the N Coast of E **New Guinea** (**Papua**), site of a Japanese landing 7/42, under Allied control by 1/43 after heavy fighting

Gondar (or **Gonder**) (**gahn**•dahr, -duhr) town in the mountains of NW **Ethiopia**, the last Italian stronghold, surrendered to the British by General Nasi 11/28/41

Gonzaga (guhn•**zahg**•uh) N coastal town on **Luzon** in the **Philippines**, site of a Japanese landing 12/41, held until the end of the war

Gorshkov, Vice-Admiral Sergei G. (gawrsh•kohv, **sair**•gay) Soviet Naval Commander of the Sea of **Azov** and **Danube** River 1941-12/44, later CiC of the Soviet Navy (1955-85)

Gort, FM Lord John -- CiC of the **British Expeditionary Force** (**BEF**) in France, directed the evacuation at **Dunkirk**. Governor and CiC of **Gibraltar** (1941-42) and **Malta** (1942-7/44)

Gothenburg (Sw **Göteborg**) (**gahth′**•uhn•**buhrg, gaht′n-**) port city in SW Sweden

Gothic Line -- the major and final German defensive position across N Italy, running N of **Florence** from Massa on the W coast to a point S of Rimini on the E coast, assaulted by Allied forces 8/44 and breached 9/44

Goumiers (US **goo•mee•ayz**, Fr goo•**myayz**) Moroccan infantrymen organized into French-led units called Goums (**goomz**), fought in Italy and France

Goutsmidt, Samuel A. (**gut**•smidt) Dutch theoretical physicist and scientific head of the **Alsos** project

Govorov, Marshal Leonid A. (**gah**•vuh•ruhv, **lay**•uh•nid, **lee-**) Soviet Commander of the **Leningrad** Front from 6/42 to 7/45

Graf Spee -- see **Admiral Graf Spee**

Grand Dorsal, the (**dawr**•suhl) a 200-mile long mountain range (E and W) in **Tunisia**, broken at one point by the **Kassarine Pass**

Granville (grahn•**veel**) French coastal town on the W side of the **Cotentin Peninsula**, successfully raided 3/9/45 by German troops occupying the **Channel Islands**

Graz (**grahts**) city in SE Austria, site of a German airfield bombed by the **Allies** during **Big Week** (2/44)

Graziani, Marshal Rodolfo (**grahts**•ee•**ahn'**•ee, roh•**dawl**•foh) led Italian forces in subjugating **Libya** and **Abyssina** in the mid-1930s, CiC Italian forces in N Africa from summer 1940 to 3/41 when, after a series of defeats by the British, he was recalled and resigned his command

Greater East Asia Co-Prosperity Sphere -- Japanese propaganda term to disguise the nature of their conquests

Great Marianas Turkey Shoot (**mair**•ee•**an'**•uhz, **mar-**) aircraft carrier battle in the **Philippine Sea** 6/19/44 in which the

Japanese lost over 300 planes while inflicting little damage on US planes or ships

Grechko, Col Gen Andrey A. (grech•**koh**, uhn•**dray**(ee)) Soviet commander of the 1ˢᵗ Guards Army from 12/43 to the end of the war, liberated **Kiev** and **Lvov**, then helped liberate Czechoslovakia

Greenglass, David -- technician at **Los Alamos**, New Mexico, who began passing atomic bomb secrets to the Soviets 9/44, imprisoned 1950-60

Greenland (**green**•luhnd, -land) Danish colony in the N Atlantic, the world's largest island, became a US protectorate 4/9/41 by agreement with the Danish government-in-exile for the duration of the war

Greim, Robert Ritter von (**grym**) appointed head of the German Air Force and FM by **Hitler** 4/45 after he dismissed **Goering**. Committed suicide 5/24/45 in a US prison at **Salzburg**

Greiser, Artur (or **Arthur**) (**gry**•zuhr, **ahr**•tur) appointed German Governor of the Poznan-Wartheland district of Poland 10/39, hanged in **Poznan** 6/20/46

Grew, Joseph C. -- US Ambassador to Japan 1932-41, Under-Secretary of State 1944-45

Grini (**gree**•nee) German concentration camp near **Oslo**

Griswold, Maj Gen Oscar W. (**griz**•wawld) Commander of the US 14ᵗʰ Corps, which liberated **Manila** from the Japanese 1-2/45

Grodno (**grahd**•noh, **grawd**- , -nuh) city in E Poland, now Hrodna (**hrawd**•nuh) in W Belarus

Gromyko, Andrei A. (gruh•**mee**•koh, groh- , US **ahn**•dray, Rus uhn•**dray**(ee)) Soviet Ambassador to the US 1943-46 and the United Nations 1946-48, became Soviet Foreign Minister in 1957 and held other high level positions until 1988

Gross-Rosen (grohs roh•zen) concentration camp in E Germany

Groves, Maj Gen Leslie R. -- Director of the **Manhattan Project** 9/42-1945

Grozny (grahz•nee, **grawz-**) city and oil center in the **Caucasus**, less than 50 miles beyond the farthest German advance, now the capital of Chechnya (**chech**•nee•uh) in SW Russia

Gruenther, General Alfred M. (grun•thuhr) succeeded **Eisenhower** as CoS 3rd Army in 1941, CoS for **Mark Clark** 1943-45, SAC in Europe 1953-56

Grynszpan, Herschel (grin′•shpan, huhr•shuhl) a 17-year-old German Jew whose assassination of a member of the German embassy staff in Paris to protest the 1938 expulsion of 10,000 Polish-German Jews to Poland provided the immediate excuse for the **Nazis** to launch **Kristallnacht** in Germany

Guadalcanal (gwahd′l•kuh•**nal′)** the largest of the **Solomon Islands**, site of heavy land, naval, and air fighting between the US and Japan from 8/42 until the final withdrawal of the Japanese 2/43

Guam (gwahm) S-most of the **Mariana Islands**, captured by the Japanese 12/8-10/41, retaken by the US 7-8/44

Gubbins, General Sir Colin McVean -- Director of Operations for the British **SOE** from 11/40, executive head from 9/43

Guderian, General Heinz W. (gu•**dair**•ee•uhn, guh-) a leading exponent of tank warfare, led German **Panzer** divisions in the invasions of Poland, France, and the Soviet Union, served as Chief of the General Staff 7/21/44-3/28/45

Guérisse, Albert-Marie (alias Pat O'Leary) (gair•**ees**, ahl•**bair**-mah•**ree**) a Belgian doctor who worked as a British agent in France operating an escape route into Spain known as the "Pat Line," captured but liberated from **Dachau** near the end of the war

Guernica (**gwair**•nih•kuh, **gair**-) Basque town in N Spain, whose destruction by German bombing in 4/37 during the **Spanish Civil War** inspired Picasso's greatest painting

Guernsey (**guhrn**•zee) second largest of the **Channel Islands,** 25 square miles, population 55,000

Gulag (an acronym in Russian) (**goo**•lahg, -lag) USSR prison system of forced labor camps, 1918-1953, primarily associated with **Stalin**

Günther, Hans F. K. (**gun**•tuhr, **hahns**) German professor and author whose racial theories became the chief support for **Nazi** racial policy and practice

Gurkhas (**guhr**•kuhz, **gur**-) Nepalese soldiers with a long tradition of ferocity in war, fought with the British in N Africa, Italy, and Burma

Gustav Line (**gus**•tahf) German defensive line S of **Rome** running across Italy through **Cassino**, broken by the **Allies** 5/44 after long resistance

H

Haakon VII, King of Norway (**haw**•kun, **hah-**) ruler of Norway since its independence in 1905, led the Norwegian resistance from his government-in-exile in London and returned to his country 6/45 to rule until his death in 1957

Habbaniya (huhb•buh•**nee**•yuh, hahb-) British air base in **Iraq** 50 miles W of **Baghdad**, attacked but not taken by **Rashid Ali** 5/2-5/41

Hácha, Emil (**hah**•**khah**, -kuh, **em**•il) elected President of Czechoslovakia 11/38, controlled by Germany from its occupation of **Bohemia-Moravia** 3/39 until the end of the war, died in prison 6/45 awaiting trial as a collaborator

Hague, The (**hayg**) capital city of Holland, site of German **V-2** launchings 11/44-3/45, now the home of the International Court of Justice

Haile Selassie (**hy**•lee suh•**las**•ee, -**lah**•see) Emperor of **Abyssinia/Ethiopia** 1930-1974, driven into exile by the Italian conquest for exactly five years, 5/5/36-5/5/41

Hainan (**hy**•**nahn**) large Chinese island off **French Indo-China** (now N Vietnam), S-most province of China

Haiphong (**hy**•**fahng**) port city in **French Indo-China** (now N Vietnam)

Halder, General Franz (**hahl**•duhr, **frahns**) German Chief of General Staff from 9/1/38 until 9/24/42, when **Hitler** dismissed him and he retired from the military. Imprisoned after the **July Bomb Plot** (6/44), he survived and lived until 1972, publishing an important war diary.

Halfaya Pass (**hahl**•fy•uh, **hal-**) (aka "hellfire") key position in NW **Egypt** near the **Libya**n border

Halifax (**hal'**•uh•**faks**) capital of **Nova Scotia**, an important port city for N Atlantic convoys

Halifax, Lord (**hal'**•uh•**faks**) (Edward Wood) British Foreign Secretary 2/38-12/40, Ambassador to the US 1/41-5/46

Halmahera (**hal**•muh•**heh'**•ruh, **hahl**•mah•**heh'**•rah) the largest of the Molucca Islands, bypassed by **MacArthur**'s army in favor of **Morotai**, leaving its 25,000 Japanese defenders stranded

Halsey, Admiral William F. ("**Bull**") (**hawl**•zee) US Carrier Commander 3rd Fleet, in the S Pacific Area from 10/42 to 6/44, then took the fleet N to the **Philippines**, **Okinawa**, and Japan

Hamar (**hah**•mahr) Norwegian town 60 miles N of **Oslo**, temporary capital of Norway following the German invasion 4/41

Hamburg (US **ham**•buhrg, Ger **hahm**•burg, -burk) major German port city bombed heavily during the war, including a firestorm the nights of 7/24-27/43 that killed over 40,000 people and caused an exodus of over a million survivors

Hammamet (**ham**•muh•met) town and gulf in N **Tunisia**

Hanford (**han**•fuhrd) a plant on the Columbia River in SE Washington State, produced **plutonium** which was used in the "Fat Man" bomb dropped on **Nagasaki**

Hanko (**hahng**•koh) naval base, town, and peninsula on the S tip of **Finland**, leased to the Soviet Union for 30 years following the Soviet victory in the **Russo-Finnish War**, 3/40, evacuated by the Soviets 12/41

Hankow (or **Hankou**) (US **hang•kow**, Chin **hahng•koh**) seat of the Chinese Nationalist government from 12/37 to 10/38, when it fell to the Japanese

Hanoi (ha•**noy**) capital of **French Indo-China** from 1887, N Vietnam from 1954, and Vietnam from 1975

Hanza (**hahn•**zah) town in **Okinawa**

Harbin (**hahr•bin**) city in **Manchuria**, chief objective of the Soviet invasion of 8/45, surrendered by the Japanese 8/20/45

Harding, General John H. -- British CoS of **Alexander**'s 15th Army Group in Italy from 1/44, commanded the 13th Corps from 12/44

Harmon, Maj Gen Ernest N. (**hahr•**muhn) US tank commander who fought in NW Africa, Italy, N France, and Germany

Harmon, Lt Gen Millard F. (**hahr•**muhn, **mil•**uhrd) commanded US land and air forces in the Pacific 1942-44, became commander of all US Pacific Air Forces 8/44, died in a plane crash 2/45

Harriman, W. Averell (har•uh•muhn, **ay•**vuh•ruhl) **Roosevelt**'s emissary to **Stalin** after the German invasion, US Ambassador to the Soviet Union 10/43-2/46

Harris, Air Chief Marshal Sir Arthur (**"Bomber"**) -- British Head of Bomber Command from 2/42, controversial advocate of massive civilian bombing, as in **Cologne**, **Hamburg**, and **Dresden**

Hartmann, Major Erich (**hahrt'•mahn**, ay•rikh) German Me-109 fighter pilot credited with 352 kills on the E Front 1942-45, the highest total of the war, imprisoned in the Soviet Union until

1955, then served in the West German Air Force until he retired in 1968

Haruna (hahr•oo•nuh) Japanese battleship attacked but undamaged at **Midway**, in action throughout the rest of the war, including **Guadalcanal** and **Leyte**, the last remaining Japanese battleship when it was sunk by US planes in 8/45

Harwood, Admiral Sir Henry H. -- Commander of the British South Atlantic Squadron, which defeated the **Admiral Graf Spee**, succeeded **Cunningham** as CiC Mediterranean Fleet 5/31/42, resigned for health reasons early in 1943

Harz Mountains (**hahrts**) German stronghold about 100 miles WSW of Berlin, encircled by US forces 4/45

Hassell, Baron Ulrich von (**hah•**suhl, **ul•**rikh) German diplomat opposed to **Hitler** who tried to initiate peace talks with Britain 2/41, then supported attempts to assassinate the **Fuehrer**. Hanged at **Plotzensee** prison 9/8/44 as a consequence of the **July Bomb Plot**

Hatab River (ha•**tahb**) stream in **Tunisia** running through the **Kassarine Pass**

Haushofer, Karl (**hows'•**hoh•fuhr) founder of the Institute for Geopolitics at the University of Munich. His ideas influenced **Nazi** ideology through a student, **Rudolf Hess**, though he himself was increasingly skeptical of Nazism. His son Albrecht was a noted German resistance figure, whose execution 4/23/45 contributed to his suicide 3/13/46

Heilbronn (**hyl•**brahn, -brawn) city in SW Germany, fire-bombed 12/4/44

Heinrici, Col Gen Gotthard (hyn•ree•kee) German specialist in defensive battles, which he led effectively on the E Front 1943-45, imprisoned after the war by the Russians until 1955

Heisenberg, Werner (US **hy'•**zuhn•**buhrg**, **wuhr•**nuhr, Ger **hy'•**zen•**bairk**, **vair•**nuhr) won the Nobel Prize for Physics 1932, director of the German atomic bomb program

Helena, USS (**hel•**uh•nuh) light cruiser damaged at **Pearl Harbor**, fought in the **Solomons** until she was sunk at **Kula Gulf** 7/6/43

Helgoland (**hel'•**goh•**land**, -**lahnt**) German island in the **North Sea**

Helldorf, Count Wolf Heinrich, Graf von (**hel•**dawrf, **vuhlf hyn•**rikh, **grahf** vahn) Chief of Police in Berlin from 1935 who turned against **Hitler**, hanged in Berlin 8/15/44 for his part in the **July Bomb Plot**

Helsinki (**hel•sing•**kee, **hel•**sing•kee) major port city and capital of **Finland**

Hendaye (ahn•**dy**) French town near the Spanish border on the Bay of **Biscay**, site of a lengthy but unproductive meeting between **Hitler** and **Franco** 10/23/40

Henderson Field (**hen•**duhr•suhn) airfield on **Guadalcanal** begun by the Japanese and completed by the Americans, focal point of the Guadalcanal campaign

Hengyang (US **heng•yang**, Chin **hung•yahng**) city in SE China, fell to the Japanese 7/44

Henlein, Konrad (**hen•**lyn) head of the German **Sudeten** Party in Czechoslovakia from 1935, figurehead Governor of **Bohemia-Moravia** from 5/1/39 to 5/10/45, when he committed suicide to avoid trial for war crimes

Hennecke, Admiral (**hehn•**nuh•kuh) German naval commander at **Cherbourg**, who ordered the destruction of all port facilities 6/26/44

Henrici, Siegfried (**hen•ree•kee, sig•**freed, **seeg-**) German Army commander, active on both the E and W Fronts throughout the war

Heraklion (or **Iráklion**) (ih•**rak•**lee•uhn, **-rahk-** , **-awn**) port city and airfield on the N coast of **Crete**, held by British-led Allied forces during the German invasion of 5/41 and used as an evacuation point

Hermes, HMS (**huhr•**meez) world's first purpose-built aircraft carrier, completed 1922 for the British navy, bombed and sunk by the Japanese at **Trincomalee** 4/9/42

Hersey, John (**huhr•**see) WWII journalist and writer, won the Pulitzer Prize in 1945 for his novel *A Bell for Adano* (1944), set in the Italian campaign. He also published the first account of **PT-109** (1944) and the first book-length study of **Hiroshima** (1946).

Hershey, Maj Gen Lewis B. (**huhr•**shee) US Director of **Selective Service** (the Draft) from 7/31/41 until 1969

Hess, Rudolf -- A friend of **Hitler** from the 1920s, when he helped him write *Mein Kampf* in prison, and Hitler's chief deputy until 9/1/39, he flew alone to Scotland 5/10/41 on an unauthorized peace mission. He was placed under arrest in England, tried at **Nuremberg**, and sentenced to life imprisonment in **Spandau Prison**, Berlin, where he committed suicide in 1987 at the age of 93.

Heusinger, Lt Gen Adolf (**hoy•**zing•guhr, **ad•**awlf) Chief of Operations of the German Army High Command (OKH) 10/1/40-6/30/44

Hewitt, Admiral H. Kent (**hyoo•**uht, -it) commanded the landings at **Casablanca** 11/42 and, as head of the US 8th Fleet, in **Sicily** 7/43, Italy 9/43, and S France 8/44

Heyde, Professor Werner (hy•duh, **vair**•nuhr) directed the
German **Euthanasia Program** from 9/39 and helped develop
gassing methods for mass executions

Heydrich, SS General Reinhard (hy•drikh, **ryn**•hahrt)
Himmler's deputy in the **SS**, drafted the **Final Solution**
endorsed at the **Wannsee Conference** 1/20/42, appointed
Governor of **Bohemia-Moravia,** assassinated in **Prague** 5/29/42
(died 6/4)

Hickam Field (**hik**•uhm) the major US airbase on **Oahu**, badly
damaged during the attack on **Pearl Harbor**

Hiei (**hee**•ay) Japanese battleship, sunk 11/13/42 by American
planes at **Guadalcanal**, the first enemy battleship in the war
sunk by US forces

Higashikuni, General Naruhiko (hih•**gah**•shuh•**koo′**•nee,
nahr•oo•**hee′**•koh) an uncle of Emperor **Hirohito**, in charge of
the Home Front Defense Command, helped remove **Tojo** from
office 7/44, became transitional PM for 50 days following
Japan's surrender

Higgins Boat -- the most versatile US amphibious landing craft
of the war, named after its designer and manufacturer, officially
designated LCVP (Landing Craft, Vehicle, Personnel)

Himmler, Heinrich (**him**•luhr, **hyn**•rikh) the most powerful
man in Germany after **Hitler** himself, head of the **SS** (from
1929), administrator of the **Holocaust**, Minister of the Interior
from 8/25/43, committed suicide when captured on 5/23/45

Hipper -- see **Admiral Hipper**

Hiranuma, Baron Kiichiro (**heer**•uh•**noo′**•muh,
kee•ee•**cheer′**•oh) President of the Privy Council from 1936,
PM of Japan 1/4/39-8/28/39, head of the Imperial Rule

Assistance Association (an organization promoting business interests) 1940-45, sentenced to life imprisonment in 1948

Hirohito, Emperor of Japan (**heer•oh•hee′•toh**) succeeded his father as Emperor 1926, played a largely passive role in the rise of Japanese militarism, forced the Japanese surrender after the atomic bombs, renounced his divinity to remain as a figurehead monarch after the war until his death in 1989

Hiroshima (**heer•oh•shee′•muh**, hih•roh•shuh•muh) Japanese industrial and port city in SW **Honshu**, target of the first atomic bomb 8/6/45

Hirota, Koki (heer•oh•tuh, **koh•**kee) Japanese Foreign Minister 1933-36 and again under **Konoye** from 6/37 to 1/39, PM from 3/36 to 6/37, hanged for war crimes 12/23/48

Hiryu (**heer•**yoo) Japanese aircraft carrier, part of the **Pearl Harbor** attack force, sunk during the Battle of **Midway** 6/42

Hitler, Adolf (**hit•**luhr, US **ay•**dahlf, Ger **ad•**awlf) leader (**Fuehrer**) of Germany 1933-45

Hiyo (**hee•**oh) Japanese aircraft carrier, sunk during the Battle of the **Philippine Sea** 6/20/44

Hobart, General Sir Percy C. S. -- divisional tank commander from 1938, developed special tanks for use by the British in the invasion of **Normandy**

Hobby, Colonel Oveta Culp -- first director of the Women's Army Corps (WAC), which reached a total strength of 100,000 by the end of the war, 7/1/43-7/12/45, became the first Secretary of HEW in 1953

Ho Chi Minh ("He who enlightens," adopted name of Nguyen Van Trahn) (**hoh chee min**) led Vietnamese resistance against the Japanese occupation and French reoccupation, ruler of North Vietnam 1954-69

Hodges, General Courtney H. -- commanded the US 1st Army under **Bradley** in **Normandy** and led it into Germany

Hoel, USS **(hool)** destroyer sunk off **Samar** in the Battle of **Leyte Gulf** 10/44

Hoepner, Col Gen Erich (US **hep**•nuhr, **air**•ik, Ger **hurp-** , **ay**•rikh) led the 4th **Panzer** Group into the Soviet Union 6-12/41, dismissed for his failure to take **Moscow** after getting within sight of it, hanged 8/8/44 for his part in the **July Bomb Plot**

Hoess, Rudolf (US **hes**, Ger **hurs**) Commandant of **Auschwitz** from 6/40, supervised its transformation into an extermination camp using **Zyklon B** cyanide gas instead of carbon monoxide. Arraigned at **Nuremberg**, tried by a Polish court, and hanged at Auschwitz 4/7/47

Hofacker, Colonel Caesar (or **Cäsar**) **von** (**hoh′•fah•**kuhr, **tsez•**ahr) one of the leaders of the **July Bomb Plot**, executed 12/20/44

Hokkaido (hah•**ky•**doh, hoh-) N-most of the four main Japanese islands

Hollandia (hah•**lan•**dee•uh, hoh-) port city on the N coast of Dutch New Guinea (now **Jayapura** (**jah•**yuh•**poor′•**uh) in Indonesia), administrative and supply base for the Japanese 18th Army, captured by US forces 4/44

Hollard, Michel (oh•**yahr(d)**, mee•**shel**) a Frenchman working as a British agent who provided much valuable information about German **V-1** sites before his arrest by the **Gestapo** 2/44

Holocaust (**hahl′•uh•kawst**) a term applied primarily to the **Nazi "Final Solution"** of the "Jewish Problem," the systematic murder of some six million Jews during the war. Sometimes extended to include an additional ten million non-combat victims, mostly Polish and Soviet civilians and POWs

Homma, General Masaharu (**hahm•uh, hoh•mah, mah•suh•hah•roo**) led the Japanese invasion of **Luzon** 12/41, replaced for incompetence 6/9/42 for allowing US and **Filipino** troops to withdraw into the **Bataan Peninsula**, executed on **Luzon** 4/3/46 for war crimes committed during the **Bataan Death March**. The justice of both the firing and the execution is questioned by some historians.

Honda, Lt Gen Masaki (**hahn•duh, mah•sah•kee**) Commander of the Japanese 33rd Army in **Burma**, led effective fighting retreats during 1944-45

Hong Kong (**hahng•kahng**) British colony on the SE coast of China, captured by the Japanese 12/41 and held until the end of the war

Honolulu (**hahn•uh•loo′loo**) capital and major city of Hawaii, on S **Oahu** E of **Pearl Harbor**

Honshu (**hahn•shoo**) largest of the four Japanese home islands

Hood, HMS -- British battlecruiser, launched 1920, sunk by the **Bismarck** in the Denmark Strait (S of **Greenland**) 5/24/41 with only three survivors from its crew of over 1,400

Hopkins, Harry L. -- friend and advisor to **Roosevelt**, served in many roles during the war, notably as a special envoy to **Churchill** and **Stalin**

Horii, Maj Gen Tomitaro (**hawr•ee, toh•mee•tahr′•oh**) led Japanese forces in taking **Guam** and **Rabaul**, failed to take **Port**

Moresby via the **Kokoda Trail** 8-9/42, drowned while retreating across a river near his base at **Buna** 11/12-13/42

Hornet, USS -- aircraft carrier which launched the **Doolittle Raid** 4/18/42, in action at **Midway** 6/42, sunk by Japanese carrier planes in the Battle of the **Santa Cruz Islands** 10/26/42

Horrocks, Lt Gen Sir Brian (hahr•iks) served as corps and army commander under **Montgomery** in N Africa and N Europe

Horthy, Admiral Miklós (hawr•t(h)ee, **mik'•lohsh**) Regent of Hungary 1920-44, allied himself with Germany while trying to minimize his commitment, forced to abdicate by **Hitler** 10/44

Horton, Admiral Sir Max -- British CiC of the Western Approaches 11/42-8/15/45, responsible for convoys and anti-submarine strategy in the N Atlantic

Hosogaya, Vice-Admiral Hoshiro (hoh•suh•gah'•yuh, hoh•**sheer**•oh) CiC Japanese Fleet Central China 12/40-7/41, CiC Northern (Pacific) Area Force 7/41-5/42, CiC **Aleutians** Area 6/42-4/43

Hoth, General Herrmann (hohth, hair•mahn) commanded the 15th **Panzer** Corps in Poland, Panzer Group Hoth in France, the 3rd Panzer Group in Operation **Barbarossa**, and the 4th Panzer Army at **Stalingrad** and **Kursk**. Dismissed by **Hitler** after the loss of **Kiev** 11/43, convicted of war crimes at **Nuremberg** in 1948 and served six years

Houffalize (oo•fa•**leez**) Belgian town where the US 1st and 3rd Armies met 1/16/45 to conclude the Battle of the **Bulge**

Hoxha, General Enver (haw•jah, -hah, **en**•vair) Soviet-trained Albanian resistance leader during the Italian (1939-43) and German (1943-44) occupations, then ruler of **Albania** until his death in 1986

Hukawng (hoo•kawng) river valley in N Burma

Hull, Cordell (hul, kawr•**del)** US Secretary of State 1933-44, chief negotiator with the Japanese 4-12/41, awarded the Nobel Peace Prize in 1945 for helping found the UN

Hump, The -- Allied air supply route over the **Himalayas** from **Assam**, India, to **Kunming**, China. Begun when the Japanese cut the **Burma Road** 4/42, it was used until the end of the war.

Huntziger, General Charles (hunt'•zig•uhr, **shahrl)** Commander of the French 2nd Army during the German invasion 5-6/40, led the Armistice delegation on 6/22/40, Minister of War in the **Vichy** government until his death in a plane crash 11/12/41, which may have been German sabotage

Huon (hoo•uhn) Peninsula and Gulf in NE **New Guinea**, controlled by the Japanese until 7/42, taken by US forces 8-9/42

Hurley, Maj Gen Patrick J. (**huhr•**lee) a troubleshooter for FDR in various Asian hot spots, including the **Philippines**, **Moscow**, Iran, and Afghanistan. The first US Ambassador to **New Zealand** from 1/43 and Ambassador to China 11/44-11/45

Hürtgen Forest (hurt•ghen, -ghin) SE of **Aachen**, the site of costly fighting from 9/44 to 12/44 as US troops tried to reach the dams on the Roer River to prevent the Germans from blowing them up

Hu Shih, Dr. (hoo•shee) Chinese Ambassador to the US 1939-45, an educator and philosopher with a Ph.D. from Columbia

Husseini, Amin el, Grand Mufti of Jerusalem (hoo•sayn•ee, hu- , ah•**meen)** During the 1930s he actively opposed the creation of a Jewish state in **Palestine**. From 10/39 to 4/41 he helped install the pro-German government of **Rashid Ali** in Iraq, fleeing to Germany when the British overthrew Ali 5/41. He spent the rest of the war raising **SS** Muslim units in **Axis-**occupied countries.

Huston, John (**hyoos•**tuhn) Hollywood director who made three classic documentary films during the war: *Report from the Aleutians* (1943), *The Battle of San Pietro* (1944), and *Let There Be Light* (1945). All three are antiwar in spirit and were rarely shown during the war.

Hvalfjordur (**vahl'•fyawrd•**uhr, **val'-**) port in W **Iceland** N of **Reykjavik**, used by Allied ships from 7/41, known unaffectionately as Valley Forge

Hyakutake, General Haruyoshi (**hyah•**koo**•tah'•**kee, **hahr•**oo**•yoh'•**shee) Commander of the Japanese 17th Army 4/42-4/45, based in **Rabaul**, in charge of operations in the **Solomon Islands** and **New Guinea**

Hydeman's Hellcats -- group of nine US submarines operating in the Sea of Japan 6/45, named for Commander E. T. Hydeman in USS Sea Dog

I

Iachino (or **Jachino**), **Admiral Angelo** (yah•kee•noh) CiC Italian Fleet 12/40-1943, personally commanded the Battle of **Cape Matapan** 3/28-29/41, a British victory

ibn Saud, Abdul-Aziz (ib•uhn sah•ood′, ahb•dool ah•zeez′) founder of **Saudi Arabia** and King 1932-53, officially neutral but pro-British during the war

Iceland (eye•sluhnd) N Atlantic island affiliated with Denmark, occupied by the British 5/10/40 after the German occupation of Denmark, then by the US 7/41, independent since 1944

Ichi-Go ("Operation Number One") **Plan** (ee′•chee **goh**) successful Japanese offensive in E China 4/18/44-early 1945

Ichiki, Colonel Kiyono (ee•chee•kee, kee•yoh•noh) played a key role in the **Marco Polo Bridge Incident** 7/37 which launched the **Sino-Japanese War**, was scheduled to lead ground forces at **Midway**, died on **Guadalcanal** in the Battle of the **Tenaru River** 8/21/42

Ickes, Harold (ik•eez) US Secretary of the Interior 1933-2/46, administrator for key raw materials during the war

Ie Shima (ee•ee shee•muh) small Japanese island off the W coast of **Okinawa**, captured by US forces 4/16-20/45

IG Farben (ee gay fahr•buhn) the largest German cartel, which flourished under the Third Reich. Prosecutions after the war for the use of slave labor were dropped, along with efforts to destroy the cartel, because of the need for industry in West Germany during the Cold War.

Iheya Islands (ee•hay•yah) N of **Okinawa**, taken by US Marines 6/3/45

Iida, General Shojiro (ee•dah, shoh•jee•roh) led the Japanese
15th Army into Burma from **Malaya** early in 1942, established a
Burmese civil government under Japanese control

Ijmuiden (eye•moy•duhn) **North Sea** port in Holland

Ijssel (eye•suhl) river in Holland which flows into the
Ijsselmeer (-**mair**), a lake created by diking the Zuider Zee

Illustrious, HMS -- name ship of a class of British aircraft
carriers, sent to **Alexandria** 6/30/40, carried torpedo bombers
which attacked the Italian fleet at **Taranto** 11/11/40, badly
damaged by German bombers 1/10/41, active in the Pacific 1/44-
4/45

Ilmen (**il**•muhn) Russian lake about 200 miles S of **Leningrad**

Ilyushin, Sergei (or -**gey**) (il•**yoo**•shin, **sair**•gay) aeronautical
engineer who designed several important Soviet planes, notably
the Il-2 fighter-bomber, of which the Soviets produced 36,000,
the highest total of any Soviet plane during the war

Imamura, General Hitoshi (im•uh•**moor'**•uh, -**myoor'**- ,
hih•**toh**•shee) commanded the Japanese 16th Army in the
conquest of **Java** (2-3/42) and the 17th and 18th Armies against
Guadalcanal from HQ in **Rabaul**, where he retained his
increasingly isolated command until the end of the war

Imphal (**imp**•huhl, **im**•pahl) city in NE India near the Burma
border, center of a British defense perimeter that withstood the
Japanese 15th Army 4-7/44, the turning point of the Burma
campaign

Indaw (**in**•dahw) town in NC Burma, site of a successful
Chindit ambush against the Japanese 3/44

Independence, USS -- name ship of a class of nine light aircraft carriers built on the hulls of Cleveland class light cruisers, all of which entered service in the Pacific in 1943

Indianapolis, USS -- US heavy cruiser, active throughout the Pacific War, carried the first atomic bomb to **Tinian** 7/45, sunk with the loss of 883 men the night of 7/29-30/45, the largest loss at sea in US history

Indian Ocean -- bounded by Africa to the W, Asia to the N, and Australia to the E, saw extensive merchant shipping and raids, but no major battles

Indochina (in•doh•chy'•nuh) SE Asian peninsula between the Bay of **Bengal** and the South China Sea, contains Burma, part of **Malaya**, **Thailand**, Laos, Cambodia, and Vietnam

Indomitable, HMS -- British aircraft carrier completed in 1941 with an armored flight deck, saw action in the **Mediterranean**, **Indian Ocean**, and Pacific

Ingersoll, Admiral Royal E. (ing'•uhr•sawl, -suhl) US CiC Atlantic Fleet from 1/42 to 11/44

Ingram, Admiral Jonas H. (ing•gruhm) Commander of the US 4th Fleet in the S Atlantic from 1942, then CiC Atlantic Fleet from 11/44

Inönü, Ismet (ih•noh•nu, is•met) Premier of **Turkey** 1923-37 under Kemal Atatürk (at'•uh•turk, kuh•mahl), whom he succeeded as President 1938-50. Maintained a policy of neutrality until severing diplomatic relations with Germany in the summer of 1944 and declaring war 2/45

Inouye, Admiral Shigeyoshi (in•oh•ay, -uh•way, shig•ee•oh'•shee) CiC Japanese 4th Fleet from 11/39, in overall command of operations at **Guam**, **Wake**, **Port Moresby**, and the Battle of the **Coral Sea**, head of the Naval Academy from 10/42,

Vice-Minister of the Navy from 8/44, member of the Supreme
War Council from 5/45

International Military Tribunal for the Far East (IMTFE) --
The Japanese counterpart to the **Nuremberg** trials began in
Tokyo 5/46 and were also held in other cities such as **Singapore**
and **Hong Kong**, eventually resulting in almost 1,000 death
sentences.

Intramoros (in•truh•**mawr**•ohs) the old Spanish city within
Manila, about 400 acres, largely destroyed 2/45 by a murderous
and suicidal Japanese defense (see **Iwabuchi**)

Intrepid, USS -- **Essex** class aircraft carrier commissioned
1943 which survived several **kamikaze** attacks and in 1982
became a museum in New York harbor

Ionian (eye•**oh**•nee•uhn) 1) a small sea within the
Mediterranean between Italy and Greece 2) a group of Greek
islands located there

Iowa, USS (eye•uh•wuh) class name ship for the last four US
battleships ever completed (1943-44) and the largest. The other
three were the **New Jersey**, **Missouri**, and Wisconsin.

Iráklion -- see **Heraklion**

Ironbottom Sound -- US nickname for the water between
Guadalcanal and Florida Island, referring to the nearly 50 ships
sunk there from 8/42 to 2/43

Iron Cross -- the highest German military decoration,
established 1813. **Hitler** added the following embellishments (in
ascending order): Knight's Cross, Oak Leaves, Swords, and
Diamonds

Ironside, FM Sir William Edmund -- served in the Boer War and WWI, appointed Chief of the Imperial General Staff 9/3/39, moved to CiC Home Forces by **Churchill** 5/40, retired 7/40

Irrawaddy (eer•uh•wahd'•ee) the major river of Burma, flowing from the N mountains S into the **Andaman Sea** near **Rangoon**

Isely (or **Isley**) **Field** -- see **Aslito**

Isère (ee•zair) river and department in SE France

Ismay, Maj Gen Sir Hastings L. (iz•may) **Churchill**'s CoS from 5/40 to the end of the war

Istria (is•tree•uh) peninsula in NE Italy bordering Yugoslavia, now part of **Croatia**

Italian East Africa -- **Abyssinia** (now **Ethiopia**), **Eritrea**, and **Italian Somailand**. Formed 1936, ended by British conquest early in the war

Ito, Vice-Admiral Seiichi (ee•toh, say•ee•chee) Commander of the **Yamato** attack force when the battleship was sunk 4/7/45

Iwabuchi, Rear Admiral Sanji (ee•wuh•boo'•chee, sahn•jee) appointed Commander of Japanese Naval Forces in **Manila** 11/44, ordered his 17,000 men to resist the invading Americans to the death. In the month-long fighting (2/45), most of the city was destroyed, along with 100,000 civilians and all but a few Japanese.

Iwo Jima (ee•woh jee•muh, -wuh) small volcanic Japanese island (eight square miles) about 800 miles S of Tokyo, taken by US Marines 2-3/45 with heavy casualties (almost 6,000 US deaths), returned to Japan 1968

J

Jackson, Robert Houghwout (**how**•uht) Supreme Court Justice (1941-54) who served as Chief US Prosecutor at the **Nuremberg Trials**

Jan Mayen (**yahn my**•uhn, -en) island between **Greenland** and Norway, annexed by Norway 1929

Jasenovac (**yah**•seh•noh•vahts) village in N Yugoslavia, now in E **Croatia**, site of a German concentration camp

Jassy (US **yah**•see) now spelled **Iaşi** (Rom **yahsh**(ee)) city in NE Romania

Java (**jah**•vuh, **jav**•uh) the most populous island in the **Dutch East Indies**, occupied by the Japanese from 3/42 to the end of the war

Java Sea, Battle of the (**jah**•vuh, **jav**•uh) Japanese naval victory over an Allied (**ABDA**) force 2/27/42

Jayapura -- see **Hollandia**

Jean Bart (zhah(n)•**bahr**) French battleship, sailed from **St. Nazaire** 6/19/40 to **Casablanca** to keep the invading Germans from seizing it, destroyed resisting the US **Torch** landing 11/8-10/42

Jedburghs (**jed**•buhr•uhs) teams of three, usually one British or American, one French, and one radio operator, who parachuted into France in 1944 to help the French resistance prepare for the **Normandy** invasion

Jefna (**jef**•nah) town in N **Tunisia**, site of a successful German ambush against British forces 11/29-30/42

Jehol (juh•**hohl**) province in NE China, incorporated into **Manchukuo** by the Japanese 1932-45

Jersey (**juhr**•zee) the largest (44 square miles) and most populous (80,000) of the **Channel Islands**

Jervis Bay, HMS (US **juhr**•vis, Brit **jahr**•vis) British armed merchant cruiser, sunk 11/5/40 by the German battleship **Admiral Scheer**, which it attacked to help 32 of the 37 ships in its convoy escape

Jeschonnek, Col Gen Hans (**yesh**•ahn•nek, yesh•**ahn**•nek) Chief of the German Air Staff 1939-43, committed suicide 8/18/43 after the successful British bombing raid on **Peenemunde**

Jesselton (**jes**•uhl•tuhn) port city and capital of North **Borneo**, now called Kota Kinabalu (**koh**•tuh **kin**•uh•buh•**loo'**) and part of Malaysia

Jinyo (**jin**•yoh) Japanese escort carrier, sunk by the US submarine Picuda 11/17/44 in the Yellow Sea

Jodl, General Alfred J. (**yohd'l, yahd'l**) Chief of the Operations Staff of the German High Command 8/39-5/45, directed all German campaigns except the USSR, which he helped plan. Signed the German surrender at **Reims** 5/7/45. Convicted of war crimes at **Nuremberg** and hanged 10/16/46

Johnson, Group Captain James (**"Johnnie"**) -- Though he missed the Battle of **Britain**, Johnson became the top scoring British RAF fighter pilot with 38 kills from 6/41 to 9/44 and survived the war

Johnston, USS -- see **Evans**

Johore Strait (juh•**hawr**, -**hohr**) narrow waterway separating **Singapore** Island from mainland **Malaya**, crossed by 5,000 Japanese troops 2/8/42

Jones, Dr. Reginald V. (R.V.) -- British physicist, scientific advisor to the War Cabinet and MI-6 on a variety of issues, including anti-submarine measures, defenses against rockets, and atomic energy

Joubert de la Ferté, Air Chief Marshal Sir Philip (zhoo•**bair** du la fair•**tay**) As CiC of RAF Coastal Command from mid-1941 to mid-1943, he played a major role in winning the Battle of the Atlantic.

Joyce, William ("Lord Haw-Haw") -- an Anglo-American British subject who broadcast propaganda from Berlin to England throughout the war, hanged for treason 1/3/46

Jud Süss ("*The Eternal Jew*") (**yood sus**) anti-semitic **Nazi** propaganda film, first shown in Berlin 9/24/40

Juin, General Alphonse (zhoo•**a(n)**, ahl•**faw(n)s,** al-) succeeded **General Weygand** as CiC N Africa under the **Vichy** French government 11/41, joined the **Allies** after the **Torch** landings 11/42, led French colonial troops in Italy, including **goumiers**, from 12/43, and became CoS of the French National Defense Committee 8/12/44

July Bomb Plot -- the most important of several attempts to assassinate **Hitler**, 7/20/44 (see **Stauffenberg**)

Juneau, USS (**joo•noh**) cruiser sunk off **Guadalcanal** 11/13/42 with the loss of almost 700 lives, including the five **Sullivan** brothers

Junkers (**yung•**kuhrz) a series of German planes produced before and during the war, including the **Ju 87** dive bomber (**Stuka**) used in the **Blitzkrieg** attacks on Poland, France, and the

Soviet Union, and the **Ju 88**, a versatile medium bomber which was produced in greater numbers than any other German plane

Juno (joo•noh) one of the five landing beaches in the **Normandy** Invasion (**D-Day**), assigned to Canadian forces

Jutland (US **juht•**luhnd, Dan **yuht-**) the mainland portion of Denmark, name of the most famous naval battle of WWI

K

Kadena (kuh•**deen**•uh) airfield on **Okinawa** near the landing beaches at Hagushi, taken by US forces on the first day, 4/1/45

Kaga (**kah**•gah) Japanese aircraft carrier, part of the **Pearl Harbor** task force, sunk in the Battle of **Midway**

Kagoshima (**kah**•goh•**shee'**•muh, -guh- , -mah) city and bay at the S end of **Kyushu**, used by the Japanese to practice for **Pearl Harbor**, projected landing site for the Allied invasion of Kyushu

Kairouan (or **Kairwan**) (kair•oo•**ahn**, kair•**wahn**) holy city in NE **Tunisia**

Kaiser, Henry J. (**ky**•zuhr) US shipbuilding magnate best known for his mass production of **Liberty** merchant ships to supply Britain, also completed 50 escort carriers between 7/43 and 7/44

kaiten (**kyt**'n) one-man suicide torpedoes, first mission 11/44, planned for use by the Japanese to defend the home islands

Kako (**kah**•koh) Japanese heavy cruiser, sunk by US submarine S-44 off **Kavieng** 8/10/42 after participating in the Battle of **Savo Island** 8/9/42

Kalach (**kah**•lahch, -lahj) Soviet town on the **Don** River about 40 miles W of **Stalingrad**, where the two arms of the giant Soviet pincer closed around **Paulus**'s 6th Army 11/22/42

Kalinin 1) **Mikhail I.** (kuh•**lee**•nin, kah- , mih•**kyl**) figurehead President of the USSR from 1938 until his death in 1946 2) Soviet city on the **Volga**, named for **Mikhail** (above) 1934-1990, before and after that called Tver (**tvair**) 3) **Kalinin Bay, USS** -- escort carrier, part of the Taffy 3 Force in the Battle of **Leyte**

Gulf, hit at least a dozen times but not sunk 4) **Kaliningrad** -- see **Königsberg**

Kállay, Miklós (**kahl•**loy, **mik•**lohsh) PM of Hungary, who tried to arrange a surrender to the Soviet Union 9/43, dismissed by **Admiral Horthy** under orders from **Hitler** 3/44

Kallio, Kyosti (**kahl•**yoh, **kyus•**tee) President of **Finland** 1937-40

Kaltenbrunner, SS General Ernst (**kahl'•**ten•**bru•**nuhr, **airnst**) Austrian **Nazi**, appointed head of the German Security Police (by this time called RSHA ("Reich Main Security Office"), an expanded version of the SD) by **Hitler** 1/30/43, supervised round-ups and deportations, replaced **Canaris** as head of the **Abwehr** 2/18/44 when it became part of the RSHA. Hanged at **Nuremberg** 10/16/46

Kamaing (kuh•**mang**, kah•**myng**) city and road in N Burma

Kamchatka (kahm•**chaht•**kuh, kam•**chat-**) large peninsula in the NE Soviet Union

kamikaze ("divine wind") (**kah•**mih•**kah'•**zee) suicide tactic by Japanese pilots attacking ships, begun 10/25/44

Kaminski Brigade (kuh•**min•**skee) Russian POWs who chose to fight with the Germans, notably during the **Warsaw Uprising** 7-10/44

Kammhuber, General Josef C. (**kahm•**hoo•buhr, **yoh•**zef) commander of German night fighter defenses 10/40-9/43

Kandy (**kan•**dee, **kahn-**) city in C **Ceylon**, **Mountbatten**'s forward HQ 1944-45

Kaneohe (**kah•**nay•**oh'•**hay) town, bay, and US naval air station on E **Oahu**

Karachi (kuh•**rah**•chee, kar•**ah**-) port city in NW India (now Pakistan), important base for the China-Burma-India (CBI) Theater

Karelia (kuh•**reel**•yuh, kah•**ray**•lyuh) an autonomous republic in NW Russia, part of **Finland** until WWII

Karens (kuh•**renz**, ka- , -**reenz**) tribes in **Burma** who waged guerrilla warfare against the Japanese

Karinhall (**kah'•rin•hahl**) **Goering**'s lavish estate N of Berlin

Karlsruhe (or **C**-) (**kahrlz'•roo**•uh, **kahrls'**-) 1) city on the **Rhine** in SW Germany 2) German light cruiser, sunk by a British submarine 4/10/40 returning from Norway

Kasbah (**kahz**•bah, **kaz**-) US name for a fort near **Mehdia** in W **Morocco**, site of heavy fighting during the Atlantic **Torch** landings

Kassala (**kah'**•sah•**lah**, **kas**•uh•luh) small city in the Anglo-Egyptian Sudan, occupied by Italian forces summer 1940, reoccupied by British forces 1/41, now in E Sudan

Kassel (US **kas**•uhl, Ger **kah**•suhl) industrial city in C Germany where aircraft and rocket production were disrupted by British bombing, including a firestorm 10/22/43

Kasserine Pass (**kas**•uh•reen) key US defensive position in WC **Tunisia**, taken by **Rommel** 2/20/43 as US troops lost their first major battle in N Africa, recaptured a few days later

Katchin (**kach**•in, ka•**cheen**) peninsula in SE **Okinawa**

Kattegat (**kat'**•ih•gat) strait between Sweden and the **Jutland** peninsula in Denmark, joining the **North** and **Baltic Seas**

Katukov (or -tyu-), **General Mikhail** (**kah'•choo•kuhv,** **mih•kyl**) commanded Soviet tank armies 1941-44

Katyn Forest (**kah•tin**, ka- , **kat'n**) near **Smolensk**, site of a massacre of 4,000 Polish POW officers by the Soviet Secret Police (**NKVD**) early April 1940. The bodies were discovered 4/43 by the Germans.

katyusha (**kah•tyoo•shuh**, -shah) Soviet multiple rocket launcher, used against the Germans (who called them **Stalin** organs) increasingly from 7/41 to the fall of Berlin

Kauffman, Commander Draper (**kawf•muhn, kahf-**) foremost US naval expert on bomb disposal during the war

Kaufmann, Henrik (**kowf•muhn**, -mahn, **hen•reek**) Danish Ambassador to Washington when the Germans occupied Denmark 4/40, organized and directed Free Denmark and encouraged the resistance movement in Denmark

Kaunas -- see **Kovno**

Kavieng (**kay•vee•eng**) Japanese stronghold in New Ireland, NW of **Rabaul**

Kawabe, General Masakazu (or **Shozo**) (**kah•wah•bay,** **mah•suh•kah'•zoo**) CoS of Japanese armies in China from 8/42, Commander of Japanese forces in Burma 1943-44, Commander of the Japanese Army Air Force 4-8/45

Kawaguchi 1) **Maj Gen Kiyotake** (**kah•wuh•goo'•chee,** **kee•oh•tah'•keh**) led Japanese forces on **Guadalcanal** 8-11/42, older brother of **General Torashiro** (**tawr•uh•sheer'•oh**), who held high-level staff positions during the war 2) a city near Tokyo

Kazakhstan (**kah•**zahk**•stahn**) Soviet Republic in Asia, a center of industrial production shifted from the W after the German invasion

Kazinets, Isai (Rus kah•zih**•nyets**, ee**•sy**) Soviet Jewish partisan leader in the **Minsk** area. Caught, tortured, and hanged by the Germans 5/7/42

Keddab (keh**•dahb**) a ridge near **El Guettar** in **Tunisia** where US forces under **Ted Roosevelt** (who was awarded the Distinguished Service Cross for his actions) stopped a German advance 3/23/43

Keitel, FM Wilhelm (**kyt'l**, **vil•**helm) Chief of the German Armed Forces High Command (**OKW**) 2/4/38-5/13/45, known for his unquestioning obedience to **Hitler**, hanged at **Nuremberg** 10/16/46

Kempeitai (**kem•pay•ty**, -**py-**) Japanese Military Police, primarily loyal to **Tojo.** An individual member is called a kempei.

Kendari (**kuhn•**dah**•ree**) port city in SE **Celebes**, the chief landing point for the Japanese invasion 1/42, made into a major naval base

Kennedy, Lt John F. -- son of **Joseph P.**, skipper of **PT** (fast patrol boat) **109**, which was rammed and sunk by a Japanese destroyer the night of 8/2-3/43 while patrolling **The Slot** in the **Solomon Islands**. President of the US 1961-63

Kennedy, Joseph P. -- father of **John F.**, US Ambassador to Britain 1937-2/41, whose isolationism and pessimism about Britain's ability to survive led to his recall

Kenney, General George C. -- CiC US Far East Air Force from 8/42, neutralized **Rabaul**, supported **MacArthur**'s land campaigns in **New Guinea** and the **Philippines**, and finished the war bombing targets on the Japanese home island of **Kyushu**

Kerama Islands (keh•rah•mah) off SW **Okinawa**, taken by US forces 3/27-31/45

Kerch (**kuhrch, kairch**) port city, peninsula, and strait on the E tip of the **Crimea**, site of an amphibious Soviet counterattack 12/26/41

Keren (**kair•en**) town in **Eritrea** surrounded by mountains, taken from the Italians by the British 4th and 5th Indian Divisions 3/27/41 after 8 weeks of fighting

Kersten, Felix (**kair•stuhn, fay•liks**) Estonian-born masseur highly valued by **Himmler**, his patient from 3/39 to 4/45, whom he persuaded to take measures saving thousands of lives in the camps and pursue secret peace negotiations during the closing months of the war

Kesselring, FM Albert (**kes•uhl•ring, ahl•bairt**) highly regarded Commander of German forces in Italy 7/43-10/44, CiC Western Front 3-5/45, spent five years in prison for debatable war crimes 1947-52

Keyes, Lt Col Geoffrey (**keez**) British commando who died while leading an attempt to assassinate **Rommel** in **Libya** 11/17-18/41

Keyes, Sir Roger (**keez**) British Director of Combined Operations (coastal commando raids) 7/40-10/41

Keynes, John Maynard (**kaynz**) eminent British economist, financial advisor to the British Treasury, and organizer of the International Monetary Fund (IMF)

Khalkhin (or **Khalkin**) **Gol** (**kahl**•kin **gahl, -keen-**) site of the final victory of Soviet forces under **Zhukov** over the 6th Japanese Army in the Soviet-Mongolian border fighting, 8/31/39

Kharkov (**kahr**•kawf, -kahv, -kuhv) a major Ukrainian city which changed hands four times before Soviet forces drove out the Germans for good 8/22/43

Khartoum (kahr•**toom**) capital of the Anglo-Egyptian Sudan, now Sudan

Khrushchev, Nikita S. (**krush**•chef, -chawf, **kroosh-** , US nih•**keet**•uh, Rus nyik•**yee**•tuh) member of the Soviet Politburo from 3/39, supervised the annexation of E Poland from 9/39, served as a political commissar on several W and SW fronts 1941-43, led purges of Ukrainian nationalists from 11/43 that helped bring the **Ukraine** under tighter Soviet control. First Secretary of the Communist Party from 1953, Premier of the USSR 1958-1964

Kido, Marquis Koichi (kee•doh, koh•ee•chee) Japanese Lord Privy Seal and closest advisor to **Emperor Hirohito** 1940-45, sentenced to life imprisonment after the war, paroled 1956

Kiel (**keel**) 1) German port city on the **Baltic** about 50 miles S of the Danish border 2) 60-mile canal in N Germany connecting the **North** and **Baltic** Seas

Kieta (**kyay**•tah) town on the SE coast of **Bougainville**, landing point for the Japanese invasion 3/30/42

Kiev (kee•ef, -ev) capital and major city of **Ukraine**, on the **Dnieper** River, taken by German forces 9/41 with huge Soviet losses, retaken by the Soviets 11/43

Kimmel, Admiral Husband E. (kim•uhl, -el) appointed CiC US Pacific Fleet, based at **Pearl Harbor**, 2/1/41, dismissed shortly after the Japanese attack on 12/7/41

King, Admiral Ernest J. -- head of the US Navy throughout the war; appointed CiC Atlantic Fleet 2/41, CiC US Fleet 12/41, and simultaneously Chief of Naval Operations (CNO) 3/42

King George V, HMS -- British battleship, completed 1940, name ship for a class that included the **Prince of Wales**, Duke of York, Anson, and Howe. As flagship of the Home Fleet, she helped sink the **Bismarck** 5/41. Transferred to the **Mediterranean** 5/43 and the Pacific 1944. Serving under US Admiral **Halsey**, she was the last battleship to fire on Japan (7/45) and the last British battleship to fire on anyone.

King, Maj Gen Edward P. (Ned) -- surrendered US forces on Bataan 4/42

King, William Lyon Mackenzie -- Liberal Party PM of Canada 1921-30, 1935-48, effectively persuaded his country to support the Allied war effort

King's African Rifles -- British regiment drawn from the E African colonies, fought in **Ethiopia** and **Madagascar**, then in Burma 1943-45 as the 11th E African Division

Kinkaid, Admiral Thomas C. (kin•**kaid**) commanded US naval groups throughout the Pacific, including **Guadalcanal**, the **Aleutians**, and **Leyte Gulf**

Kinugasa (kee•noo•**gah'**•suh) Japanese heavy cruiser, sunk at **Guadalcanal** 11/14/42 by land and carrier based US planes

Kippenberger, General Howard K. -- led **New Zealand** forces in Greece, **Crete**, Syria, N Africa, and Italy until losing both feet to a land mine 3/2/44, then took charge of repatriating New Zealand POWs and editing the official New Zealand war histories

Kiribati -- see **Gilbert Islands**

Kirishima (keer•ih•shee•muh, -ee-) Japanese battleship, sunk 11/14-15/42 by the USS Washington during an attempt to land Japanese troops on **Guadalcanal**, the only time in the Pacific war that one battleship sank another

Kiriwina (kih•rih•wee•nuh) largest of the **Trobriand Islands**, site of a US Marine landing 6/23/43

Kirkenes (khir•ken•es) port in N Norway near the Soviet border

Kirponos, Col Gen Mikhail (keer•pahn•ohs, mik•hyl) Soviet commander of the **Kiev** military forces when the Germans invaded the USSR, refused permission by **Stalin** to retreat from Kiev until 9/41, killed 9/20 trying to break out of a German encirclement that took about 650,000 prisoners

Kiska (kis•kuh) one of the W **Aleutian Islands**, occupied by Japanese forces 6/42 in an unsuccessful attempt to draw US ships away from **Midway**, abandoned 7/43

Kislovodsk (kis•lah•**vuhdsk)** town in the **Caucasus** Mountains in **Georgia**, occupied by German forces 8/17/42

Kita, Nagao (kee•tah, -tuh, nah•**gow)** Japanese consul and spy in Hawaii, provided Tokyo with reports on **Pearl Harbor** throughout 1941 which were decoded but ignored by US Intelligence

Kleist, FM Ewald von (klyst, ay•vahlt) commanded **Panzer** groups in France, Yugoslavia, and the Soviet Union, and from 11/42 to 3/44 Army Group A in the **Caucusus** and **Ukraine**. Died in prison in the Soviet Union 10/5/54

Klopper, Maj Gen Hendrik -- South African commander of **Tobruk**, who surrendered the British garrison to **Rommel** with 30,000 men 6/21/42

Kluge, FM Hans Günther (or **Guen-**) **von** (kloo•guh, hahns gun•tuhr) led the German 4th Army in Poland and France, and Army Group Center in the Soviet Union from 12/41 to 6/44, replaced **Rundstedt** as CiC W Front 7/1/44, was himself replaced by **Model** 8/17/44, committed suicide 8/19/44 under pressure for his acquaintance with members of the **July Bomb Plot**

Knight's Cross -- see **Iron Cross**

Knin (kneen) NW Yugoslav town near the **Dalmatian** coast, site of the first Allied air raid (from bases in S Italy) in support of **Tito**'s partisans 3/2/44

Knipping, Max (nip•ping) head of the French **Milice** in N France, executed 1947

Knochen, SS Colonel Helmut (naw•khen, nah- , hel•moot) helped organize a kidnapping of two British Intelligence agents in Holland (the **Venlo** incident) 11/9/39, **Gestapo** chief of Paris from 6/40, sentenced to death in 1954 but released in 1963

Knochlein, SS Captain Fritz (nawkh•lyn, nahkh-) ordered a massacre of about 100 British prisoners on the **Dunkirk** perimeter 5/27/40, for which he was tried in **Hamburg** and hanged 1/28/49

Knox, William Franklin (**"Colonel Frank"**) -- 1936 Republican Vice-Presidential candidate who served as Secretary of the Navy from 6/19/40 until his death on 4/23/44.

Kobe (koh•bee, -bay) Japanese port city in S **Honshu**, bombed in the **Doolittle Raid** 4/42 and several times thereafter

Koch, Erich (US **kahk, air•ik**, Ger **kawkh, ay•rikh**) German Governor of the **Ukraine** 10/41-4/44, died while serving life imprisonment in Poland 1986

Koch, Colonel Karl (US **kahk,** Ger **kawkh**) **SS** commandant of **Buchenwald** from the time it opened in 1937 until 1944, when he was removed by the **SS** and hanged early in 1945. His wife Ilse earned her own notoriety for sadism at the camp and committed suicide in 1967 while serving life imprisonment

Koeltz, General Louis-Marie (**kurltz**, loo•ee-ma•**ree**) Commander of the French 19th Corps in **Tunisia** after the **Torch** landings 11/42

Koenig, General Marie-Pierre (**kur•**nig, mah•**ree**-pee•**air**) joined **DeGaulle** in England 1940, commanded the **Free French** Brigade in **Egypt** and **Libya** 1941-42, winning acclaim for his defense of **Bir Hacheim** 5/27-6/10/42, represented the resistance on **Eisenhower**'s staff before **D-Day**, took command of the French Forces of the Interior 6/44, became military governor of Paris after its liberation, commanded French occupation forces in Germany 1945-49

Koga, Vice-Admiral Mineichi (**koh•gah**, **mee•**nay•**ee'•**chee) succeeded **Yamamoto** as CiC Japanese Combined Fleet after the latter's death 4/17/43, killed in an aircraft accident 3/31/44

Kohima (koh•**hee•**muh) town in NE India about 60 miles N of **Imphal**, held by British and Indian forces against the Japanese 31st Division 4/44, a turning point in the Burma campaign

Koiso, Lt Gen Kuniaki (koh•ee•soh, koo•nee•**ah'•**kee) became Japanese PM 10/44 after the fall of **Tojo**, had no base of support and little influence, resigned 4/45, sentenced to life imprisonment after the war

Kokoda Trail (kuh•**koh•**duh) mostly a muddy path running 150 miles over the Owen Stanley Mountains of E **New Guinea**, from **Buna** on the N coast to **Port Moresby** on the S coast. A Japanese force landing at Buna 7/21/42 was stopped 30 miles from Port Moresby by an Australian force, which then drove the

Japanese back to Buna. Considered by many the worst fighting terrain of the war.

Kokuba (koh•koo•buh) town in SW **Okinawa**

Kokura (koh•kur•uh, -koor- , -ah) Japanese city on the N coast of **Kyushu**, the primary target for the second atomic bomb, which was dropped instead on **Nagasaki** because of poor visibility over **Kokura**

Kola Peninsula (koh•luh) located in NW Russia between the **Barents** and **White** Seas

Kolberg (kohl•bairg) (now Kolobrzeg (koh•**wohb**•zeeg) in Poland) German **Baltic** port city in **East Prussia**, which held out against Soviet forces until 3/18/45. Its heroic and successful resistance during the Napoleonic campaign in 1807 was the subject of the most expensive film made in Nazi Germany, titled *Kolberg* and shown from 1/30/45 to inspire the remaining German strongholds.

Kolombangara (kohl•uhm•buhn•**gahr′**•uh, -bahn-) one of the **Solomon Islands**, the site of a night naval battle 7/12-13/43 as US ships tried unsuccessfully to prevent Japanese ships from reinforcing their garrison on the island. Skipped over 8/43 by US forces advancing from **New Georgia** to **Vella Lavella**.

Komandorski Islands (kahm•uhn•**dawr′**•skee) Soviet-owned group between the peninsula of **Kamchatka** and the W-most **Aleutian** island of **Attu**. Site of a naval battle 3/26/43 when US ships prevented a Japanese convoy from delivering reinforcements to their base on Attu.

Komura, Rear Admiral Keizo (koh•**moor**•uh, kuh- , kay•ee•zoh) After participating in battles from **Pearl Harbor** to the **Philippine Sea**, he commanded the 1st Carrier Division in the Battle of **Leyte Gulf**

Kondo, Vice-Admiral Nobutake (kohn•doh, noh•bu•tah′•kee)
commanded the Japanese Southern Fleet, whose land-based
bombers sank the **Repulse** and **Prince of Wales** off **Malaya**
12/10/41, commanded the **Midway** Occupation Force 6/42, was
active throughout the **Guadalcanal** campaign (8/42-1/43), then
served in administrative posts

Konev, Marshal Ivan S. (koh•nev, -nyev, ih•vahn) led Soviet
armies from the defense of **Moscow** in 1941 to the fall of Berlin
in 5/45, with major victories in the **Ukraine** 1943-44 and the
subsequent captures of **Prague** and **Dresden.** CiC Warsaw Pact
armies 1955-60.

Kongo (kohn•goh) Japanese battleship in action at
Guadalcanal and **Leyte Gulf**, sunk by a US submarine N of
Formosa 11/44

Königsberg (kur′•nigz•buhrg, -nikhs•bairk) German city and
naval base in **East Prussia**, now **Kaliningrad**
(kuh•lee′•nin•grad, -grahd) in Russia, captured by Soviet forces
4/9/45 with huge German losses

Konoye (or Konoe), Prince Fumimaro (kuh•noy•ee, -noh•ay,
foo•mee•mahr′-oh) PM of Japan 6/37 to 1/38 and 7/22/40 to
10/16/41, when he was replaced by **Tojo**, his Minister of War.
Though he was considered a leader of the peace faction, the US
threatened to try him as a war criminal and he poisoned himself
12/16/45.

Korea (kuh•ree•uh) ruled by Japan from the end of the Russo-
Japanese War in 1905 to the end of WWII

Korsun (kawr•soon, -sun) village in SW **Ukraine** where some
30,000 German troops escaped an encirclement in the Cherkassy
Pocket early in 1944 while many more were killed or captured

Korten, Günther (or **Guen-**) (**kawr•**tuhn, gu(r)n•tuhr)
succeeded **Jeschonnek** as Chief of the German Air Staff 8/43,
killed in the **July Bomb Plot** explosion 7/44

Kos (or **Cos**) (**kahs, kaws**) Greek island in the SE **Aegean Sea**,
occupied by the Germans from 10/4/43 to the end of the war

Kosovo (**kaw•**suh•voh, **kah-** , **koh-**) province in S Yugoslavia,
incorporated into **Albania** by Italy 1941, autonomous after the
war, annexed by Serbia in 1990, now a province of South Serbia
and **Montenegro**

Kosygin, Alexei N. (kuh•**see•**ghin, uh•**lek•**say) one of three
members of the **Evacuation Council** established in **Moscow**
6/23/41 to organize the transfer of over 1,500 factories and plants
from W to E Soviet Union. Premier of the Soviet Union (USSR)
1964-1980

Kota Bharu (**koh•**tuh **bahr•**oo) E Malayan port city and
airfield 350 miles N of **Singapore**, site of a Japanese landing
12/8/41

Kouri Shima (**koor•**ee **shee•**mah, -muh) island off NW
Okinawa, occupied by US forces 4/45

Kovno (**kawv•**nuh) city in **Lithuania**, now **Kaunas** (**kow•**nahs,
-nuhs)

Koyanagi, Rear Admiral Tomiji (**koh•**yuh•**nah′•**ghee,
koy•uh- , toh•**mee•**jee) **Kurita**'s CoS in the Battle of **Leyte
Gulf**

Kozhedub (or **Kosh-**), **Maj Gen Ivan N.** (**koh•**zheh•**doob**,
-sheh- , ih•**vahn**) top Soviet fighter ace of the war, credited with
shooting down 62 German planes, including an ME-262 jet
fighter, between 7/43 and the end of the war

Kra, Isthmus of (**krah**) the narrow S part of **Thailand** where Japanese forces landed 12/8/41 to start their drive to **Singapore**

Krakow -- see **Cracow**

Kramer, Josef (**krah**•muhr, **yoh**•zef) Commandant of **Birkenau**, transferred to **Belsen** 12/44 where he became known as "the Beast of Belsen," tried and executed 11/45

Krancke, Admiral Theodor (**krahn**•kuh, **tay'**•oh•dohr) drafted the initial plan for the German invasion of Norway. In 11/40, commanding the pocket battleship **Admiral Scheer**, he sank 5 merchant ships of the 37 in the N Atlantic convoy HX84 along with its armed escort, the **Jervis Bay,** then continued a five-month raiding expedition through the West Indies, the S Atlantic, and the **Indian Ocean**, returning at the end of March 1941.

Krasnodar (US **kras'**•nuh•**dahr**, Rus kruh•snuh•**dahr**) Soviet city in the W **Caucasus**, on the **Kuban** River, captured by the Germans 8/9/42, retaken 2/12/43, site of the first Soviet war crimes trial against the Germans beginning 7/14/43

Krebs, General Hans (**krebz**) succeeded **Guderian** as Chief of the German General Staff 4/1/45, committed suicide a month later after failing to negotiate a surrender of Berlin following **Hitler**'s suicide

Kreipe, Maj Gen Karl-Heinrich-Georg (**kry**•puh, **kahrl-hyn**•rikh-**ghay**•awrg) German commander of **Crete**, kidnapped 4/26/44 by British agents and Greek partisans, who took him to **Egypt** as a POW

Kreisau Circle (**kry**•zow) a group of about 20 prominent Germans opposed to **Hitler**, which was formed in 1933 by **Count Helmuth von Moltke** and met at his estate in Kreisau, **Silesia**. On 8/9/43 they drafted a document titled *Basic Principles for the New_Order.*

Kretschmer, Lt Commander Otto (krech•muhr) the most successful **U-boat** commander of the war, sank about 300,000 tons of Allied shipping before he was captured by British destroyers 3/27/41

Kristallnacht (US **kris′•tuhl•nahkt,** Ger kree•shtahl•nahkt) (Crystal Night, or the Night of Broken Glass, 11/9/38) a **Nazi**-led attack on German Jews which destroyed about 200 synagogues and 7,500 stores and warehouses

Kristiansand (US **kris′•chuhn•sand,** Nor **kris•chen-sahn)** S-most port in Norway, occupied by the Germans 4/9/40

Kronstadt (US **krahn•**stat, -staht, Rus krun•**shtaht)** Russian island and naval base in the Gulf of Finland, considered part of **Leningrad**, remained in Soviet hands throughout the war

Krueger, General Walter (kroo•guhr) led the US 6th Army in the Pacific under **MacArthur** from early 1943, culminating with the liberation of the **Philippines**, where he finished the war as a full (four-star) general

Krupp family (**kruhp, krup**) German munitions dynasty, founded 1810 in **Essen. Gustav**, heading the company between the wars, supported **Hitler**'s rise to power. His son **Alfried** (**ahl•**freed), assuming control in 1942, was imprisoned from 1948 to 1951 for using slave labor during the war, then resumed his career.

Ksaira (k'sair•ah) key hill (djebel) at **Faïd Pass** in **Tunisia**

Kuantan (kwahn•tahn) port city on the E coast of **Malaya** about 150 miles N of **Singapore**, site of a Japanese landing 12/10/41 which the **Repulse** and **Prince of Wales** were hoping to prevent when Japanese planes sank them

Kuban (koo•**ban,** -**bahn)** river in the W **Caucasus**, flowing through **Krasnodar** and into the Sea of **Azov**

Kube, Wilhelm (koo•buh, vil•helm) German Commissar of White **Ruthenia**, assassinated with a bomb 9/43

Kubis, Jan (koo•bish, **yahn**) Czech resistance fighter whose grenade mortally wounded **Reinhold Heydrich** 5/27/42, betrayed and killed 6/16/42

Kuechler (or **Küchler**), **FM Georg von** (ku(r)sh•luhr, **gay**•awrg) CiC German Army Group North in Russia 1/42-1/44, sentenced to 20 years at **Nuremberg**, freed 1953

Kuibyshev (kwee•buh•shef, -shev) Soviet city on the **Volga** River about 600 miles ESE of **Moscow**, temporary location for government offices and diplomatic missions evacuated from **Moscow** in the autumn of 1941, called Samara (suh•**mahr**•uh) before 1935 and since 1991

Kukum (ku•**koom**) coastal village on N **Guadalcanal** near **Lunga Point**

Kula Gulf (koo•lah) located between **Kolombangara** and **New Georgia** in the **Solomon Islands**, site of a night battle 7/5-6/43 in which a US naval force failed to prevent a Japanese force from reinforcing its garrison on Kolombangara

Kuman (koo•mahn) mountain range in Burma

Kunishi Ridge (koo•nee•shee, -nish•ee) final Japanese defensive position on the S tip of **Okinawa**, overcome about 6/20/45

Kunming (kun•ming) Chinese city, capital of **Yunnan** province, terminus of the **Burma Road**, and after the Japanese closed the road 4/42 terminus of the "**Hump**," an air supply route over the **Himalayas**

Kuomintang (kwoh•min•tang, -tahng, gwoh-) Chinese Nationalist Party founded by Sun Yat-sen in 1912, led by **Chiang Kai-shek** after Sun's death in 3/25

Kure (kur•ee, -ay, koor-) Japanese city and naval base near **Hiroshima**, heavily bombed 7/45

Kuribayashi, Lt Gen Tadamichi (kur•uh•bah•yahsh′•ee, tah•duh•mee′•chee) Japanese commander of **Iwo Jima,** died at the end of the campaign (3/22-24/45) under uncertain circumstances

Kurile (or Kuril) Islands (ku•reel, kur•il, kyur-) Japanese chain running from **Hokkaido** to **Kamchatka**, occupied by Soviet forces during 8/45 and ceded to the Soviet Union as agreed at **Yalta**

Kurita, Admiral Takeo (kur•ee•tuh, tah•kay•oh) Active throughout the Pacific war, he led the main Japanese fleet (the 1st Striking Force) in the Battle of **Leyte Gulf** (10/44), where his failure to exploit a temporary advantage ended his career, though he lived until 1977

Kurland -- see **Courland**

Kuroshima, Captain Kameto (koor•uh•shee′•muh, kuh•met•oh) Yamamoto's senior operations officer, who devised the battle plan for **Midway**

Kursk (kursk) city in Russia which gives its name to the **Kursk** salient and the battle that occurred there 7/43, the largest tank battle in history, which ended in defeat for Germany

Kurusu, Saburo (kur•oo•soo, suh•bur•oh) A career diplomat, he served as Japanese ambassador to Italy and Germany in the late 1930s, signing the pact that brought Japan into the **Axis**. In 11/41, he was sent to Washington to assist **Nomura** in peace negotiations, both of them apparently unaware that the Japanese were already committed to the **Pearl Harbor** attack.

Kusaka, Rear Admiral Ryunosuke (koo•**sah**•kuh, ree•**ah**•nuh•**soo**•kee, -kay) As **Nagumo**'s CoS from 4/41 to 11/42, he played a major role in the planning for **Pearl Harbor** and **Midway**, became CoS of the Combined Fleet under **Toyoda** 4/44

Kuznetsov, Admiral Nikolay (or **-lai**) (kuz•**net**•sawf, -suhv) CiC Soviet Navy throughout the war

Kuznetsov, Col Gen Vasily (kuz•**net**•sawf, -suhv, vah•**see**•lee) Excessively blamed for the fall of **Kiev** 10/41, he regained a command at **Stalingrad** and led armies on to Berlin.

Kwai (**kwy**) river in **Thailand** where the Japanese forced prisoners to build a bridge as part of the Burma-Thailand railway under appalling conditions, subject of the 1957 film *Bridge on the River Kwai*

Kwajalein (**kwah**'•juh•**layn**, -luhn) an atoll in the **Marshall Islands**, taken from the Japanese by US forces 2/1-6/44

Kwantung Army (**kwahn**•tung, **gwahn**•dung) name of the Japanese Army in **Manchuria** 1919-45. A force of 700,000 Japanese was overwhelmed by a million Soviet troops 8/45 when the Soviet Union declared war on Japan as agreed at **Yalta**.

Kyoto (kee•**oh**•toh, -aw, **kyoh**•toh, **kyaw**-) Japanese city considered for an atomic bomb target but spared because of its religious and cultural importance

Kyushu (**kyoo**•shoo) the S-most of the four main Japanese islands, whose invasion by the **Allies** was scheduled for 11/1/45

L

Laborde, Admiral Jean de (lah•bawrd, zhah(n) du) Commander of the French Mediterranean Fleet at **Toulon**, who ordered the scuttling of over 50 warships 11/27/42 as the Germans took over **Vichy** France

Labuan (lah•boo•ahn', luh•boo•uhn) island off the NW coast of **Borneo**, taken by the Japanese 1/42, retaken by Australian forces 6/45, part of Malaysia since 1963

Laconia (luh•koh•nee•uh) British troopship sunk by German submarine U-156 on 9/12/42. An attack on the **U-boat** by an American plane during rescue operations led **Admiral Dönitz** to issue the "Laconia Order" forbidding any future rescue operations.

Ladoga (lah•duh•guh, la-) the largest lake in Europe (7,000 square miles), NE of **Leningrad**, which provided the main supply line to the city, mostly when frozen, from 11/41 to 1/43

Lae (lah•ay, lay•ee) port city in NE **New Guinea**, occupied by the Japanese 3/8/42, retaken by Australian forces 9/43

Laffey, USS (laf•ee) the name of two US destroyers, the first sunk 11/13/42 in the Naval Battle of **Guadalcanal**, the second damaged but not sunk by **kamikazes** off **Okinawa** 4/16/45

Lambiridi (lam•buhr•ee'•dee) town just W of **Algiers**

Lammers, Hans Heinrich (lah•muhrs, hahns hyn•rikh) Chief of the Reich chancellery 1933-45, one of Hitler's closest advisors, tried at **Nuremberg** 1949 and imprisoned until 1952

Lampedusa (lam•pih•doo'•suh, -zuh) small Italian island between **Tunisia** and **Malta**, taken by British forces 6/12/43 to prepare for the invasion of **Sicily**

Lancaster (**lang**•kuh•stuhr) the leading British heavy bomber of the war, began service 3/42

Lancastria (lang•**kas**•tree•uh) British passenger liner sunk by a German bomber while evacuating 5,000 people from **St. Nazaire** in France to England 6/17/40. About 3,000 died.

Langsdorff, Hans (**lahngz**•dawrf, **hahns**) Captain of the **Admiral Graf Spee**, committed suicide two days after scuttling his ship in **Montevideo** harbor 12/17/39

La Pallice (lah pah•**lees**) Atlantic port in France, used by the Germans as a submarine base

La Sénia (lah sayn•**yah**) airfield near **Oran**, captured by US forces 11/9/42

Lashio (**lahsh**•yoh, **lash**•ee•oh) town in N Burma, the Allied end of the **Burma Road** into China, taken by Japanese forces 4/29/42 and not recaptured by the **Allies** until 3/45

La Spezia (lah **spayt**•see•uh, **spet**- , -tsyuh) coastal city and naval base in NW Italy

de Lattre de Tassigny, General Jean-Marie (du **laht**(ruh) du **tahs**•een•**yee**, **zhah(n)**-mar•**ee**) led the 14th Infantry Division against the Germans in 1940, served with the small **Vichy** Army until arrested for resisting the German takeover of unoccupied France in late 1942, escaped from a German prison in 1943 and joined the **Free French** in **Algiers**, led the French 1st Army from the 8/44 landings in S France into Germany, signed the German surrender for France 5/9/45.

Latvia (**lat**•vee•uh) one of the three **Baltic States**, annexed by the Soviet Union 7-8/40, occupied by Germany 7/41-10/44, independent since 8/91

Laval, Pierre (luh•val, lah- , la- , -vahl) pro-**Nazi** Premier of **Vichy** France, tried and shot for treason 10/15/45

Laycock, Maj Gen Robert ("Lucky") -- British Commando leader 1940-43, succeeded **Mountbatten** as Chief of Combined Operations 1943-47 and helped plan the **Normandy** invasion

Layton, Captain Edwin T. (layt'n) Head of US Navy code-breaking efforts against the Japanese throughout the war, stationed at **Pearl Harbor**, highly regarded by **Admiral Nimitz**

LCVP -- see **Higgins Boat**

League of Nations -- ineffectual predecessor of the United Nations, 1919-46

Leahy, Fleet Admiral William D. (lay•hee) US Chief of Naval Operations (CNO) from 1/37 until reaching the mandatory retirement age of 64 in 8/39, then became Governor of Puerto Rico (6/39) and Ambassador to **Vichy** France (1/41). From 7/42 to 3/49 he served as CoS to **Roosevelt** and **Truman** (a newly created position) and liaison to the Joint Chiefs of Staff (JCS) of which he was a member. Promoted to the newly created five-star rank of Fleet Admiral 12/44.

Lebanon (leb•uh•nuhn, -nahn) small Christian Arab country on the E **Mediterranean** coast, French mandate from 1920, taken from **Vichy** French control by British and **Free French** forces 6-7/41, gained independence 9/44

Lebensraum ("living space") (lay'•buhnz•rowm) **Hitler**'s view that Germany was entitled to additional land in the east

Leclerc, Maj Gen Philippe (luh•klair, fee•leep) nom de guerre of Jacques Philippe de Hautecloque (oht•kluhk). Led **Free French** troops against **Rommel** at the **Mareth Line** in **Tunisia** 3/43, then formed the 2nd French Armored Division which landed in **Normandy** 7/31/44 and liberated Paris 8/25/44

Ledo Road (lee•doh) a 300-mile military link from Ledo in India to the **Burma Road** N of the Japanese-controlled section. Begun late in 1942, it was used to retake Burma in 1944-45 and resupply China starting 1/45.

Lee, Vice-Admiral Willis A., Jr. (**"Ching"**) -- the leading US battleship group commander in the war, served throughout the Pacific

Leeb, FM Wilhelm Ritter von (**layb**, **vil**•helm **rit**•uhr) German Commander of Army Group North, which besieged **Leningrad**, relieved by **Hitler** at his own request 1/16/42, retiring at age 65

Leese, Lt Gen Sir Oliver (**lees**) succeeded **Montgomery** as CiC British 8th Army in Italy 1/44-10/44, then CiC Allied Land Force SE Asia 1944-45

Le Havre (US luh **hah**•vruh, Fr luh **ah**•vr) French coastal city on the **English Channel**

Leigh-Mallory, Sir Trafford (lee-**mal**•(uh)•ree) CiC British Fighter Command 11/42-10/44

Leipzig (**lyp**•sig, -sik) German city 100 miles SSW of Berlin, site of aircraft production, heavily bombed by the **Allies**, especially during **Big Week** 2/44

Le Kef (luh **kef**) key town in NW **Tunisia**, **Rommel**'s objective (unrealized) after breaking through the **Kassarine Pass**, now El Kef or Al Kaf (both el **kef**)

LeMay, Maj Gen Curtis (luh•**may**) directed US bombing campaigns against German and Japanese cities 1943-45

Lend-Lease -- US program of military aid to allies, primarily Britain, 3/41-8/45

Leningrad (**len'•in•grad**) Russian city on the E tip of the Gulf of Finland, besieged by German forces 9/41-1/44, causing about a million civilian deaths

Leopold III, King of Belgium (1934-1951) (**lee'•uh•pohld**) His policy of neutrality before the German invasion and his sudden and controversial decision to surrender to the invading Germans 5/28/40 led to his repudiation by the Belgian people.

Léros (**leh•rohs**) one of the **Dodecanese Islands**, a group off SW **Turkey** belonging to Italy from 1911 to 1945, occupied by the British after the Italian surrender 9/43, then by the Germans 11/43-5/45, now part of Greece

Lexington, USS (**lek•sing•tuhn**) aircraft carrier sunk in the Battle of the **Coral Sea** 5/8/42. A second Lexington, an **Essex**-class carrier, joined the Pacific Fleet in 1943 and survived the war.

Ley, Robert (**ly**) As head of the German Labor Front, **Nazi** dictator of German labor from 1934 to the end of the war. Committed suicide 10/25/45 while awaiting trial at **Nuremberg**

Leyte (**lay•tee**) Gulf in the **Philippines**, site of the largest naval battle in history 10/23-26/44 when the Japanese Fleet tried unsuccessfully to prevent US landings on the island of Leyte, which was taken 12/44

Liberty Ships -- over 2,700 standardized, partly pre-fabricated cargo vessels made in the US 1941-45

Libreville (US **lee'•bruh•vil**, Fr **lee•bruh•veel**) capital of **Gabon** in **French Equatorial Africa**, taken from **Vichy** control by **Free French** forces 11/13/40

Libya (**lib•ee•uh, -ah**) an Italian colony in N Africa since 1912, scene of heavy fighting in the Desert War 1940-43 between British-led and **Axis** forces, independent since 1951

Licata (lih•**kaht**•uh) town in **Sicily**, landing point for **Truscott**'s 3rd Division (US 7th Army) in Operation **Husky**, 7/10/43

Liddell Hart, Basil (**lid**'l **hahrt**, **baz**•uhl, **bay**•zuhl) British advocate of mobile tank warfare between the wars, who had more influence on Germans like **Guderian** and **Rommel** than on the British military

Lidice (**lee**'•duh•chay, -tsay, **lid**•uh•see) Czech village near **Prague** destroyed by the **SS** 6/10/42 as a reprisal for the assassination of **Reinhard Heydrich**

Liège (lee•**ezh**, -**ayzh**) heavily fortified industrial city in Belgium which slowed the German advance in both world wars. After being liberated by US forces 9/44, it was attacked by **V-1** and **V-2** missiles, and on 12/24/44 suffered the first jet bomber attack in history

Lille (**leel**) city in N France near the Belgian border

Lindbergh, Charles A (**lind**•buhrg, **lin-**) leading spokesman for the isolationist American (sic) First Committee, which disbanded after **Pearl Harbor**

Lindemann, Frederick A. -- see **Cherwell, Lord**

Lingayen Gulf (**ling**•gah•yen, **ling**'•ghy•uhn, lin-) the main invasion point on **Luzon** (NW coast) for both the Japanese in 12/41 and the US in 1/45

Lingga Roads (**ling**•guh) Japanese naval base near **Singapore**, starting point for two of the three task forces heading for **Leyte Gulf** 10/44

Linlithgow, Lord (Victor A. Hope) (lin•**lith**•goh) British Viceroy of India 1935-43

Linz (lints) city on the **Danube** in N Austria

Liri Valley (leer•ee) the main invasion route from **Cassino** to Rome

Lisbon (liz•buhn) capital of neutral Portugal, a center for espionage and intrigue

Liscome Bay, USS (lis•kuhm) escort aircraft carrier sunk by a Japanese submarine during the invasion of the **Makin** atoll near **Tarawa** 11/24/43

List, FM Wilhelm (list, vil•helm) led German armies in Poland, Belgium, and France (1939-40), CiC Southeast **(Balkans)** 6-10/41, CiC Army Group A (South) Soviet Union from 7/15/42 until dismissed by **Hitler** 9/9/42. Sentenced to life imprisonment at **Nuremberg** 2/46, released 12/52

Lithuania (lith•oo•ay′•nee•uh) one of the three **Baltic States**, independent since 1920, annexed by the Soviet Union 8/3/40, occupied by Germany 6/41-7/44, regained independence 1990

Littorio (leet•tohr•yoh) Italian battleship completed in 1940, put out of commission for almost a year by the British aerial torpedo attack on **Taranto** harbor 11/12/40, damaged by German air attack while heading for **Malta** after the Italian surrender 9/43, interned in **Egypt** by the British for the remainder of the war

Litvinov, Maxim (lit•vee•nuhf, -nuhv, mak•seem) pro-Western Soviet Commissar for Foreign Affairs 1930-39, Soviet Ambassador to the US 11/41-8/43

Liuchow (or Liuchou) (lyoo•choh), also **Liuzhou (lyoo•joh)** city in SE China

Liverpool (liv′•uhr•pool) the major port city and Atlantic convoy terminus in W England

Livorno (US lih•**vawr**•noh, It lee•**vohr**•noh) 1) coastal city in NW Italy 2) the best and only fully mobile Italian division in **Sicily** to meet the Allied invasion 7/43

Ljubljana (US **loo**•blee•**ah′**•nuh, -nah) capital of **Slovenia**, then part of Yugoslavia, near the Italian border

Lockwood, Vice-Admiral Charles A., Jr. -- Commander of the US Pacific Submarine Fleet from 1942 to the end of the war

Lodz (US **lahdz**, Pol **luj**, **looj**) Polish city 70 miles WSW of **Warsaw**

Lofoten Islands (**loh•fut′•n**) off the NW coast of Norway, an important source of fish products for Germany, successfully raided by the British 3/4/41 and 12/26-28/41

Lohse, Heinrich (**loh•**zuh, **hyn•**rikh) German Governor of the **Baltic States** and **Belorussia** 1941-44, with HQ in **Riga**, imprisoned for war crimes 1948-51

Loire (**lwahr**) the longest river in France, flowing 630 miles W into the Atlantic

Longstop Hill -- key point in **Tunisia** for control of the **Medjerda** valley, assaulted by Allied forces 12/42 but not taken until 4/43

Lord Haw Haw -- see **William Joyce**

Lorient (law•**ryahn**) French Atlantic seaport used as a submarine base by Germany

Los Alamos (laws **al′•uh•mohs**, lahs-) town in New Mexico NW of Santa Fe where the final planning and assembly of the atomic bomb took place before the successful test 50 miles NW of **Alamogordo**, a few hundred miles to the S

Los Negros (lohs **neg**•rohs, -**nay**•grohs) a small island in the **Bismarck Archipelago**, part of the **Admiralty Islands**, occupied by US forces 2/29/44

Lothian, Lord (Philip Henry Kerr) (**loathe**•ee•uhn) British Ambassador to the US from 8/39 to 12/12/40, when he died unexpectedly at 57, played a key role in starting the **Lend Lease** program

Louvain (loo•**va(n)**) Dutch name **Leuven** (loo•vuhn), cathedral city in C Belgium

LST (**Landing Ship, Tank**, aka Large Slow Target) -- versatile US craft used for amphibious landings

Lübeck (**lu**•bek) **Baltic** port city in Germany, site of the first large-scale British incendiary bombing raid 3/28/42, which damaged about half the city

Lublin Committee (aka **Lublin Poles**) (**loo**•blin, -bleen) a group of Communist-dominated, Soviet-backed Poles who replaced, starting in 1943, the London-based Polish government-in-exile (aka London Poles) as the de facto government by the end of the war. Named for a city in E Poland where they established HQ 7/44

Lucas, Maj Gen John P. (**loo**•kuhs) US commander of the **Anzio** landing 1/22/44, replaced 2/23/44 by **Truscott** for failing to move inland before German reinforcements contained the beachhead

Lucy -- see **Rudolf Rösseler**

Ludendorff Bridge (lood'n•dawrf) -- see **Remagen**

Luftwaffe (**luft'**•vahf•uh) name for the German Air Force during the **Nazi** era

Lunga Point (**luhn•**guh) US escort carrier, named for a key coastal position on **Guadalcanal** near **Henderson Field**

Lungling (**luhng•ling**) ancient Chinese city on the **Burma Road**, occupied by the Japanese 1942, retaken by Chinese forces 6/44

Lütjens, Vice-Admiral Günther (**lu•**tyenz, **gu(r)n•**tuhr) German fleet commander from 4/40, led the Atlantic commerce raiding expedition by the **Gneisenau** and **Scharnhorst** 1/21-3/22/41, went down with the **Bismarck** 5/27/41

Luzon (loo•**zahn**) the N-most and major island of the **Philippines**, taken by the Japanese 12/8/41-5/6/42, retaken by US forces 1/9/45-8/45

Lvov (l'**vawf**, l'**vuhv**) city in SE Poland, annexed by the Soviet Union 9/29/39, occupied by the Germans 6/29/41-7/27/44, retained by the Soviet Union after the war, now part of **Ukraine**

Lyon, or **Lyons** (lee•**oh(n)**, **lyaw(n)**)) city in SE France on the **Rhône** river

Lys River (**lees**) main line of defense in Belgium 5/40, crossed by the Germans 5/24-25

M

Maas (**mahs**) -- see **Meuse**

Maastrikht (**mahs**•trikt) city on the **Maas** river in SE Holland

Macao (muh•**kow**) port city in SE China, W of **Hong Kong**, a Portuguese colony occupied by the Japanese during the war, reverted to Chinese sovereignty 1999

MacArthur, General Douglas (muh•**kahr**•thuhr, mik•**ahr-**) first in his class at West Point 1903, Superintendent of West Point 1919-22, CoS of the Army 1930-35, chief military adviser to Philippine President **Manuel Quezon** 1935-41, Supreme Commander SW Pacific Area from 4/42, Supreme Allied Commander of occupation forces in Japan 9/45-4/51, commanded US and UN forces in **Korea** from 7/50 until relieved by **Truman** for insubordination 4/51

Macassar (or **Mak-**) **Strait** (muh•**kas**•uhr) between **Borneo** and **Celebes**, named for a port city on the SW coast of Celebes where the Japanese maintained a prison camp for most of the war, site of an early and successful US naval attack on Japanese shipping by four destroyers 1/24/42

Macedonia (**mas**•ih•**doh**′•nee•uh, -**dohn**′•yuh) an ethnic area in SE Yugoslavia, SW Bulgaria, and N Greece, part of Yugoslavia 1946-1991, became an independent country during the 1990s

Machinato Line (**mahch**•ih•**nah**′•toh, -ee-) Japanese air base and defense line in **Okinawa**, taken by US forces 4/25/45 after three weeks of heavy fighting

MacIntyre, Captain Donald (**mak**′•in•**tyr**) outstanding British destroyer captain and escort commander against German U-boats in the N Atlantic 1941-44, killing **Joachim Schepke** and capturing **Otto Kretschmer**, the two top German submarine aces, in his first convoy escort 3/41

Mackensen, Col Gen Eberhard von (mak′•en•sen, ay′•buhr•hahrt) commanded the German 14th Army at **Anzio**

Maclean, Brigadier Fitzroy (muh•**klayn**, mak•**layn**) British MP turned commando, **Churchill**'s personal liaison with **Tito** 9/43-3/45, led a team that included Churchill's son Randolph

Madagascar (mad•uh•gas′•kuhr, -kahr) the fourth largest island in the world, off the SE coast of Africa, a French colony since 1896, taken from **Vichy** control by British and South African forces 5/5/42-11/8/42. In 1940 the **Nazis** considered the forcible resettlement of European Jews there, but the plan was soon dropped.

Madang (mahd′•ahng) Japanese-held port and air base on the NE coast of **New Guinea**, destination of a 200-mile retreat through the jungle by 20,000 Japanese 1/44, of whom only about half survived, taken by Australian forces 4/44

Madeira (muh•deer•uh, -dair-) archipelago consisting of one large and seven small Portuguese islands about 400 miles off the NW coast of Africa

Madras (muh•dras, -drahs) port city on the E coast of India, now called Chennai (chuh•**ny**)

Magadan (mah•guh•dahn′) Soviet naval base and convoy port on the Sea of **Okhotsk** in Siberia

Magdeburg (mag′•duh•buhrg, mahg′-) German city on the **Elbe** about 80 miles WSW of Berlin, taken by US forces 4/18/45

Magic -- combined effort of US Army and Navy Intelligence to break Japanese diplomatic and military codes, begun 1939 and greatly expanded after **Pearl Harbor**, leading to success for the rest of the war, notably at **Midway**

Maginot Line (mazh′•uh•noh, maj′-) the most formidable defensive fortification ever constructed, running the entire length of the French border with Germany and Luxembourg. Since it was not continued along the Belgian border to the **North Sea**, the Germans were able to go around it in conquering France 5-6/40

Mahan (muh•han) 1) **USS** name ship for a class of 16 destroyers, sunk 12/7/44 in **Ormoc Bay** off **Leyte** in a **kamikaze** raid, named for 2) **Rear Admiral Alfred Thayer Mahan**, military theorist whose belief in the "decisive battle" featuring the battleship was widely accepted in the 1930s, but proved to be obsolete in WWII

Maidanek -- see **Majdanek**

Maikop (my•kawp) Soviet oil fields in the **Caucasus** named for a nearby city, taken by German forces 8/9/42, but with the oil wells blown up and unusable

Maingkwan (mang•kwahn) village in N Burma, Japanese stronghold

Mainz (mynts) city on the **Rhine** in WC Germany, taken by US forces 3/22/45

Maisky, Ivan M. (my•skee, ee•**vahn)** highly regarded Soviet ambassador to Britain 1932-43, Chair of the 1945 Allied Reparations Commission in **Moscow**

Majdanek (or **Mai-**) (**my′•**duh•nek, my•**dahn•**ik) German extermination camp in Poland outside **Lublin** where an estimated million and a half people were killed before it became the first death camp to be liberated, by Soviet forces, 7/23/44

Majorca (US), **Mallorca** (Sp) (muh•**jawr**•kuh, mah•**yawr**•kah) the largest of the **Balearic Islands** off the E coast of Spain

Majuro Atoll (mah•**joor**•oh, muh- , -**jur**-) part of the **Marshall Islands**, about four square miles, occupied by US forces 1/31/44

Makin Atoll (see also **Butaritari Island**) (**may**•kin) N-most part of the **Gilbert Islands**, occupied by Japanese forces 12/9/41, taken by US forces 11/20-23/43

Maknassy (now **Mek-**) (mak•**nas**•see, mik-) key pass in C **Tunisia**, also a nearby town

Malacca, Strait of (muh•**lahk**•uh, -**lak**-) (now spelled **Melaka**) a key waterway between **Sumatra** and the Malay (muh•**lay**, **may**•lay) peninsula

Malaya (muh•**lay**•uh) strategically and economically the most important British colony in the Far East, taken by the Japanese in a 500-mile drive S down the peninsula 12/41-1/42, culminating in the fall of **Singapore** 2/15/42. Now part of Malaysia (muh•**lay**•zhuh), an independent country since 1957

Maldives (**mawl**•deevz, **mal**- , -dyvz) a British protectorate in the **Indian Ocean** SW of **Ceylon** (now **Sri Lanka**) consisting of about 1,200 islands, an independent country since 1965

Maleme (mah•**leh**•mee, mal•**em**) port town in NW **Crete**, site of a key airfield which, when taken by German paratroopers 5/20-21/41, assured the success of their invasion against British, Australian, and **New Zealand** defenders

Malenkov, Georgy (or **-gi**) **M.** (Rus muh•**len**′•kawf, US **mah**•luhn•kawf) A close crony of **Stalin** from 1927, he played a leading role in the Great Purges of 1937-38. One of the five original members of the Soviet State Defense Committee (GKO), which included Stalin, formed eight days after the German invasion. Ruled the Soviet Union briefly after Stalin's death in 1953, but lost control to **Khrushchev** by 1955.

Malinovsky, Marshal Rodion (mah•len•ahv′•skee, **mal•in-** , **awf′-** , US **roh**•dee•ahn, Rus rah•**dyawn**) commanded an army at **Stalingrad** and fronts in the **Ukraine** and E Europe, then led the Transbaikal (**tranz•by•kahl**) Front against the Japanese 8/45. Soviet Minister of Defense 1957-67.

Malmédy (**mal•may•dee**) town in the Belgian **Ardennes**, site of a massacre of at least 70 American soldiers captured by an **SS** unit led by **Lt Col Joachim Peiper**, 12/17/44

Malmö (**mal•**moh, **mahl-** , Sw **mahl•**mu) S-most city in Sweden, opposite **Copenhagen**

Maloelap (**mah•loh•eh•lahp**) one of the Japanese-held **Marshall Islands**, about four square miles, attacked by US carrier planes 1/31/42 in the first US offensive carrier action of the war, but bypassed two years later by land forces taking control of the Marshalls

Malöy (or **Maalöy**) (now **Måløy**) (**mohl•**ohy) German naval base on the SW coast of Norway, successfully raided by British commandos 12/27/41

Malraux, Andre (US mal•**roh**, Fr mahl- , **ahn•**dray) French writer who fought with the Underground and the French 1st Army in 1944, then became Minister of Information under **DeGaulle**

Malta (**mawl•**tuh) British island and vital military base about 60 miles S of **Sicily**. Its 280,000 inhabitants were collectively awarded the George Cross for civilian bravery 4/42 after enduring over a year of continuous bombardment from **Axis** planes, which only abated late in 1942.

Maly (now **Malyy**) **Trostenets** (**mah**•lee trohs•tuh•**nets,** trahs-)
German concentration camp near **Minsk** in Russia, opened 6-
7/41, turned into an extermination camp 5/42 with the use of gas
vans, liberated by the Soviet Army early in July 1944

Manado (or **Menado**) (muh•**nah**•doh) city on the N tip of
Celebes, captured 12/11/41 by the Japanese, who then declared
war on the **Dutch East Indies**

Manchuria (man•**chur**•ee•uh) the NE region of China,
annexed by Japan 4/32 as a puppet regime renamed **Manchukuo**
(man•**choo**•kwoh, -koo•oh), invaded by Soviet forces 8/8/45 and
conquered in about two weeks, returned to China after the war

Mandalay (**man**•dl•ay) city in C Burma, second largest in the
country, taken by the Japanese 5/42 from Allied troops led by US
General Stilwell, retaken by troops led by British **General Slim**
3/20/45

Mandel, Georges (man•**del, zhawrzh**) named French Minister
of the Interior by **Paul Renaud** 5/18/40, opposed surrender and
left for N Africa 6/40, arrested in **Meknès** (**Morocco**) 9/41 and
finally executed by the French **Milice** near Paris 7/7/44

Manhattan Project (man•**hat**'n) code name for the US atomic
bomb program, officially begun under the direction of **Maj Gen
Leslie R. Groves** 9/23/42

Manila (muh•**nil**•uh) **Philippine** capital, on the island of
Luzon, entered by Japanese forces unopposed 1/2/42, retaken by
US forces 2/45

Mannerheim, FM Baron Carl Gustav (or **-taf**) **von**
(**man**'•uhr•**hym, mahn**'- , **kahrl gus**•tahv, -tahf) Finland's
greatest military and political leader, recalled from retirement in
1939, at age 72, to lead the inspired but finally unsuccessful
defense against the Soviet invasion. Joined **Hitler** in attacking
the Soviet Union in 1941 to regain territory lost in the **Russo-**

Finnish War, but withdrew on favorable terms in 1944. President of **Finland** 8/4/44-3/4/46.

Mannerheim Line (**man'•uhr•hym**, **mahn'-**) 60-mile defense line across the **Karelian Isthmus** built under **Mannerheim**'s direction in the 1930s, proved highly effective in the **Russo-Finnish War** of 1939-40

Manstein, FM Erich von (**mahn•**styn, -shtyn, **ay•**rikh) considered by many the greatest German general of WWII, devised the **Ardennes** strategy (Manstein Plan) for invading France. His successes in the Soviet Union included the capture of the **Crimea** (9/41-6/42) and the recapture of **Kharkov** (3/43). Dismissed by **Hitler** 3/30/44, sentenced to 18 years imprisonment for war crimes in 1949, freed 5/6/53

Manteuffel, General Baron Hasso von (**mahn•**toy•fuhl, **hah•**soh) German tank commander who served with distinction in the Soviet Union (1941-42, 1943-44), **Tunisia** (1943), France (1944), and Germany (1945)

Manus (**man•**uhs, **mahn•**us) the largest of the **Admiralty Islands**, taken from the Japanese 3/15-26/44 by US forces, who then used Seeadler Harbor as a major fleet base

Maoris (**mow•**reez, ma•**awr•**eez) native New Zealanders who fought with British Commonwealth troops in N Africa and Italy

Mao Tse-tung (**mow•**tsuh•**tung**, -tsuh- , -dzuh•**dung**, -dzuh-) now written **Mao Zedong** (**mow•**zuh•**dung**, -dzuh- , **-dzuh-** , **-dahng**) Chairman of the Chinese Communist Party from 1931 until his death in 1976, formed an alliance with **Chiang Kai-shek**'s **Kuomintang** in 1937 to resist the Japanese invasion. After Japan's defeat, he won a Civil War against Chiang in 1949.

Maquis (or **maquis**), **the** (mah•kee) the French resistance movement against German occupation, from 4/43, also applied to units and/or individuals (who were also called **maquisards**) within the movement

March, Juan (**mahrch, (h)wahn**) wealthy Majorcan, supporter of **Franco**

Marcks, Maj Gen Erich (**mahrks, ay'•rikh**) headed the group which prepared the initial plans for the German invasion of the Soviet Union

Marco Polo Bridge Incident -- a skirmish in **Peking** 7/7/37 used by the Japanese to justify escalating their invasion of China into the **Sino-Japanese War**

Marcus Island (**mahr•kuhs**) US protectorate about 1,000 miles E of **Iwo Jima**, occupied by the Japanese throughout the war

Mareth Line (**mar•eth, mahr-**) a defense line in SE **Tunisia** originally built by the French utilizing a dry river bed (the **Wadi Zigzaou**) as an anti-tank obstacle. **Rommel**'s army withstood frontal attacks by **Montgomery**'s 8th Army here 3/20-27/43.

Mariana Islands (or **Marianas**) (**mar•ee•an'•uh, mair-** , **mahr•ee•ahn'•uhz**) a C Pacific group including **Saipan**, **Tinian**, and **Guam**, taken by US forces 6/15/44-8/10/44, providing the first bases close enough to bomb Japan

Mariupol (**mar•ee•ooh'•puhl**) Soviet city on the Sea of **Azov**, taken by German forces 10/8/41, retaken by Soviet forces 9/10/43, called **Zhdanov** (**zhdah•nuhf, zhuh•dah-**) 1948-1989

Mariveles (mah•ree•veh•lehs, -rih-) **MacArthur's** HQ on the S end of **Bataan** until his evacuation 3/11/42

Market-Garden, Operation -- see **Arnhem**

Marne (**mahrn**) French river E of Paris, crossed by German forces 6/12/40

Marpi Point (mahr•pee) the N tip of **Saipan**, where hundreds of Japanese civilians died jumping from high cliffs, though there is doubt about how many were suicides

Marquesas Islands (mahr•kay•zuhz, -suhz, -suhs) one of several French colonies in the S Pacific occupied by the **Free French** from 1941

Marrakesh (Fr -kech) (mar•uh•kesh′, mar′•uh•kesh) resort city in **Morocco** near the Atlas Mountains, 150 miles SSW of **Casablanca**, visited by **Roosevelt** and **Churchill** 1/24-25/43 after the Casablanca Conference. Site of a meeting between Churchill and **DeGaulle** 1/12/44

Marsala (mahr•sah•luh) small port city and river in W **Sicily**

Marseilles (mahr•say) the second largest city in France, on the **Mediterranean** coast, liberated by Allied forces 8/28/44

Marshall, General of the Army George C. -- US Army CoS from 9/1/39, Chairman of the Joint Chiefs of Staff from 12/41 to the end of the war. As Secretary of State (1947-49), he inaugurated the **Marshall Plan** in 1947 to aid the economic recovery of Europe, for which he received the Nobel Peace Prize in 1953.

Marshall Islands -- Japanese mandate group in the C Pacific from 1920, including **Kwajalein**, **Eniwetok**, **Majuro**, **Roi**, and **Namur**, taken by US forces 2/44. US Trust Territory 1945-1986, independent in association with the US since 1986.

Martinique (mahrt′n•eek′) French island colony in the **Caribbean Sea**, part of the West Indies, joined the **Allies** 1943

Maryland, USS (mair•uh•luhnd) one of a class of three battleships that also included the **West Virginia** and Colorado, commissioned 1921-23. Lightly damaged at **Pearl Harbor**

12/41, torpedoed at **Saipan** 6/44, heavily damaged by a
kamikaze attack at **Okinawa** 4/45, decommissioned 1946

Masaryk, Jan G. (**mas•uh•rik**, **mah•sah•rik**, **yahn**) Czech
Ambassador to Britain 1925-38, Foreign Minister of the
government-in-exile in London under **Benes** 1940-45 and the
post-war government in Czechoslovakia, died 3/10/48 in Prague,
possibly murdered for his anti-communist stance

Massawa (mah•sah•wah) now **Mitsiwa** (mit•soo•uh) (Both
names have variant spellings.) Italian naval base on the Red Sea,
whose capture by the British 4/8/41 marked the final defeat of
the Italians in **Eritrea**

Mast, Charles E. (US **mast**, Fr **mahst**) a senior **Vichy**
commander in **Algiers** who, with the help of US diplomat
Robert Murray, initiated a secret meeting with **Mark Clark**
10/22/42 in the nearby fishing village of Cherchel (or -chell)
(shair•shel) to arrange French cooperation with the **Allies** in their
invasion of NW Africa. The meeting was a confused affair in
which Clark was almost captured.

Matanikou (or -**kau**) (muh•**tahn**•ih•kuh, -kow) river and
coastal village in **Guadalcanal**, a few miles W of **Henderson
Field**

Matapan, Cape (**mat'•uh•pan**) (now Cape Taínaron
(**tay'•nuh•rawn**, **teh'•nah-**)) cape on the S tip of Greece which
gives its name to the **Battle of Matapan**, a major defeat for the
Italian navy at the hands of the British 3/28/41

Mateur (ma•**tuhr**) key Tunisian town 20 miles SSW of
Bizerte, taken by Allied forces 5/3/43

Matmata (or -**tah**) **Hills** (met•meh•**tah**, maht•mah•**tah**,
maht•**mah**•tah) the inland (W) end of the German **Mareth Line**
in **Tunisia**, used by **Montgomery** to go around the line 3/43.
Also the name of a town in that area.

Matsuda, Rear Admiral C. (mat•soo•duh, maht-) commanded one of the two groups of the Japanese North Force in the Battle of **Leyte Gulf** 10/44

Matsui, General Iwane (maht•soo•ee, ee•**wah**•nee, -ay) formulated the plan to invade **Shanghai** 8/37 and nominally led the Japanese advance 170 miles up the **Yangtze** river to take **Nanking**. Though the resulting atrocities were contrary to his intention, he was hanged as a war criminal 12/23/48.

Matsuoka, Yosuke (**maht**•soo•**oh′**•kuh, -kah, yoh•**suk**•eh, -ay) led the dramatic Japanese withdrawal from the **League of Nations** 2/33 when the League condemned Japan for its 9/31 invasion of **Manchuria**. Headed the South Manchurian Railway 1935-39, served as Foreign Minister under **Konoye** from 7/22/40 to 7/41, during which time he concluded the **Tripartite Pact** with Germany and Italy (9/27/40), recognized a puppet regime in **Nanking** under **Wang Ching-wei** 11/40, and signed a neutrality treaty with the Soviet Union 4/14/41. Coined the name **Greater East Asia Co-Prosperity Sphere**. Died while awaiting trial for war crimes 6/27/46

Mauldin, Sgt William H. (Bill) (**mawl**•din, -duhn) infantry cartoonist who created the anti-heroic characters Willie and Joe as US forces moved through **Sicily**, Italy, France, and Germany

Mauritius (maw•**rish**•uhs, -ee•uhs) small island in the **Indian Ocean** about 500 miles E of **Madagascar**, a British colony until 1968, independent since 1992. Some of its mostly Indian population fought in the Middle East, notably at **Bir Hakeim**; others helped garrison **Madagascar** from 1/44.

Mauser (**mow**•zuhr) German small arms manufacturing company which provided the standard German rifle of the war and many other weapons

Mauthausen (**mowt′**•**how**•zen) German concentration camp in Austria, E of **Linz**. Although not officially an extermination camp, it produced a death toll estimated at 180,000, including 36,000 recorded executions.

Maya (my•uh, mah•yah) Japanese heavy cruiser, in action at **Guadalcanal** (10/42) and the **Aleutians** (3/43), sunk 10/23/44 by the US submarine **Dace** in the Battle of **Leyte Gulf**

McAuliffe, Brig Gen Anthony (mik•aw•lif) commander of US forces surrounded in **Bastogne** during the Battle of the **Bulge**, on 12/22/44 rejected a German surrender demand with the famous reply "Nuts!" Held out until relieved by **Patton**'s 3rd Army 12/26

McCloy, John J. -- US Assistant Secretary of War 4/41-11/45

McClusky, Lt Com Clarence Wade, Jr. -- led the **USS Enterprise** Air Group at **Midway**, credited with sighting the four Japanese carriers that were sunk

McCollum, Commander Arthur H. (mik•**kuhl**•luhm) Head of the Far East Section of the Office of Naval Intelligence (ONI) before and during the **Pearl Harbor** attack, alleged by some to have prepared a plan to goad Japan into the attack

McCreery, General Sir Richard -- as CoS to **Alexander** from 8/42 helped plan the Second Battle of **El Alamein**, served as a Corps Commander in the 8th Army in Italy from 9/43 and as Commander of 8th Army from 11/44 to the end of the war

McNair, Lt Gen Lesley J. (mak•**nair**, **les**•lee, **lez**-) overall commander of Army Ground Forces 7/40-6/44, in charge of training US troops. Died 7/25/44 while observing in **Normandy**

McNarney, General Joseph Taggart (mik•**nahr**•nee) Deputy US CoS from 3/42 representing the Army Air Corps, Deputy SAC in the **Mediterranean** from 10/44, succeeded **Eisenhower** as Commander of US Army forces in Europe 3/7/45 to 1947

Medal of Honor -- the highest US military award, given only for bravery in combat

Médenine (mayd•neen) town in SE **Tunisia**, SE of the **Mareth Line**, scene of **Rommel**'s last defeat, 3/6/43, before leaving N Africa three days later

Mediterranean (med•ih•tuh•ray′•nee•uhn) the most strategically important sea in the world, lying between S Europe and N Africa

Medjerda (med•jer•dah′) river valley in NE **Tunisia**

Medjez-el-Bab (med•jez el bahb, meh-) key town in NC **Tunisia**

Mehdia (may•dyah, meh-) French Moroccan resort town at the mouth of the **Sebou** river on the Atlantic coast 80 miles N of **Casablanca**, landing area for **Truscott**'s 9,000 troops in Operation **Torch**, 11/8-10/42, who had to overcome resistance from its **Vichy** French defenders

Meiktila (mayk•tih•lah, mek•tih•luh, mik•tee•luh) Japanese transportation and administration center 90 miles S of **Mandalay** in Burma, taken by the British 17th Indian Division 2/28-3/3/45 in conjunction with the British advance on Mandalay

Mein Kampf ("My Struggle") **(myn kahmf) Hitler**'s autobiography and political program, written 1924-26

Meitner, Lise (myt•nuhr, lee•zuh) Austrian-born theoretical physicist who helped calculate the potential power of splitting the atom. Because she was Jewish, she left Germany for Sweden in the 1930s and her work benefited the **Allies** rather than Germany.

Meknès (mek•nes) city in NW French **Morocco**

Mekong (may•kawng, -kahng) the major river of SE Asia, flowing 2,600 miles S from SE China through the vast **Mekong Delta** in S Vietnam into the S China Sea

Memel (may•muhl, mem•uhl) Lithuanian port city, part of **East Prussia** before WWI, annexed by Germany 3/39, taken by Soviet forces 1/45, now **Klaipeda (kly•pih•duh)** in **Lithuania**

Memphis Belle (mem•fis bel) an American bomber flying missions from Britain against German-occupied Europe, subject and title of a documentary film directed by William Wyler, shot 5/43, released 4/44

Mendès-France, Pierre (US men•dis frans, Fr mahn•dez frah(n)z', pyair) French Undersecretary of the Treasury who joined the **Free French** in N Africa and served as Minister of the Economy under **DeGaulle** 9/44-4/45. Premier of France 1954-55

Mengele, Dr. Josef (or Joseph) (Fritz) (men•guh•luh, meng- , yoh•zef) chief **Nazi** doctor at **Auschwitz** from 5/43, infamous for condemning thousands to death and conducting sadistic medical experiments. Escaped prosecution after the war and is thought to have died in South America in the early 1980s

Menzies, Sir Robert Gordon (men•zeez) PM of Australia 4/39-8/41, 1949-1966, a strong supporter of **Churchill** and British war policy

Menzies, Maj Gen Sir Stewart (ming•is) (sic) succeeded Admiral Hugh Sinclair as Chief of MI-6 (the major branch of the British Secret Intelligence Service) 11/28/39 and served until 1952

Meretskov, Marshal Kirill (or Kiril) A. (Rus meh•ret•skahv, kyir•yeel) commanded the Soviet 7th Army in the **Russo-Finnish War**, led various N fronts against the Germans, and the 1st Far Eastern Front against the Japanese 8/45

Merrill, Maj Gen Frank D. (**mair•**il) led **Merrill's Marauders** in guerrilla warfare behind Japanese lines in Burma from 2/44, became Deputy US Commander in Burma-India 8/44

Mersa Matruh (**muhr•**suh maht**•roo**) Eygptian port town and railhead, British 8th Army defensive position taken by **Rommel** 6/27 as the 8th Army retreated to **El Alamein**

Mers-el-Kébir (**mehrs** el kay**•beer**) French naval base near **Oran** on the coast of **Algeria**, where a major portion of the French fleet was attacked by British ships 7/3/40 to prevent the **Vichy** government from letting it fall into German hands

Mersey (**muhr•**zee) British river flowing into the Irish Sea at **Liverpool**

Messe, Marshal Giovanni (**meh•**say, jyoh**•vahn•**nee) After commanding Italian forces in **Ethiopia** (1935-36), **Albania** (1939), Greece (1940), and the Soviet Union (1941-1/43), he led the Italian 1st Army in **Tunisia** until the **Axis** surrender of N Africa 5/43. Army CoS under **Marshal Badoglio's** government from Italy's surrender 9/43 until 1945

Messerschmitt, Willi (or **Willy**) (**mes'•**uhr**•shmit, vil•**ee) designer and builder of the most famous German planes during the war, including the standard single-seat fighter (Me-109) and the first jet (Me-262)

Messervy, Gen Sir Frank W. (**mes•uhr•**vee) After divisional commands in N Africa (1941-42), he was sent to India, where he led the 7th Indian division at **Kohima** (1944) and from 10/44 the 4th Corps, which took **Meiktila** in Burma 2-3/45

Messina (**meh•see•**nuh) city on the NE tip of **Sicily** and the narrow strait separating the island from the toe of Italy. Allied forces entered the city 8/17/43 but failed to prevent the Germans from evacuating up to 60,000 troops and most of their equipment across the strait during the preceding week. The **Allies** began crossing the strait 9/3/43

Metaxas, General Ioannis (John) (muh•**tak**•suhs, meh- , US yoh•**an**•uhs, Gr yaw•**ahn**•yees) dictator of Greece from 8/4/36 until his death 1/29/41, led the successful Greek resistance to the Italian invasion which started 10/28/40 from **Albania**

Metz (**mets**) city in NE France, liberated by **Patton**'s 3rd Army in late November 1944

Meuse (US **myooz**, Fr **mu(r)z**) river flowing from NE France through Belgium and Holland (where it is called the **Maas**) into the **North Sea**

Mexico (**mek′•**sih•**koh**) entered the war on the Allied side 5/42

Mezzouna (mez•oo•**nah**) town in EC **Tunisia**, site of a German airfield

Mga (m'**gah**) key railroad town ESE of **Leningrad**, held by German forces from 9/1/41 to 1/15/44

Michael, King of Romania (**my**•kuhl, roh•**may**•nee•uh, -**mayn**•yuh) became king 9/6/40 at the age of 19 after his father, **Carol II** (**kar**•uhl), abdicated. He was forced to cede power to the pro-German **Marshal Antonescu**, but when Soviet troops entered Romania 8/22/44, he arrested Antonescu on 8/23 and joined the **Allies**. Abdicated 12/30/47 rather than lead a communist regime.

Michelier, Vice-Admiral Francois Félix (mish•el•**yay**, frah(n)•**swah** fay•**leeks**) **Vichy** naval commander of N Africa, in **Casablanca** 11/42 where he ordered resistance to the Allied **Torch** landings

Middleton, Maj Gen Troy H. -- commanded the US 45th Infantry Division in **Sicily** and Italy, and the 8th Corps in the Battle of the **Bulge** and the final advance into Germany

Midway -- US atoll with two small islands 1,300 miles NW of **Hawaii**, which gives its name to the Battle of **Midway**, 6/3-6/41, the first major US victory over Japan and the turning point of the Pacific War

Mignano (min•**yahn**•oh) town and gap in Italy about 10 miles SE of **Cassino**

Mihailović (or -**haj**-), **General Draža** (mih•**hy**•luh•vich, **drah**•zhuh) led the Serbian nationalist resistance forces known as **Chetniks** against the Germans following the fall of Yugoslavia 4/41, but increasingly fought **Tito's** communist partisans instead, with Italian and German help, and was shot for treason 7/17/46

Mikawa, Vice-Admiral Gunichi (mih•**kah**•wuh, gu•**nee**•chee) After participating at **Pearl Harbor** and **Midway**, he became CiC at **Rabaul**, from where he led a group of Japanese cruisers which sank four Allied cruisers (three US and one Australian) in the Battle of **Savo Island** 8/8-9/42 with no losses

Mikolajczyk, Stanislaw (**mik**•ih•**ly**•chik, **mee**•koh- , **stan'**•is•lahv, stah•**nee**•slahf) headed the Polish government-in-exile in London after the death of **Sikorski** 7/14/43 until he resigned 11/44. Deputy PM of the postwar government until he was defeated in the 1/47 elections, emigrated to the US 10/47

Milan (mih•**lan**, -**lahn**) the major city of N Italy, under German control from the Italian surrender 9/43 until late April 1945

Milch ("Milk") **cows** (**milsh**) German submarines used as tankers for other **U-boats** from 4/42

Milch, FM Erhard (**milsh**, **air**•hahrt) operational head of the German Air Force (and air production from 11/41) under various titles and with some political setbacks, from the mid-1930s to 1944. Imprisoned for war crimes 1947-55

Mili (**mee**•lee) atoll in the **Marshall Islands**, Japanese air base bypassed by advancing US forces 2/44

Milice (mee•**lees**) the secret police of **Vichy** France, working with the **Gestapo**

Milne Bay (**miln**) Allied air base located on the E tip of **New Guinea**, the site of an unsuccessful Japanese landing aimed at **Port Moresby**, repulsed by Australian forces 8/26-9/6/42, the first Allied land victory against the Japanese

Mindanao (**min**•duh•**now**′, **-nah**′•oh) second largest and S-most of the main **Philippine Islands**, scene of fighting between the Japanese 35th Army and the US 8th Army from 4/45 until the end of the war

Mindoro (min•**dawr**•oh, **-dohr**•oh) Philippine island S of **Luzon**, taken by US forces 12/44 as a base to support the invasion of Luzon

Minsk (**minsk**) city in W Russia, now the capital of **Belarus**, in German hands from 7/41 to 7/44

Missouri, USS (mih•**zur**•ee, -uh) the last battleship built for the US Navy (commissioned 6/44), used for the signing of the Japanese surrender in Tokyo Bay 9/2/45

Mitscher, Vice-Admiral Marc A. (**mich**•uhr) an expert on naval aviation, commander of the **USS Hornet** for the **Doolittle Raid** (4/42) and the Battle of **Midway** (6/42), from 1/44 Commander of Fast Carrier Task Force 38/58, which played a major role in the Pacific War

Mitsubishi (mit•su•bee′•shee, -bih-) leading manufacturer of
Japanese aircraft during the war, of which the A6M (**Zero**) is the
best known

Mitterand, François (mee•tuh•rahn′, frah(n)•**swah)** French
resistance leader, President of France 1981-1995

Mius (mee•yoos) river in S Russia, used as a German defense
line against a Soviet counter-attack 11-12/41

Mizukami, Maj Gen Genzu (meez•oo•kahm′•ee, ghen•soo)
Japanese commander at **Myitkyina** in Burma, committed suicide
when the town fell 8/1/44

Model, FM Walther (Walter) (mohd'l) a German staff officer
in Poland (1939) and France (1940), he led the 3rd **Panzer**
Division in the invasion of the Soviet Union (1941), then the 9th
Army 1/42-1/44. From 1943 to 8/44 his success in stabilizing
various fronts in the USSR earned him the nickname "**Hitler**'s
Fireman." He was transferred to France 8/44 as CiC Western
Front, then commanded Army Group B in Belgium 9/44,
directing the successful defense of **Arnhem** and the Battle of the
Bulge. Always loyal to Hitler, he committed suicide 4/21/45
when his army was trapped in the **Ruhr** pocket.

Mogadishu (moh•guh•dee′•shoo, -dish′•oo, maw-) port on the
Indian Ocean and capital of **Italian Somaliland**, taken by
British-led Allied forces 2/25/41, now the capital of Somalia

Mogami (moh•gahm•ee) name ship for a class of four Japanese
heavy cruisers, damaged at **Midway**, sunk in the Battle of **Leyte
Gulf** 10/25/44

Mogaung (moh•gahng, -gowng) key railroad town and river
valley in N Burma, the first town in Burma to be liberated from
the Japanese by Allied forces, 6/26/44

Möhne Dam (mu(r)•nuh) one of two German dams destroyed by the British with innovative "bouncing bombs" 5/16-17/43

Molde (mohl•duh) coastal town in C Norway

Mölders (or Moelders), Colonel Werner (mel•duhrz, **vair•nuhr)** a leading **Luftwaffe** fighter pilot who was the first recipient of the Diamonds added to the **Knight's Cross** before dying in a non-combat crash 11/22/41

Molotov, Vyacheslav M. (mahl'•uh•tawf, moh'•luh•tahf, vyih•chis•**lahf)** Soviet Foreign Minister 1939-49, 53-56, signed the **Molotov-Ribbentrop Pact** with Germany 8/23/39, including a secret protocol which provided for the division of Poland and Soviet annexation of the **Baltic States**

Moltke, Count Helmuth von (mohlt•kuh, **mawlt-** , **hel•**moot) German leader of the anti-**Nazi Kreisau Circle**, named for his family estate in **Silesia**, hanged 1/23/45 at the age of 37

Mongolia (mahng•**goh•**lee•uh, mahn-) in mid-1939 the site of a decisive victory by tank forces led by Soviet **General Zhukhov** over Japanese forces invading from **Manchuria (Manchukuo)**

Mönichkirchen (mur'•nish•**keer•**shuhn) village in SE Austria, **Hitler**'s base for directing the **Balkan** campaign from 4/12 to 4/26/41

Monowitz (mahn•uh•vits, **mawn-**) site of the Buna works, an **IG Farben** factory in S Poland for synthetic rubber and oil, using slave labor from nearby **Auschwitz**, from 5/42

Monrovia, USS (muhn•**roh•**vee•uh) a cargo ship converted into an amphibious attack transport, **Admiral Hewitt**'s flagship for the **Sicily** landings 9/43, active in the Pacific from **Tarawa** (11/43) to **Okinawa** (4-6/45)

Monte Cassino -- see **Cassino**

Montecorvino (**mahn•**tay•kawr•**vee•**noh) key airfield SE of **Salerno**

Montenegro (**mahn•tuh•nay'•**groh, **-nee'-**) a province (now a constituent republic) in the SC part of Yugoslavia

Montevideo (**mahn•tuh•vih•day'•**oh, **-vid'•**ee•**oh**) the capital of Uruguay, site of the **Graf Spee** incident

Montgomery, FM Sir Bernard Law (mahnt•**guhm•**uh•ree, **-guhm•**ree, US buhr•**nahrd**, Brit **buhr•**nuhrd) active throughout WWII, best known for leading the British 8th Army to victory over **Rommel** at **El Alamein** 10/23-11/4/42

Moran, Lord Charles (**mawr•**in) **Churchill**'s personal physician

Moravia -- see **Bohemia-Moravia**

Morell, Dr. Theodor (mawr•**el**, **tay'•**oh•**dohr**) **Hitler**'s personal physician 1936-45, widely regarded as a self-serving fraud

Morgan, Lt Gen Sir Frederick E. -- CoS for the planning of the **Normandy Invasion** from 4/23/43

Morgenthau, Henry, Jr. (**mawr'•**ghen•**thaw**, **-thow**) US Secretary of the Treasury 1/34-7/45, author of the **Morgenthau Plan**, presented at the second **Quebec Conference** 9/44, to convert Germany from an industrial to an agrarian country after the war

Morison, Samuel Eliot (**mawr•**uh•suhn, **mahr•**ih-) Harvard history professor who served on eight ships as a member of the US Naval Reserve and wrote the Navy-sponsored *History of*

United States Naval Operations in WW II (15 volumes, 1950-62)

Morocco (muh•**rahk**•oh) -- see **French North Africa**

Morotai (**mawr'**•uh•**ty**) island between **New Guinea** and the **Philippines**, taken by the Japanese 1/42, retaken by American forces 9/15/44 for its airfield

Morrison, Herbert Stanley (**mawr**•uh•suhn, **mahr**•ih-) British Labour Party leader who helped force **Chamberlain's** resignation 5/8/40, then served in **Churchill's** coalition government as Minister of Supply (5-10/40) and then as Home Secretary and Minister of Home Security (10/40-1945), joining the War Cabinet in 1941

Morshead, Lt Gen Sir Leslie J. -- commanded the 9th Australian Division in N Africa (including **Tobruk** and **El Alamein**) 1941-42 and the Far East (including **Lae**) 1943-44, then became overall commander in **New Guinea** (1944) and **Borneo** (1945)

Mortain (**mawr•teh(n)**) a town in **Brittany** where Allied forces halted a German counterattack aimed at the coastal town of **Avranches**, ten miles to the W at the base of the **Cherbourg Peninsula** 8/7-14/44

Moscow (**mahs**•koh, -kow) capital of the Soviet Union, which the Germans failed to capture after getting within 20 miles in late November, 1941

Mosel (**moh**•zuhl) a river flowing from NE France into the **Rhine** in Germany, called the **Moselle** (moh•**zel**) in France

Moskalenko, Col Gen Kirill S. (**mahs**•kuh•**leng'**•koh, kyir•**yeel**) led various Soviet forces in the SW Front throughout the war, notably at **Kharkov**, **Kursk**, and **Kiev**

Mosley, Sir Oswald E. (**mohz•**lee) British Fascist leader, in custody 1940-43

Mosquito -- versatile high-speed British plane in service from 1942 as a bomber, fighter, and reconnaissance aircraft

Moulin, Jean (code name **"Max"**) (moo•**leh(n)**, **zhah(n)**) French resistance leader who succeeded in uniting most groups into the Conseil National de la Résistance (CNR), loyal to **DeGaulle**. Captured by the Germans 6/21/43, he died early in July from extended torture.

Moulmein (mool•**mayn**, mohl-) port city in S Burma at the mouth of the **Salween River**, captured by Japanese forces 1/31/42 and held until the end of the war

Mountbatten, Admiral Lord Louis (mownt•**bat'**n) in action as a destroyer captain off Norway (5/3-4/40) and **Crete** (5/23/40), planned the raids on **St. Nazaire** (3/42) and **Dieppe** (8/42), became CiC Allied Forces SE Asia 10/43, where he initiated a successful land campaign against the Japanese in Burma led by **General Slim**, received the surrender of 750,000 Japanese at **Singapore** 9/45. A popular and respected first cousin of Queen Elizabeth, he was assassinated in an IRA terrorist car bombing 8/27/79.

Mozhaisk (now -**ysk**) (moh•**zhysk**) railroad town about 70 miles W of **Moscow**

Mrs. Miniver (min•uh•vuhr) The Oscar-winner for Best Picture of 1942, this popular and patriotic British drama culminates with the evacuation of **Dunkirk** as experienced by the Minivers

Mufti of Jerusalem -- see Amin el-**Husseini**

Mukden (muk•den, mook-) the major city of **Manchuria**, site of an explosion on the Southern Manchurian Railway (the **"Mukden Incident"**) staged by Japanese **Kwantung Army**

officers 9/18/31, which led to the Japanese establishing the puppet state of **Manchukuo** 2/32 and withdrawing from the **League of Nations** when it censured them early in 1933. The city was captured by Soviet forces 8/45 and is now Shenyang (**shuhn•yahng**), capital of the Liaoning (**lyow•ning**) province in NE China.

Mulberries (US **muhl′•bair•**eez, Brit **muhl•**buhr•eez) two artificial harbors towed from England to the **Normandy** beachhead immediately after **D-Day**. The one in the US sector at St. Laurent (sa(n) law•**ren**) was rendered unusable by a storm on 6/19/44; the other, in the British/Canadian sector at **Arromanches**, survived the storm and delivered supplies to the **Red Ball Express** until 12/44.

Müller (or **Mueller**), **SS Lt Gen Heinrich** (**mur•**luhr, **myoo-** , **hyn•**rikh) Chief of the **Gestapo** from 10/39 and the leading administrator of deportations of Jews to **Auschwitz**, disappeared after visiting **Hitler'**s Berlin bunker 4/45

Munda Point (**mun•**duh) key Japanese airfield on the **Solomon** island of **New Georgia**, captured by US forces early in 8/43 after a difficult month-long land campaign

Munich Pact (or **Agreement**) (**myoo•**nik) Concluded in Munich 9/29-30/38 by **Chamberlain**, **Daladier**, **Hitler**, and **Mussolini**, the agreement allowed Hitler to annex the German-speaking **Sudetenland** portion of Czechoslovakia in return for renouncing further territorial claims. **Chamberlain** thought they had achieved "peace in/for our time," but Hitler seized the rest of Czechoslovakia 3/39.

Murmansk (mur•**mahnsk**, -mansk) Soviet port on the **Kola** (**koh•**luh) Inlet of the **Barents Sea** (Arctic Ocean) near the **Finland** border, winter terminus for British and US supply convoys after the German invasion 6/41

Murphy, Audie (aw•dee) won the **Medal of Honor** while fighting as a 20-year-old lieutenant in Germany on 1/26/45, was featured on the cover of *Life* magazine as the most decorated soldier of the war, and became a movie star

Murphy, Robert D. -- **Roosevelt**'s political representative in **French North Africa** 1941-43, helped prepare for the Allied landings in Operation **Torch** 11/42

Musashi (moo•sah•shee) Japanese battleship, with its sister ship **Yamato** the most powerful ever built, sunk by US carrier planes in the Battle of **Leyte Gulf** 10/44

Mussolini, Benito (moo•suh•lee′•nee, mus•uh- , beh•nee•toh) founder of Fascism and leader of Italy 1922-43 (dictator from 1928), known as Il Duce ("The Leader") (eel **doo•**chay), forced from office 7/25/43, shot by Italian partisans 4/28/45

Mutaguchi, Lt Gen Renya (moo•tuh•goo′•chee, **rehn•**yuh) one of three divisional commanders in the successful Japanese invasion of **Malaya** and **Singapore** (1941-42), led the unsuccessful invasion of NE India in 1944

Myitkyina (**mich•**ih•nuh, -nah, mih•**chee-**) key railroad and river town in N Burma, taken by Japanese forces 5/8/42, retaken by Allied forces 8/3/44

N

Nadzab (**nad•zab**) Japanese airfield on NE **New Guinea** suitable for heavy bombers, taken by a US paratroop assault 9/5/43

Naga(s) (**nah•**guh(z)) hill tribes in N Burma who fought against the Japanese

Nagano, Osami (nah•**gah•**noh, nuh- , oh•**sah•**mee) Chief of the Japanese Naval General Staff and Deputy Minister of the Navy 4/9/41-2/21/44

Nagasaki (**nag•**uh•**sak′•**ee, **nah•**guh•**sah′•**kee) industrial port city on the W end of **Kyushu**, target of the second atomic bomb, 8/9/45, which caused about 35,000 deaths and convinced Emperor **Hirohito** to insist that his government surrender

Nagato (nah•**gah•**toh, nuh-) Japanese battleship, damaged in the Battle of **Leyte Gulf** (10/44)

Nagoya (nah•**goy•**uh, nuh- , -ah) Japanese port city about 200 miles SW of Tokyo, heavily damaged by US firebombing 3/10-11/45, the night after the great raid on Tokyo

Nagumo, Vice-Admiral Chuichi (nah•**goo•**moh, nuh- , choo•**ee•**chee) led the Japanese attack on **Pearl Harbor** 12/7/41 and commanded the same 1st Carrier Fleet at **Midway** 6/42, led the newly formed 3rd Carrier Division during the **Guadalcanal** campaign, committed suicide 7/6/44 on **Saipan** after commanding the Central Pacific Fleet in the unsuccessful defense of the **Mariana Islands**

Naha (**nah•**hah) capital of **Okinawa** and W coast anchor of the Japanese **Shuri** defensive line across the S end of the island

Nakagawa, Colonel K. (**nahk**•uh•**gow**•uh, **nak-**) commanded the 10,000 Japanese defenders of **Peleliu** against US forces 9/15-25/44, committing suicide after their defeat

Nakajima, Lt Gen Kesago (**nah**•kuh•**jee′**•muh, **nak-** , keh•**sah**•goh, kay-) a former head of the Japanese secret police with a reputation for savagery, he led troops in the Rape of **Nanking** and probably escaped execution for war crimes only because he died of illness 10/28/45

Namsos (**nahm**•sus) port in C Norway, scene of fighting between British and German forces 4/40, evacuated by the British 5/2/40

Namur (nah′**mur**) a province of S Belgium and its capital

Namur Island (nuh•**muhr**, na•**moor**) part of the **Kwajalein** atoll in the **Marshall Islands**, taken from Japan by US forces 2/1-2/44

Nancy (US **nan**•see, Fr nah(n)•**see**) city in NE France, base of the German 1st Army, taken without opposition by **Patton**'s 3rd Army 9/15/44

Nanking (**nan**•king, **nahn-**) now Nanjing (**nahn**•jing) city on the **Yangtze** River, capital of China from 1928 to 11/20/37, when it was captured by the Japanese, who then murdered an estimated 250,000 civilians during the Rape of Nanking. In 1940 they installed a puppet government under **Wang Ching-wei.**

Nanning (**nahn**•ning, **nan-**) city in S China, taken by Japanese forces 11/24/44, retaken by the Chinese 5/26/45

Nantes (Fr **nahnt**, US **nants**) French port city at the mouth of the **Loire** on the Bay of **Biscay**, entered by German forces 6/19/40, reached by US forces 8/13/44

Naples (**nay•**puhlz) port city in SW Italy, liberated from German control by Allied forces 10/1/43

Narev (also **Narew**) (**nah•**ref) river N of **Warsaw**, a German defense line in 1944-45

Narvik (US **nahr•**vik, Nor **-veek**) seaport in N Norway occupied 4/9/40 by about 2,000 German troops, then 5/28 by British and French forces, who were soon evacuated as German forces gained control of the country and the Norwegian army surrendered 6/9

Naujocks, Alfred Helmut (**now•**yawks, **-yahks, ahl•**frayt, **hel•**mut) **SS** officer who directed the staged "Polish" attack on the **Gleiwitz** radio station 8/31/39 and the kidnapping of two British agents near **Venlo** in Holland 11/9/39

Nauru (nah•**oo•**roo, Aus **now•**roo) small Pacific island W of the **Gilberts**, formerly Pleasant Island, administered by Australia from 1914, a Japanese air base bypassed by US forces, an independent republic since 1968

Nazi (**naht•**see, **nat-**) the standard abbreviation for the National Sozialist party and its members

Nazi-Soviet Pact -- see **Molotov-Ribbentrop Pact**

N'Djamena -- see **Fort-Lamy**

Negros (**nay•**grohs, **neg•**rohs) island in the C **Philippines** which saw heavy guerrilla fighting by **Filipino** troops after the Japanese occupation in 1942 and during the reconquest by the US 40th Division 3-6/45

Nehring, General Walther K. (**nair•**ing, **vahl•**tuhr) German tank commander active throughout the war in N Africa and the Eastern Front

Nehru, Jawaharlal (**nay**•roo, **nair**•oo, juh•**wah'**•huhr•**lahl**)
head of the National Congress Party in India, which demanded
independence from Britain, imprisoned 10/42-6/45 for anti-war
activity, became the first PM of India 1947-64

Neisse (**ny**•suh) river in E Germany with two branches, the W
branch and the **Oder** becoming the postwar boundary between
Germany and Poland

Nelson, Donald M. -- controversial but effective chairman of
the US War Production Board (WPB) 1/42-8/44, with almost
total control of US industrial production

Nettuno (net•**too**•noh) Italian coastal town and airstrip two
miles E of **Anzio**, **Lucas**'s command post

Neuengamme (**noy'**•uhn•**gah**•muh) German concentration
camp NW of **Hamburg**, notorious for its medical experiments,
which contributed to its estimated 82,000 deaths

Neurath, Baron Constantin (or **Kon-**) **von** (**noy**•raht)
German Foreign Minister 1932-38, Reich Protector of **Bohemia-
Moravia** 3/39-9/41. Sentenced to 15 years at **Nuremberg**,
released 1954

Neva (US **nee**•vuh, Rus nyeh•**vah**) river flowing 40 miles from
Lake Ladoga through **Leningrad** to the Gulf of Finland

New Britain -- large island (about 300 by 50 miles) NE of **New
Guinea**. The W end, including **Rabaul**, was held by the
Japanese from 1/42 to the end of the war, while the E end was
taken by US forces starting 12/26/43

New Caledonia (**new** kal•ih•**doh**•nee•uh, -**dohn**•yuh) island
about 800 miles E of Australia, **Free French** territory from
7/40, US base from 3/42

Newfoundland (**new'•fuhnd•land, new•**fuhn•luhnd) a large island in E Canada vital to Allied shipping across the N Atlantic

New Georgia (**new jawr'•**juh) largest (about 50 by 20 miles) of a group of the **Solomon Islands** taken from the Japanese by US forces 6-8/43

New Guinea (**new ghin'•**ee) second largest island in the world (after **Greenland**), N of Australia, scene of intense fighting between Japanese and Allied (US and Australian) forces from 7/42 until the **Allies** ended organized resistance 5/44

New Hebrides (**new heb'•rih•deez**) island group ENE of Australia under British and French control, since 1980 the independent country of **Vanuatu** (**vah•noo•ah'•too, van•oo•at'•oo**)

New Jersey, USS -- US battleship commissioned in 1943, **Halsey**'s flagship in the Battle of **Leyte Gulf** 10/44

New Zealand (**new zee'•luhnd**) an independent member of the British Commonwealth from 1931, located SE of Australia, whose troops fought with distinction, primarily in N Africa and S Europe

Nicaragua (**nik•uh•rah'•gwuh**) a staunch Central American ally of the US, declared war on the three **Axis** powers 12/9/41

Nice (**nees**) a French resort city on the **Mediterranean**, occupied by Italy from 6/25/40 and by Germany from the Italian surrender 9/43 until the Allied landings in S France 8/44

Nicobar Islands (**nik'•uh•bahr**) an island group belonging to India, NW of **Sumatra** in the Bay of **Bengal**, occupied by Japan from 5/42 to the end of the war

Nicosia (**nik•uh•see'•uh**) the capital of **Cyprus**, in the NC part of the island, site of a British air base

Niemöller (or **-moeller**), **Martin** (**nee′•mu(r)•**luhr)
pastor of the Berlin-Dahlem Church and leader of the
Confessional Church, imprisoned from 1937 to the end of the
war for his opposition to **Hitler**

Nijmegen (**ny′•may•**guhn) town in Holland where Allied
paratroopers landed 9/17/44 as part of an unsuccessful operation
(**Market-Garden**) to capture a bridge across the **Rhine** at
Arnhem, about 10 miles to the N, subject of the book (1974) and
movie (1977) *A Bridge Too Far*

Nikopol (nih•**kaw•**puhl, nee•kuh•puhl) city in the SE **Ukraine**
on the **Dnieper** River, site of manganese mines important to the
German steel industry

Nimitz, Admiral Chester W. (**nim•**its) CiC US Pacific Fleet
12/31/41-9/11/45, Chief of Naval Operations (CNO) 12/15/45-
11/47, after which he retired from active duty at age 62

Nippon (**nip•**ahn, nih•**pahn**) Japanese name of Japan. Nip was
used in the same derogatory sense as Jap.

Niscemi (nih•**shay•**mee, nee-) key Sicilian town about 10
miles inland (NE) from **Gela**

Nisei (Eng **nee•**say, Jap nee•**say**) a second-generation
Japanese-American immigrant

Nishimura, Vice-Admiral Shogi (**nish•**uh•**moor′•**uh,
nee•shee- , **shoh•**ghee) Commander of the Southern Japanese
Force in the Battle of **Leyte Gulf**, defeated and killed at **Surigao
Strait** by US ships under Rear Admiral **Oldendorf** 10/25/44

Nishizawa, Chief Warrant Officer Hiroyoshi
(**nish•**ih•**zah′•**wuh, -ee- , -wah, **heer•**uh•**yoh′•**shee) the leading
Japanese fighter ace of the war, recording over 100 kills from
2/3/42 at **Rabaul** to his death in **Luzon** 10/26/44

Nissen Huts (nis•uhn) prefabricated half-cylindrical shelters made of corrugated metal, named for their British designer Lt Col Peter N. Nissen (1871-1930)

NKVD (or N.K.V.D.) Narodnyi Kommissariat Vnutrennikh Del (People's Commissariat for Domestic Affairs) -- the Soviet Secret Service, which operated with increasingly expanded power along with the NKGB (People's Commissariat of Public Safety) and GRU (Central Intelligence Administration) throughout the war

Noble, Admiral Sir Percy -- British CiC Western Approaches 2/41-11/42, in charge of protecting Atlantic convoys

Noemfoor (or -for) (now spelled **Numfoor**, or **-for) (num•foor)** small circular island about 12 miles in diameter off NE **New Guinea**, taken easily for use as an air base by US forces after a landing 7/2/44

Noguès, General Auguste P. (noh•ghes, -ghez, aw•gust, oh-) CiC French Army North Africa under the **Vichy** regime 11/42 when Anglo-American landings began, persuaded by **Admiral Darlan** to cease resistance, subsequently became French Governor-General of **Morocco** before retiring 6/43

Nomura, Admiral Kichisaburo (nuh•mawr•uh, noh•mur•uh, kee•chee•sa•boor•oo) Japanese Foreign Minister 9/39-1/40 and Ambassador to Washington 2-12/41

Nordhausen (nawrd′•how•zuhn) town in C Germany, site of a German underground factory to manufacture **V-2** rockets 1943-45

Norfolk (nawr•fuhk) city in Virginia, the major E coast naval base

Normandy (**nawr•muhn•dee**) province (département) in NW France, including the S coast of the **English Channel**, where Allied forces landed on **D-Day** (6/6/44)

Norsk Hydro (**nawrsk• hy•**droh) a Norwegian hydroelectric plant capable of producing large amounts of "heavy water" for a German atomic bomb, successfully raided by British and Norwegian commandos several times in 1943

North Sea -- the part of the Atlantic Ocean between Britain and NW Europe

Nouméa (noo•**may•**uh) capital of **New Caledonia**, site of an excellent harbor and a US air base

Nova Scotia (**noh•**vuh **skoh•**shuh) province in SE Canada consisting of a mainland peninsula and Cape Breton (**bret'**n, **brit'**n) Island to the NE

Novgorod (**nahv'•**guh•**rahd**) historic Russian city about 80 miles SSE of **Leningrad** on the N end of Lake **Ilmen** (**il•**muhn), held by German forces 8/41-1/44

Novikov, Marshal Alexander A. (**nahv•**ih•**kahf**, -**kawf**) CiC of the Soviet Air Force from 4/42 to 3/46, awarded the designation Hero of the Soviet Union (HSU) twice in 1945, held in custody from 4/46 until **Stalin**'s death in 1953, after which he continued to hold high positions

Novorossiisk (or -**ssisk**) (Rus **noh•**vuh•ruh•**seesk'**, US nahv•**rah•**sik) Soviet city and naval base on the NE coast of the **Black Sea**, taken by German forces 9/6/42, retaken by Soviet forces 9/16/43

Nowotny, Walther (noh•**vaht•**nee, **vahl•**tuhr) fifth-ranked German fighter ace with 255 kills on the Eastern Front, killed in action in N Europe 11/8/44 in an Me-262 jet fighter at age 23

Noyes, Rear Admiral Leigh (Noyz, Lee) survived the sinking
of his carrier USS **Wasp** off **Guadalcanal** on 9/15/42, but had
no further combat command

Nuremberg (nur′•uhm•buhrg, nyur-) Ger **Nürnberg
(nurn′•behrk**) historic city in **Bavaria** in SE Germany, site of
10 **Nazi** rallies held in August or September from 1923 to 1938.
The **Nuremberg Laws**, aimed at removing Jews from public life
in Germany, were introduced by **Hitler** at the 1935 rally. The
Nuremberg Trials of 22 prominent Nazis for war crimes lasted
from 11/45 to 10/46, and were followed by others.

Nye, General Sir Archibald (ny) Vice-Chief of the Imperial
General Staff under **FM Sir Alan Brooke** 1941-46

**Nygaardsvold, Johan (US nee•gahr(d)s•vohld, Nor
ny′•gawrs•vawl**) PM of Norway from 1935, head of the
Norwegian government-in-exile in London 6/40-6/25/45

O

Oahu (oh•ah•hoo) one of the Hawaiian islands, which includes **Honolulu** and **Pearl Harbor**

Oak Ridge -- area in E Tennessee on the Clinch River, site of the first Uranium-235 production facility for the atomic bomb. Construction started 2/43 and the complex eventually employed over 80,000 people

Obersalzberg (oh•buhr•sawls•buhrg) mountain in S Germany (6,400 feet) near **Berchtesgaden** where **Hitler** built his fortified retreat (the **Berghof**)

Oboe -- code name for a British radar bombing system first used at the end of 1942 and subsequently improved several times

O'Connor, General Sir Richard -- British Commander of the Western Desert Force in **Egypt** under **Wavell** from 6/40, defeated Italian forces invading from **Libya** 12/40 and advanced into Libya, where he was captured 4/41 by German forces under **Rommel** and imprisoned in Italy. Escaping 12/43, he commanded 8th Corps in **Normandy**.

Odense -- see **Embry**

Oder (oh•duhr) a river in E Germany flowing N into the **Baltic Sea**, part of the **Oder-Neisse Line** (which also included the W **Neisse** River) agreed upon at the **Potsdam Conference** (7-8/45) as the postwar boundary between Germany and Poland

Odessa (oh•des•uh) Soviet city on the N coast of the **Black Sea**, taken by German and Romanian forces 10/41 and annexed to Romania, retaken by Soviet forces 4/44

ODESSA (oh•des•uh) acronym for a **Nazi** escape network at the end of the war whose main terminus was Buenos Aires (**bway**•nuhs **eye**(uh) •riz) in **Argentina**

O'Donnell -- Japanese POW camp in N **Luzon**, destination of the **Bataan** Death March

Oglala, USS (oh•**glah**•lah, uh- , -luh) minesweeper sunk at **Pearl Harbor**

O'Hare, Lt Cmdr Edward H. ("Butch") -- the first US naval fighter ace, won the **Medal of Honor** for a battle at **Bougainville** 2/42, killed in action 11/26/43 in the **Gilbert Islands**, namesake for Chicago's O'Hare Airport

Ohka (oh•kah) ("Cherry Blossom") Japanese manned suicide bomb, developed late in the war and intended for the defense of the home islands

Ohlendorf, Otto (oh'•len•dawrf) Commander of an **SS** extermination unit (**Einsatzgruppen** D) in the Soviet Union from 6/41 to 7/42, during which time he supervised the killing of an estimated 90,000 people, mostly Jews. Sentenced to death at **Nuremberg** 4/10/48, executed 6/8/51

Ohm (Uncle) Krüger (**ohm kru(r)**•guhr) anti-British historical epic film released in Germany 4/41, starring Emil Jannings as a hero of the Boer War

Ohrdruf (**awr**•druhf) concentration camp in C Germany whose discovery by American troops 4/4/45 shocked British and American leaders, including **Eisenhower**, who visited the camp 4/12 with **Bradley** and **Patton** and reported its conditions to **Churchill**

Oikawa, Admiral Koshiro (oh•ee•**kow**•uh, koh•**sheer**•oh) Japanese Navy Minister from 9/40 to 10/41, followed by other high-level positions including Chief of Naval Staff 8/44-5/45

Oise (wahz) a river in N France flowing S from the Belgian border about 180 miles into the **Seine** W of Paris

O'Kane, Commander Richard H. -- a leading submarine captain in the Pacific whose ship, the **USS Tang**, was sunk 11/25/44 near **Formosa**. Taken prisoner by the Japanese, he survived the war.

Oka River -- see **Orel**

Okhotsk, Sea of (oh•**kahtsk**) an arm of the Pacific jutting into Russia N of Japan

Okinawa (oh•kuh•nah'•wuh, -now'•uh) the largest of the **Ryukyu Islands** S of Japan and from 4/1/45 to 6/22/45 the scene of the largest land battle of the Pacific war, with a total death toll of over a quarter million

OKW (Oberkommando der Wehrmacht) -- High Command of the Armed Forces of the Third Reich

Olbricht, General Friedrich (**ohl**•brikht, **free**•drikh) a leader of the **July Bomb Plot** against **Hitler**, executed a few hours after the plot failed

Oldendorf, Vice-Admiral Jesse B. (**ohl'**•duhn•**dawrf**) US naval commander who played a major role in the Battle of **Leyte Gulf** at the **Surigao Strait**, then took part in the liberation of the **Philippines** and the **Okinawa** campaign

Olomouc (oh'•loh•mohts, aw'•law-) a city in Czechoslovakia, scene of heavy fighting between German and Soviet forces during the last week of the war

Omaha (oh'•muh•haw, -hah) one of the two US beaches in the **Normandy** invasion (**D-Day**) 6/6/44 and the one of the five that proved to be the most difficult

Omori, Rear Admiral S. (ah•**mawr**•ee, oh-) Commander of
the Japanese task force at the Battle of **Empress Augusta Bay**
11/2/43

Onega (oh•**neh**•guh) the second largest lake in Europe, about
150 miles E of **Leningrad**

Onishi, Vice-Admiral Takijiro (oh•**nee**•shee,
tah•kuh•**jeer′**•oh) Japanese naval air specialist who helped plan
the attack on **Pearl Harbor** and directed the attack on **Clark
Field** in the **Philippines**. Later in the war, he created the first
kamikaze corps (10/44) and committed suicide after the
broadcast of Emperor **Hirohito's** surrender proclamation.

Oppenheimer, J. Robert (**ahp′**•uhn•**hy**•muhr) American
nuclear physicist, scientific head of the atomic bomb project
from 1942 and director of the laboratories at **Los Alamos** from
1943

Oradour-sur-Glane (oh•rah•**door′**-sur-**glahn**) a village in C
France where the entire population of about 700 was killed and
the buildings destroyed 6/10/44 by the German 2^(nd) **SS Panzer**
division (Das Reich) as a reprisal for French Resistance attacks
elsewhere. The village remains abandoned, maintained as a
memorial.

Oran (aw•**rahn**, -ran, oh•**rahn**, -ran) port city in **Algeria**, site
of the French naval base **Mers-el-Kébir**, where French ships
were attacked and some sunk by a British task force 7/3/40 after
they refused to take action to insure that they would stay out of
German hands. On 11/8/42, Oran was one of three landing sites
for the Allied invasion of NW Africa, Operation **Torch**.

Oranienburg (oh•**rah′**•nee•en•**buhrg**, awr•**rahn′**•yen-) town
N of Berlin where atomic bomb research and development was
halted 3/15/45 by a heavy US bombing raid. On 4/10/45 US
pilots shot down 14 German jet fighters over the town.

Ordzhonikidze (**awr**•jahn•uh•**kid′**•zuh) S Russian city in the **Causasus**, the farthest point reached by German forces (11/6/42) in their drive toward the oil fields of **Baku** and the **Caspian Sea**, now **Vladikavkaz** (**vlad**•ih•kahf•**kahz′**)

Orel (aw•**rel**, oh-) city in Russia about 250 miles SSW of **Moscow** on the **Oka** (oh•**kah**) **River**, captured by German forces 10/41, played an important role in the battle of the **Kursk** salient (7-8/43), retaken by Soviet forces 8/4/43

Orléans (awr•lay•**ah(n)**) French city on the **Loire** about 60 miles S of Paris, captured by German forces 6/16/40, retaken by **Patton**'s 3rd Army 8/17/44

Ormoc (**awr**•mahk) town and bay on W **Leyte**, Japanese landing site 10-12/44, US landing site 12/44

Oroku (awr•**oh**•koo) peninsula in SW **Okinawa**

Orote Field (**awr′**•oh•tay, oh•**roh**•tay) US airbase on **Guam**, named for the **Orote Peninsula**, played a major role in the **Great Marianas Turkey Shoot** 6/19/44

Osaka (oh•**sah**•kuh, -kah) Japanese coastal city in S **Honshu** about 300 miles SW of Tokyo, heavily damaged by US firebombing 3/45

Oshima, General Count Hiroshi (oh•**shee**•muh, -mah, heer•**oh**•shee) Japanese ambassador to Germany 1938-39, 1941-45

Oslo (**ahz**•loh, **ahs**-) capital of Norway, taken by German forces 4/9/40 and held until **V-E Day**

Osmeña, Sergio (ahz•**may**•nyuh, **suhr**•jee•oh) Vice-President of the **Philippines** under **Manuel Quezon**, President from Quezon's death (8/1/44) until he was defeated in the first post-war election 4/46

OSS (Office of Strategic Services) -- US foreign intelligence agency 7/42-9/45, forerunner of the CIA (Central Intelligence Agency)

Ostend (ahs•**tend**, **ahs**•tend) coastal city in Belgium

Oster, Maj Gen Hans (**ah**•stuhr, **oh**- , **hahns**) CoS of German Military Intelligence (the **Abwehr**) under **Canaris** 1938-43 and a leader of the resistance to **Hitler**'s National Socialist regime. Arrested after the **July Bomb Plot** and executed 4/9/45

Ousseltia (oo•sel•tee•**ah**, -t'**yah**) town and valley in NC **Tunisia**

Overlord -- operation code name for the Allied invasion of **Normandy** beginning on **D-Day** 6/6/44

Overstraeten, General Raoul van (**oh**•vuhr•**strayt**•uhn, ra•**ool**) chief military adviser to **King Leopold** of Belgium before and during the German invasion of 5/40, criticized by some historians for his lack of cooperation with France and Britain

Owen Stanley Mountains -- see **Kokoda Trail**

Ozawa, Vice-Admiral Jisaburo (oh•**zah**•wuh, -**zow**- , jee•sah•**boor'**•oh, -suh- , -uh) succeeded **Nagumo** as Commander of the Japanese 3rd (Mobile) Fleet 11/42, commanded the Battle of the **Philippine Sea** 6/19-21/44, successfully used his carrier fleet as a decoy to lure **Halsey**'s fleet away from the Battle of **Leyte Gulf** (10/44), succeeded **Toyoda** as Commander of the Japanese Fleet 5/45

P

Paasikivi, Juho K. (pah•suh•**kee**•vee) key negotiator for **Finland** in the treaties that ended the fighting against the Soviet Union in 1940 and 1944, became PM of Finland 11/44 and was President from 3/46 until his death in 1956

Padang (pah•**dahng**) port city and island in WC **Sumatra**, held by the Japanese throughout the Pacific War

Padua (**paj**•oo•uh) city in NE Italy, liberated by US forces a few days before the German surrender

Paestum (**pes**•tuhm) coastal city and airfield about 20 miles S of **Salerno**

Pahang (pah•**hahng**, puh- , -**hang**) river and state in C **Malaya**

Pahlavi (**pah′**•luh•vee) 1) **Reza Shah** (rih•**zah**) ruler (shah) of **Persia** (**puhr**•zhuh) 1925-41, changed its name to Iran (ih•**ran**, -**rahn**) 1935 (both names were used during the war), resigned under pressure from the Allied powers due to his tacit support of Germany 2) **Muhammad** (or -**ed**) **Reza** -- his son, who succeeded his father at age 22 and maintained a pro-Western policy until he was deposed in 1979 by an Islamic fundamentalist regime

Palau (puh•**low**, pah- , pa-) a group of about 200 islands in the W **Carolines** about 500 miles E of **Mindanao**, which includes **Peleliu** and **Angaur**

Palawan (pah•**lah**•wahn, puh•**lah**•wuhn) island in the SW **Philippines**, site of a Japanese POW camp

Palembang (pah•lem•**bahng′**) city in SE **Sumatra**, site of important oil fields under Japanese control from 2/42 to the end of the war

Palermo (puh•**lair**•moh, -**luhr**-) the capital of **Sicily**, on the NW coast, taken by **Patton**'s 7th Army 7/22/43

Palestine (**pal'**•uh•**styn**, -ih-) the biblical Holy Land, governed by Britain from 1923 to 1948 under a **League of Nations** mandate, part of which then became the independent state of Israel

Palmyra (pal•**my**•ruh) 1) island about 1,000 miles S of **Oahu**, part of the US supply line to Australia and **New Zealand** 2) city in C Syria bombed by the RAF 5/41 as part of a successful campaign against the **Vichy** French

Panay (pah•**ny**, puh- , pa-) 1) island in the C **Philippines**, surrendered to the Japanese by US forces 5/42, but increasingly controlled by Philippine guerrillas until US forces returned 3/45 2) a US gunboat on the **Yangtze River** sunk by Japanese planes 12/37 after rescuing the last Americans from the US embassy in **Nanking**

Pangsau Pass (**pang**•sahw) a notch in the **Patkai** mountain range crossed by the **Ledo Road**

Pantelleria (pan•**tel**•uh•**ree'**•uh, **pan**-) small Italian island between **Sicily** and **Tunisia**, heavily defended but surrendered to Allied forces 6/11/43 after an air bombardment

Panther -- German medium tank developed to counter the Soviet T-34. The first of over 5,000 built entered the fighting in 1943, overcoming initial defects evident at **Kursk** (7/43) and elsewhere to play an important role for the rest of the war.

Panzer (US **pan**•zuhr, Ger **pahnt**•suhr) the German word for armor, usually applied to tank units

Papagos, Marshal Alexander (-dros) (**pah'**•puh•**gohs**) as CiC Greek Army when the Italians invaded from **Albania** 10/28/40, he successfully counterattacked and drove them back into

Albania. In April 1941 a combined Greek-British army was defeated by German and Italian forces and **Papagos** became a German captive until freed from **Dachau** by US forces in 1945. He returned to his post as CiC and in 1952 became PM of Greece until his death in 1955.

Papandreou, George (Georgios Andreas) (pahp•ahn•dray′oo, -an-) Premier of the Greek government-in-exile in **Cairo** from 4/26/44 and head of the Provisional Administration in Athens from 10/44 to 1/4/45

Papen, Franz von (pah•puhn, frahns) helped **Hitler** become Chancellor in 1933, served briefly as Vice-Chancellor, then as special envoy to Austria 1934-39 and ambassador to **Turkey** 1939-44, acquitted of war crimes at **Nuremburg**

Papua (pap•yoo•uh, pah′•poo•ah) the SE portion of **New Guinea**, an Australian trusteeship territory which became independent in 1975 as part of Papua New Guinea

Park, Air Vice-Marshal Sir Keith -- commanded Number 11 Group (SE coast) RAF Fighter Command during the evacuation of **Dunkirk** and the Battle of **Britain**, then commanded air forces based in **Egypt**, **Malta**, the Middle East, and SE Asia

Parnu (pahr•noo) port city, bay, and river in **Estonia**

Pas de Calais (pah•duh•cal•ay′) the French name of the Strait of **Dover**, and the land area between **Calais** and **Boulogne**, the closest point in France to England. Before the **Normandy** invasion, the **Allies** persuaded the Germans that the invasion might occur there.

Pash, Lt Col Boris T. (pahsh) appointed by **Leslie Groves** in late 1943 to head the **Alsos** project

Pasig (pah•sig, pa-) river flowing through **Manila**

Patch, Lt Gen Alexander -- commanded US land forces on **Guadalcanal** 12/9/42-2/9/43 and the 7th Army from the landing in S France 8/15/44 to S Germany

Patkai (pat•ky) mountain range on the India-Burma border

Patterson, Robert P. -- US judge who became Assistant Secretary of War 7/30/40 and assumed the newly created position of Under Secretary of War 12/20/40, serving until 9/27/45 when he became Secretary of War under **Truman** until 7/47. Responsible for industrial mobilization and munitions procurement for the army and air force during the war.

Pattle, Marmaduke T. -- South African pilot whose probable total of 41 kills in N Africa and Greece puts him just ahead of **Richard Bong** (40) as the leading Allied fighter ace in the war against Germany. Killed in action 4/20/41

Patton, General George S. (pat'n) flamboyant and controversial US tank general, known to many from George C. Scott's performance in the 1970 movie, both of which won Oscars. Led armies with great success in N Africa, **Sicily**, and N Europe.

Paul, Prince Regent of Yugoslavia -- joined the **Axis** under pressure 3/25/41, deposed two days later by the armed forces, who chose to fight Germany and its allies with disastrous results

Paulus, FM Friedrich von (pow•lus, free•drikh) Commander of the German 6th Army from 1/42, surrendered at **Stalingrad** 1/31/43, the day after **Hitler** made him a Field Marshal

Paveliç (-ich), Ante (pah•vel•ich) Croat fascist who proclaimed **Croatia**'s independence from Yugoslavia after the Germans captured **Zagreb** 4/10/41 and remained its ruler, with **Hitler**'s backing, until the end of the war

Pavlov, Col Gen Dimitry (or **Dm-**) (**pav•**lahf, -lawf, **pahv-** , dih•**mee•**tree) Soviet Commander of the Western Military District (facing N Poland) when the Germans invaded 6/22/41, replaced by **Yeremenko** 6/29/41, executed for incompetence 7/41 along with eight other high-ranking officers

Pearl Harbor -- US naval base and Pacific Fleet HQ on **Oahu** island in Hawaii, target of a successful surprise Japanese air attack 12/7/41 which brought the US into the war

Peenemünde (**peen•**uh•**mun•**duh) the center of German research and development of the **V-1** and **V-2** rockets, located on the **Baltic** island of Usedom (**ooz'•**uh•**duhm**, -**dahm**) about 100 miles N of Berlin. Heavy bombing raids by Britain (8/17-18/43) and the US (8/4/44 and 8/25/44) set back production by several months.

Peierls, Rudolf -- see **Frisch**

Peiper, SS Lt Col Joachim (py•puhr, yoh•ahkh•im) Commander of a **Waffen-SS** task force group which committed several massacres of prisoners and civilians during the Battle of the **Bulge,** the most notorious being the shooting of 71 American captives near **Malmédy** on 12/17/44

Peipus (**py•**puhs) a lake on the border of Russia and **Estonia** extending 90 miles NS

Peirse, Air Chief Marshal Sir Richard (**puhrz**) CiC British Bomber Command from 10/25/40 to 2/22/42, later CiC Eastern Air Command (India/Burma) 12/43-11/44

Peking (**pee•king, pay-**) the capital city of China, now Beijing (**bay•jing**), known as Peiping (**pay•ping**) from 1928 to 1949

Peleliu (**pel•**eh•**lyoo**) one of the **Palau Islands** in the W **Carolines**, about seven square miles, taken by US forces 9/15/44-11/27/44 at a cost of about 1,500 killed and 6,000

wounded. Nearly all of the 10,000 Japanese defenders died. In
retrospect, it seems that the island could and should have been
bypassed.

Peloponnesus (**pel•uh•puh•nee′•**suhs) the large S peninsula of
Greece, occupied by German forces following the surrender of
the Greek army 4/23/41, abandoned by them 9/44

Penang (US) (**pih•nang, -nahng**) **Pinang** (Malay)
(**pee•nahng**) island off the W coast of **Malaya**, capital city
George Town (or Georgetown), site of a demoralizing
evacuation of European residents 12/16-17/41 as the Japanese
began their drive to **Singapore**

Peniakoff, Vladimir ("Popski") (pen•ee•ah•kahf, -kawf,
pen•yah- , **vlad′•uh•meer**) a Belgian of Russian parentage, he
led commando missions for the British army in **Libya** 1940-42.
In 11/42 he formed Popski's Private Army, which operated
successfully in **Tunisia** and Italy.

Percival, Lt Gen Arthur E. (**puhr•suh•vuhl**) assumed
command of British forces in **Malaya** 5/41, which remained
badly prepared for the Japanese invasion that began 12/8/41.
Surrendered **Singapore** on 2/15/42, was imprisoned in
Manchuria, and attended the Japanese surrender ceremony on
the **USS Missouri** 9/2/45

Persia -- see **Pahlavi**

Persian Gulf (**puhr•zhuhn guhlf**) vital waterway between
Arabia and Iran, remained in Allied control throughout the war

Petacci, Clara (peh•tah•chee, **klar•uh**) **Mussolini**'s mistress
from 1936 until they were both shot by partisans in N Italy
4/28/45

Pétain, Marshal Henri Philippe (pay•ta(n), ah(n)•ree
fee•**leep**) a French hero of WWI, became Premier on 6/16/40 as

France fell to the Germans, accepted an armistice 6/22 and established a new government at **Vichy** in the unoccupied S part of France, which was occupied 11/42 after the Allied invasion of NW Africa. His sentence of death for treason 4/45 was commuted by **DeGaulle** to life imprisonment. He died in 1951 at 95.

Petrov, Gen Ivan Y. (US **pet•**trahf, -trawf, **eye•**vuhn, Rus **pyay•**truhf, ih**•vahn**) Soviet general best known for his defenses of **Odessa** (1941) and **Sevastopol** (1942)

Petsamo (pet'•suh•moh) ice-free Arctic port in N **Finland** 1920-1944, before and after that period part of Russia and named Pechenga (**pyeh•**chin**•**guh)

Philippines (fil'•uh•peenz, fil•uh•peenz') a group of over 7,000 islands SE of China, a US Protectorate from 1898, self-governing since 1934. Invaded by the Japanese 12/8/41, surrendered 5/6/42, liberated by US forces 10/20/44-8/45, became fully independent 7/4/46.

Philippine Sea, Battle of the (fil'•uh•peen) the last major carrier battle between the US and Japan, 6/19-20/44, launched by Japan in an unsuccessful attempt to prevent the US capture of **Saipan.** The one-sided victory by US planes is often called the **Great Marianas Turkey Shoot.**

Pichon (pee•shaw(n), pee•chah(n)) town in NC **Tunisia**, now called Haffouz (ha**•fooz**)

Pick, Lt Gen Lewis A. (pik) US director of construction of the **Ledo Road**, which is sometimes referred to as "**Pick's Pike**"

pika-don (pee•kah-dahn) ("flash-bang") what the residents of **Hiroshima** and **Nagasaki** called the initial blast of the atomic bomb, often just **pika**

Pile, General Sir Frederick A. -- CiC British Antiaircraft Command 1939-45

Pilsen (**pil**•zuhn, -zen) German name for a city in W Czechoslovakia (Bohemia), whose Czech name is **Plzeń** (**puhl′•zen**•y(uh))

Pindus Mountains (**pin**•duhs) a range in the center of mainland Greece

Pire, Jules (**"Pygmalion"**) (**peer**, **zhool**) a Belgian general at the time of the German invasion (5/40), he joined the resistance movement and by 1944 was head of the Belgian Legion, a secret army of over 50,000 which worked with the **Allies** before and during the **Normandy** invasion

Pius XII (Eugenio Pacelli) (**py**•uhs) succeeded his mentor Pius XI as Pope 3/39 and served until his death 10/9/58. He remains controversial for not taking a stronger position against the **Holocaust**.

Placentia Bay (pluh•**sen**•shuh, -shee•uh) on the S coast of **Newfoundland**, site of the first summit conference (aboard ship) between **Roosevelt** and **Churchill** (8/9-12/41), which produced the **Atlantic Charter**

Plate – see **River Plate**, **Battle of the**

Platt, General Sir William -- British commander of the **Sudan** Defense Force 1939-41, CiC East African Command 1941-45

Ploesti (US ploh•**es**•tee, Rom plaw•**yesht**) city in Romania about 35 miles N of **Bucharest**, surrounded by oil fields which were vital to the German war effort, bombed by the US from 6/42, notably on 8/1/43, without shutting them down, captured by Soviet forces 8/44

Plötzensee (**pluts**•en•zay) a prison in Berlin, the site of many executions, especially following the **July Bomb Plot** of 7/44

plutonium (ploo•**toh**•nee•uhm) a man-made chemical element (1941), named for the recently (1930) discovered planet Pluto (no longer considered a planet), used in the **Nagasaki** atomic bomb Fat Man

Po (**poh**) a river in N Italy flowing E into the **Adriatic Sea**

Pohl, Oswald (**pohl, ahs**•vahlt, **aws-**) a general in the **Waffen-SS** whose chief responsibility was the disposition of the belongings of prisoners killed in the concentration camps, including melting down gold from teeth. He was tried by a US military tribunal 11/3/47 and hanged 6/8/51.

Poindexter, Joseph B. (poyn•**dex**•tuhr, **poyn**•dex-) Governor of Hawaii at the time of the attack on **Pearl Harbor**

Pointe du Hoc (or **Hoe**) (**point**•duh•**hahk'**, -**hohk'**, -**hoh'**) German fortification overlooking **Omaha Beach**

Polish Corridor -- a strip of land attached to N Poland after WWI to provide access to the **Baltic Sea**, separated **East Prussia** from the rest of Germany and became the catalyst for WWII

Poltava (puhl•**tah**•vuh) Ukrainian city WSW of **Kharkov** where German bombers destroyed about 50 US B-17 bombers on the ground 6/21-22/44, discouraging future plans for Allied shuttle bombing of Germany

Pomerania (pahm•uh•**ray'**•nee•uh, -**rayn'**•yuh) the NE region of Germany, transferred to Poland after the war

Ponape (**poh**•nuh•pay) Japanese-held island between **Truk** and **Eniwetok**, heavily bombed but not invaded 2/44

Ponte Olivo (**pahn**•tee, pohn- , -tay, **oh**•lih•voh, oh•**lee**•voh)
key airfield about five miles NNE of **Gela**, taken by US forces
on D + 2 (7/12/43) of the **Sicily** invasion

Pontine Marshes (**pahn**•teen, -tyn) a large area E and NE of
Anzio, some of which was drained in the 1930s to produce
farmland

Popov, Gen Markian M. (US **pahp**•awf, -awv, Rus puh•**pohv**,
mahr•**kh'yawn**) commanded Soviet forces at **Leningrad**
(1941), **Stalingrad** (1942), the **Bryansk** Front (**Ukraine**) (1943),
and the **Baltic** Front (1944)

Popski -- see **Peniakoff**

Portal, Air Chief Marshal Sir Charles -- highly regarded
British Chief of Air Staff 10/40-12/45

Port Arthur -- port city on the S tip of **Manchuria**, taken from
the Japanese by Soviet forces 8/23/45, returned to China after the
war, now called Lüshun (**lyu•shyun**)

Port Lyautey (US lee•**oh**•tay, Fr **pawr** lee•oh•**tay**) key airfield
NE of **Rabat** in **French Morocco**, seized by US forces in the
Torch landings

Port Moresby (**mawrz**•bee) the capital of **Papua New Guinea**,
on the S coast, attacked from land and sea by Japanese forces
5/42 to 9/42, successfully defended by Australian forces

Potsdam (**pahts**•dam) German city 15 miles SW of Berlin, site
of the final Allied conference of the war 7/17/45-8/2/45. The
Potsdam Declaration offered Japan a choice between
unconditional surrender and massive destruction (via the
unmentioned atomic bomb).

Pound, Admiral Sir Dudley -- British First Sea Lord from 6/39 until illness forced his resignation 9/43, a month before his death

Pownall, Rear Admiral Charles A. (**pow**•nuhl) commanded US carrier forces in the C Pacific

Pownall, General Sir Henry ("Harry") R. (**pow**•nuhl) Director of British Army Intelligence 1938-41; CiC Far East 1941-42, **Ceylon** 1942-43, **Persia** and Iraq 1943; CoS **SEAC** 1943-44

Poznań (US **pohz**•nan, -nahn, Pol **pawz'**•**nahn**•y(uh)) Ger **Posen** (**poh**•zuhn, -zen) city in W Poland, ceded to Poland by Germany at the end of WWI, returned again to Poland after WWII

Prien, Günther (**preen, gun**•tuhr) Commander of the German submarine U-47, famous for entering **Scapa Flow**, the home base of the British Navy, and sinking the battleship **Royal Oak** 10/13-14/39, died 3/7-8/41 when U-47 was sunk while attacking an Atlantic convoy.

Prince of Wales, HMS -- British battleship sunk off E **Malaya** 12/10/41 by Japanese aircraft

Princeton, USS -- US light aircraft carrier sunk by a Japanese dive-bomber 10/24/44 during the Battle of **Leyte Gulf**

Prinz Eugen (prins **oy**•guhn) German heavy cruiser which helped the **Bismarck** sink the **Hood** 5/24/41, ended the war as the only major German ship to survive

Pripet Marshes (**prip**•et, **pree**•pet) a huge area in W Russia (now in S **Belarus** and NW **Ukraine**) whose inhospitable terrain aided resistance operations after the German invasion

Prussia (pruhsh•uh) a powerful state which created the German Empire in 1871 and remained the dominant military province in Germany until dissolved in 1947

Pskov (pskawf) a city and lake in NW Russia about 200 miles SW of **Leningrad**

PT-109 -- see **Kennedy, John**

Puyi, Henry (poo•yee) the last emperor of China from age four to seven (1908-1912) and puppet emperor of **Manchukuo** under Japanese rule 1934-45, subject of the Oscar-winning film *The Last Emperor* (1987)

Pyle, Ernie (pyl) the most famous American war correspondent, killed 4/18/45 by Japanese machine gun fire on **Ie Shima**, off NW **Okinawa**, after covering the **Blitz** in London and US campaigns in N Africa, Italy, and France

Pyrenees (peer′•uh•neez) mountain range dividing France and Spain

Q

Qattara Depression (kuh•tahr•uh, kah-) a vast no man's land below sea level in the desert S of **El Alamein**

Quebec (Eng kwih•bek) Fr **Québec** (kay•bek) Canadian province and its capital city, the site of two Allied conferences headed by **Roosevelt** and **Churchill**. The first, code named Quadrant, took place 8/43; the second, code named Octagon, 9/44.

Queen Elizabeth -- the largest ship in the world when she entered service in 1940. A British passenger liner, she was used for troop transport throughout the war.

Queen Elizabeth, HMS -- one of two British battleships badly damaged in **Alexandria** harbor 12/19/40 by Italian manned torpedoes

Queen Mary -- the largest ship in the world when she entered service as a British passenger liner in 1936. Used for troop transport throughout the war, she is now a hotel complex in Long Beach, CA.

Quesada, Maj Gen Elwood R. ("Pete") (kay•sah•dah) innovative US air commander who provided support for ground forces in **Tunisia, Sicily, Corsica**, Italy, and **Normandy**

Quezon, Manuel (kay•zahn, -sohn, -sawn) President of the Philippine Islands from 11/15/35 until his death on 8/1/44. Left the **Philippines** 2/20/42 after the Japanese invasion, forming a government-in-exile in the US 5/42, where he died a few months before his good friend **MacArthur** launched the US invasion and liberation of his homeland.

Quincy, USS -- US heavy cruiser, sunk with the loss of 370 lives during the Battle of **Savo Island** off **Guadalcanal** 8/8-9/42

Quisling, Vidkun (**kwiz**•ling, **vid**•kun) from 1933 leader of the Norwegian National Fascist (**Nazi**) party, he encouraged **Hitler**'s invasion of Norway 4/9/40, led a fascist government from 9/25/40, was demoted to puppet PM 2/1/42 under the real authority of **Nazi** governor **Josef Terboven**. He was executed in **Oslo** 10/24/45 and his name has become synonymous with traitor.

Quonset hut (**kwahn**•sit) a multi-purpose, prefabricated, semicylindrical metal structure used by US forces during the war

R

Rabat rah•**baht**, ruh-) Moroccan city on the Atlantic, the capital of **Morocco** since its independence in 1956

Rabaul (ruh•**bowl**, ra-) town at the NE end of **New Britain**, the major Japanese naval and air base in the Pacific, taken from Australian control 1/42 and held until the end of the war, though isolated and ineffectual from early 1944

Rabi (**rah**•bee) town in SE **New Guinea**, site of a Japanese landing 8/25/42 which was repulsed by Australian forces during the next two weeks, the first Japanese land defeat of the war

Radolfi, Alexander (**"Rado"**) (rah•**dahl**•fee) director of a Soviet spy network in Switzerland until it was discovered and terminated 10-11/43

Radom (**rahd**•uhm, **rah**•dawm) city in C Poland and administrative area during the German occupation

Raeder, Grand Admiral Erich (**ray**•duhr, **ay**•rikh) CiC German Navy 6/35-1/43, sentenced to life imprisonment at **Nuremberg** 1946, released 1955

Ramillies, HMS (**ram′•ih•leez**) British battleship torpedoed by Japanese midget submarines in **Diego Suarez** harbor (**Madagascar**) 1942, later supported the **Normandy** invasion (6/44) and the Allied invasion of S France (8/44)

Ramree Island (**rahm**•ree) a large island off the W coast of **Burma**, taken from the Japanese 1-2/45 for use as an airbase to support the attack on **Rangoon**

Ramsay, Admiral Sir Bertram Home (**ram**•zee) organized the evacuation of **Dunkirk**, Navy CiC for the **Normandy** invasion, died in a plane crash 1/2/45

Rangoon (rang•**goon**) capital city and major port of **Burma**, taken by the Japanese 3/42 and held until 5/45, now Yangon (yang•**gahn**, -gawn)

Rape of Nanking -- see **Nanking**

Rapido River (rap•ee•doh, **rap**•ee•doh) part of the German **Gustav Line** running through **Cassino** in Italy, breached with great difficulty by Allied forces 1-2/44, finally overrun by the British 13th Corps 5/11/44

Rashid Ali (rah•**sheed**, ra- , ah•**lee**, **al**•ee) anti-British Iraqi general who seized power 3/2/41, defeated and driven out 5/30/41

Rastenburg (**rah'**•sten•**boorg**) location of **Hitler**'s field HQ (**Wolf's Lair**) in **East Prussia**, scene of the **July Bomb Plot** assassination attempt 7/20/44, now Ketrzyn (**kehn**•tshin) in Poland

Ravensbruck (Ger **rah'**•vuhnz•**bruk**, US **ray**•venz-) concentration camp for women about 50 miles N of Berlin, established 1938, liberated 4/25/45

Rawalpindi, HMS (rah•wuhl•**pin'**•dee) British armed merchant cruiser which was sunk 11/23/39 while engaging the **Scharnhorst** and **Gneisenau**, causing them to abort their Atlantic convoy raiding mission, named for a city in NW India, now in NE Pakistan

Rawlings, Admiral Sir Bernard (**raw**•lingz, US buhr•**nahrd**, Brit **buhr**•nuhrd) commander of a rescue expedition 5/26-27/41 to take 4,000 British troops from **Heraklion** in **Crete** to **Alexandria** in **Eygpt**

Red Ball Express -- an American truck delivery system of supplies from the **Normandy** coast to the front lines, begun after the **Normandy** breakout 8/25/44 and concluded 11/16/44, primarily staffed by African-Americans

Red Orchestra Ger **Rote Kapelle** (**roh**•tuh kuh•**pel**•uh) Soviet-directed spy ring in Germany, broken up by the end of 1942

Regensburg (US **ray**′•guhnz•**buhrg**, Ger **ray**′•ghenz•**burk**) German city on the **Danube** where **Messerschmitts** were made, heavily bombed by American planes based in Britain 8/17/43 and again during the **Big Week** raids of 2/20-26/44

Reggio (di) Calabria (**rej**•yoh (dee) kuh•**lah**•bree•uh) Italian city, mainland terminus of the ferry system to **Sicily**, bombed by Allied forces 5/6/43, landing site for **Montgomery**'s 8th Army crossing from **Sicily** 9/3/43

Reichenau, FM Walther von (**rykh**′•uh•**now**, **vahl**•tuhr) commanded the German 10th Army in Poland (1939) and the 6th Army in Belgium and France (1940) and the Soviet Union (1941). He was given command of Army Group South 12/41, but died of a stroke 1/17/42

Reichstag (US **ryks**•tahg, Ger **rykhs**•tahk) the German legislative body and the building housing it, which was burned 2/27/33 (the **Reichstag Fire**) under circumstances still debated by historians

Reichswald, Battle of the (US **ryks**•wawld, Ger **rykhs**•vahlt) an advance through a W German forest 2/45 by British and Canadian troops, made necessary because the Germans had flooded the areas to the N and S

Reims -- see **Rheims**

Reinhardt, Col Gen Georg Hans (**ryn**•hahrt, gay•**awrkh hahns**) German **Panzer** (tank) commander who worked his way up to command Army Group Center (from 8/44) and Army

Group North (1/45) on the Eastern Front, where **Hitler** removed
him after just two days

Reitsch, Hanna (**rych**, **hah**•nuh, -nah) German test pilot and
glider specialist, awarded the **Iron Cross** (1942), flew into
Berlin with General von **Greim** to visit **Hitler** in his bunker
4/26-29/45

Remagen (US ruh•**mah**•guhn, Ger **ray'**•**mah**•ghen) site of the
first Allied crossing of the **Rhine** (3/7/45) when American troops
found that German explosive charges had failed to destroy the
Ludendorff bridge

Remer, Major Otto (**ray**•muhr) a decorated **Nazi** officer on
the Eastern Front in 1943, he commanded the battalion guarding
Berlin at the time of the **July Bomb Plot** (7/44) and helped
prevent a coup d'etat by refusing to act without proof of **Hitler**'s
death

Rendova Island (ren•**doh**•vuh) part of the **New Georgia** group
in the **Solomon Islands**, taken from the Japanese 7/43, site of a
PT Boat base that included **John Kennedy**'s **PT-109**

Rennell Island, Battle of (ren•uhl) Japanese air attacks 1/29-
30/43 that sank the US heavy cruiser **Chicago** 1/30/43 as she
was headed for **Guadalcanal**

Rennes (ren) French city in **Brittany**, liberated by US forces
8/4/44

Renown, HMS -- sister ship of the **Repulse**, active in the
Atlantic and **Mediterranean** throughout the war

Repulse, HMS -- British battle cruiser sunk by Japanese planes
along with the battleship **Prince of Wales** off the E coast of
Malaya 12/10/41

Reuben James, USS -- destroyer which became the first US warship sunk in the war on 10/31/41 while escorting a supply convoy to Britain

Reykjavik (**ray•**kyuh**•**vik, **-veek**) capital and chief port of **Iceland**

Reynaud, Paul (ray**•noh**) A consistent advocate of stronger measures against Germany during the 1930s, he became PM of France 3/21/40, resigned 6/16/40 after the German breakthrough, and was imprisoned by the **Vichy** government and then Germany until the end of the war

Reza Pahlavi -- see **Pahlavi**

Rheims (or **Reims**) (US **reemz**, Fr **ra(n)s**) city in N France occupied by German forces 6/11/40, retaken by US forces 8/29/44, became HQ for **Eisenhower** and **SHAEF** early in 1945, site of the final German surrender signed by General **Jodl** on 5/7/45

Rhine (**ryn**) a river in W Germany, the final German defensive position in the W, breached by Allied forces 3/45

Rhineland, the (**ryn•**land, -luhnd) a portion of W Germany demilitarized under the Treaty of **Versailles**, reoccupied by **Hitler** 3/36

Rhodes (**rohdz**) a strategically valuable island in the **Aegean Sea** which **Churchill**, but not **Roosevelt**, wanted to seize after the Italian surrender. It remained in German hands.

Rhône (**rohn**) a river flowing from the Swiss Alps through SE France into the **Mediterranean Sea**

Ribbentrop, Joachim von (**rib'•**uhn**•trahp**, **yoh•**ahkh**•**im) German Ambassador to Britain 1936-38 and Foreign Minister from 2/4/38 to 1945, best known for signing the **Molotov-**

Ribbentrop Pact with the Soviet Union 8/23/39, which secretly included the partition of Poland, tried at **Nuremberg** and hanged 10/16/46

Richardson, Admiral James D. -- CiC US Fleet from 1/40 to 2/41, when he was relieved by **Roosevelt** for his opposition to basing the fleet at **Pearl Harbor**

Richelieu (US **rish′•uh•loo**, Fr reesh•(uh)•**lyu**) French battleship in the **Vichy**-controlled Atlantic port of **Dakar** in NW Africa, which fought off a landing attempt by British and **Free French** forces 9/23/40

Richthofen, FM Wolfram, Baron von (**risht′•hoh•**fuhn, **rikht′-** , **vawl•**frahm) German airman who flew with his cousin Manfred (the "Red Baron") in WWI, served as CoS of the **Condor Legion** in the **Spanish Civil War**, commanded bomber groups on both the W and E fronts in WWII, and died of a brain tumor 7/12/45 while in US custody

Rickenbacker, Edward V. ("Eddie") (**rik′•uhn•bak•**uhr) the leading US fighter ace in WWI, served as a special observer in WWII

Ridgway, General Matthew B. (**rij•**way) commanded airborne infantry operations in Italy, then in NW Europe from **D-Day** to the **Elbe** river crossing in Germany (4/45)

Riefenstahl, Leni (**ree′•**fuhn•stahl, -shtahl, leh•nee, lay-) A German actress turned director, she made two classic documentaries that enhanced **Hitler**'s worldwide prestige: *Triumph of the Will* (1936), a record of the 1934 **Nazi** party rally in **Nuremberg** (the largest ever held), and *Olympiad* (1938), the official record of the 1936 Olympic games held in Germany.

Riga (**ree•guh**) the capital city of **Latvia** with a naval base on the **Baltic Sea**, taken by German forces 7/1/41, retaken by Soviet forces 10/13/44

Rimini (**rim•uh•nee**) Italian port city S of the **Rubicon** river, E end of the Allied line across N Italy from **Pisa** 9/44

Rio de Janeiro, Conference of (**ree′•oh day** zhuh•**nair′•oh**) meeting of foreign ministers of all Western Hemisphere countries 1/42 to coordinate military and economic planning

Riom Trial (**ree•oh(n)**) a show trial organized 2/42 by the **Vichy** government to blame pre-war French leaders for negligence, ended 4/42 after the defense proved too effective

Ritchie, Lt Gen Sir Neil M. (**rich•ee, neel**) Commander of the British 8th Army in N Africa 11/26/41-6/25/42, replaced by **Auchinleck** after suffering a major defeat from **Rommel**, including the fall of **Tobruk** 6/42

River Plate, Battle of the (**playt**) Sp **Rio de la Plata** (**ree•oh** day lah **plah•tah**) naval battle near **Montevideo**, Uruguay, 12/13/39, in which three British cruisers drove the German pocket battleship **Admiral Graf Spee** into the harbor, and on 12/17 she was scuttled in the estuary of the river

Rizal Stadium (**ree•zahl**) Japanese stronghold in S **Manila** during the US liberation 2/45

Rjukan (**ryoo•kuhn, -kahn**) site of a German heavy water plant in Norway. Repeated sabotage efforts by the British **SOE** prevented the Germans from ever using the heavy water for nuclear bomb research.

Rochefort, Commander Joseph J. (**rohch•fuhrt, -fawrt**) head of US Navy code breaking at **Pearl Harbor**, whose team correctly predicted the impending Japanese attack on **Midway**

Roi Island (**roy**) part of the **Kwajaleen** atoll in the Pacific, taken from the Japanese 2/1/44 by US forces, who quickly made use of its large airfield

Rokossovsky, Marshal Konstantin K. (US **rahk•uh•sahv′•skee**, Rus ruhk•uh•**suhv**•skee) one of the greatest Soviet generals, led armies at **Moscow** (1941), **Stalingrad** (1942), and **Kursk** (1943), and in Poland (1944) and Germany (1945)

Roma (**rohm•ah**, -uh) Italian battleship sunk by German bombers 9/9/43 as it tried to reach **Malta** after Italy's surrender

Romania -- see **Michael, King of**

Rommel, FM Erwin (**rahm•uhl**, US **uhr•win**, Ger **air•veen**) led **Axis** forces in N Africa 2/12/41-3/9/43, where he earned the nickname "The Desert Fox"; commanded Army Group B in France from 1/44, strengthening coastal defenses; forced to commit suicide 10/14/44 for withholding his knowledge of the **July Bomb Plot**

Roosevelt, Eleanor (**roh′•zuh•velt**) The most active and influential First Lady in history, she traveled the world on behalf of humanitarian causes, playing a major role in the **United Nations** after the death of her husband Franklin.

Roosevelt, Franklin Delano (**roh′•zuh•velt, del′•uh•noh**) 32nd President of the US, 1933-45, and the only one to serve more than eight years

Roosevelt, Brig Gen Theodore, Jr. ("**Ted**") (**roh′•zuh•velt**) the son of President Teddy, he fought with flair and courage in NW Africa and in the **Normandy** invasion before dying of a heart attack 7/12/44

Rosenberg, Alfred (**roh′•zuhn•buhrg**) the leading National Socialist (**Nazi**) ideologue and a rabid anti-semite, a colleague of **Hitler** from 1921, nominally Reich Minister of the Eastern Occupied Territories from 7/17/41, tried at **Nuremberg** and hanged 10/16/46

Rosenthal, Joe -- Associated Press (AP) photographer who took the Pulitzer Prize-winning shot of six marines raising the American flag on top of Mount **Suribachi** on **Iwo Jima** 2/23/45

Rösseler, Rudolf ("Lucy") (**ru(r)**•suh•luhr, **roo**•dawlf) a German living in Switzerland whose contacts in the German High Command, together with British **Ultra** intelligence, enabled him to provide valuable information to the **Allies**, especially the Soviets, until 11/43, when **Radolfi**'s Swiss spy network, of which he was a part, was broken up

Rostock (**rahs**•tahk) German port city near the **Baltic Sea**, heavily bombed by the British 4/24 and 4/27/42

Rostov (or **Rostov-on-Don**) (US **rah**•stahf, Rus ruh•**stawf**) city on the **Don** river in S Russia which changed hands four times between 11/21/41 and 2/14/43

Rota (**roh**•tah, -tuh) island in the S **Marianas**, held by the Japanese until 9/2/45

Rotmistrov, Marshal Pavel A. (ruht•**mees**•truhv, **pah**•vel, -vuhl) commanded Soviet tank armies at **Stalingrad** (1942), **Kursk** and **Kharkov** (1943), and the **Baltic** states (1944)

Rotterdam (**raht′**•uhr•**dam**) port city in SW Holland, heavily bombed 5/14/40 and then occupied by Germany until the end of the war

Rouen (US roo•**ahn**, Fr -**ah(n)**) French city on the **Seine** WNW of Paris, whose railroad yards were the first US bombing target in Europe, 8/17/42

Roxas y Acuña, Manuel (**roh•**ahs ee ah•**coon•**yah, US **man'•**yuh•**wel**, Sp mahn•**wel**) **Filipino** political leader with close ties to **MacArthur**, elected first president of the newly independent **Philippines** 7/4/46, died during his second year in office

Royal Oak, HMS -- British battleship sunk at **Scapa Flow** 10/13-14/39 by **Günther Prien's** submarine U-47

Rubicon (**roo'•**bih•**kahn**) river on the NE coast of Italy, made famous by Caesar's southward crossing in 49 B.C., crossed 10/11/44 by **New Zealand** troops heading the opposite direction

Rudder, Lt Col James E. (**ruh•**duhr) led the successful US Ranger assault on **Pointe du Hoc** on **D-Day**

Rudel, Hans Ulrich (**roo•**duhl, **hahns ul•**rikh) German fighter pilot, the most highly decorated German soldier in WWII, credited with over 2,500 missions, the most of any pilot in the war

Rudenko, Sergei I. (US roo•**den•**koh, **sair•**gay) Commander of the 16th Soviet Air Army from 9/42 to the end of the war, supporting army offensives from **Stalingrad** to Berlin

Ruge, Maj Gen Otto (**roo•**geh) promoted to CiC Norwegian Army 4/11/40, two days after the German invasion, captured by German forces 6/40, liberated by Allied forces in Germany 4/45

Ruhr, the (**rur**) an industrial area in W Germany, named for the **Ruhr river**, whose dams were repeatedly attacked by the **Allies** with little success. On 5/16-17/43 the **Möhne** and **Eder** dams were destroyed, but with less damage to the **Ruhr valley** than expected

Rundstedt, FM Gerd von (US **rund•**stet, Ger **runt•**shtet, **gairt**) led German armies in Poland (1939), France (1940), and the Soviet Union (1941), then CiC Army Group West from 3/1/42 to 3/45

Russell Islands (ruhs•uhl) two large islands 30 miles NW of **Guadalcanal**, taken unopposed by US forces 2/21/43

Russo-Finnish War (11/30/39-3/12/40) The USSR's invasion of **Finland** ended with a treaty under which Finland ceded territory while preserving its independence. The poor performance of Soviet forces helped persuade **Hitler** to invade the USSR in 1941.

Russo-German Non-Aggression Pact -- see **Ribbentrop**

Rust, Bernhard (**rust**, **bairn**•hahrt) German Minister for Science, Education, and Culture 1933-45, committed suicide 5/45

Ruthenia (roo• **thee**•nee•uh, -**theen**•yuh) the E-most region of Czechoslovakia, ceded to the Soviet Union at the end of the war, now part of **Ukraine**

Rybalko, General Pavel S. (ruh•**bahl**•kuh, **pah**•vel, -vuhl) Soviet tank army commander from summer 1942, eventually liberating Prague 5/9/45

Ryder, Maj Gen Charles W. (ry•duhr) commanded the US 34th Infantry Division from the **Torch** landings in NW Africa (11/42) through the Italian campaign, returning to the US 7/44 and assuming command of the 9th Corps 9/44

Rydz-Smigly -- see **Smigly-Rydz**

Ryti, Risto (ru•ty) President of **Finland** from 12/19/40, replaced 8/4/44 by **Mannerheim**, who revoked Ryti's commitment to **Hitler** (made under duress) and signed a treaty with the Soviet Union 9/19/44

Ryuho (ryoo•hoh) Japanese aircraft carrier, fought at the Battle of the **Philippine Sea** (6/44), finally put out of action 7/24-28/45 near mainland Japan

Ryujo (ryoo•joh) Japanese aircraft carrier, hit in the **Doolittle** raid 4/42 while in dry dock at **Yokosuka**, sunk in the Battle of the **Eastern Solomons** 8/24/42

Ryukyu Islands (ree•oo•kyoo, **ryoo-**) S-most island group of Japan, whose principal island is **Okinawa**

Rzhev (r'zhev) Russian city about 200 miles W of **Moscow**

S

Saar, the (sahr, zahr) (also **Saar Basin**) a coal producing region in W Germany, named for the **Saar** (Fr Sarre) river, under the economic control of France 1919-35, 1945-57

Saarbrücken (sahr•**bruk**•uhn, zahr-) the capital of **Saarland**

Saarland (US **sahr**•land, Ger **zahr**•lahnt) a German state in the **Saar** river valley

Sabang (sah•bahng) a town and bay on **We** (or **Weh**) **Island** (**way**) off the N tip of **Sumatra**, a Japanese stronghold throughout the war

Saburov, Alexander (sah•**boo**•ruhv) Soviet partisan leader operating in and around the **Pripet Marshes** from late 1942

Sachs, Alexander (saks) Russian-born American economist who met with **Roosevelt** 10/11/39, bearing a letter from **Einstein**, to explain the possibility of developing an atomic bomb

Sachsenhausen (Ger **zahk**•zen•**how**•zuhn, US **sahk**•suhn-) German concentration camp N of Berlin, where over 100,000 died 1933-45

Safi (also **Saffi**) **(saf•ee)** Atlantic port city in French **Morocco**, W end of a 1,300 mile stretch of coast in NW Africa captured in **Operation Torch** 11/7-10/42

Sahara Desert (suh•har•uh, chiefly Brit **-hahr-**) crosses all of N Africa with an area of about 3 ½ million square miles

Saidor (sy•dawr) Japanese stronghold on the NE coast of **New Guinea**, captured by US forces 1/2/44 in an amphibious landing

Saigon (sy•**gahn**) city in **French Indo-China**, entered by Japanese forces 7/41 with the reluctant consent of the **Vichy** government, occupied by Japan until the end of the war, capital of South Vietnam 1954-76, now **Ho Chi Minh** City

St. Cloud (sa(n) **cloo**) 1) a suburb of Paris 2) a town 15 miles E of **Oran**, where French forces successfully resisted the initial **Torch** landings 11/42

St. Denis (**sa(n)** duh•**nee′**) marshalling yards outside Paris, bombed by the **Allies** 4/21/44 with a heavy death toll of French

Saint-Leu-d′esserient (sa(n) **lu** des•ree•**ah(n)′**) a cavern near Paris, site of a British bombing attack 7/4/44 which destroyed 2,000 V-1 flying bombs

St. Lo (sa(n) **loh**) fortress town and German HQ in **Normandy**, about 12 miles inland from **Omaha Beach**, captured by the US 1st Army 7/18/44

St. Lo, USS (saynt **loh**) American aircraft carrier sunk by a **kamikaze** attack 10/25/44 during the Battle of **Leyte Gulf**, the first appearance of the suicide pilots

St. Mâlo (or **Saint Malo**) (**sa(n)** ma•**loh′**, mah-) seaport in N **Brittany** where Canadian troops were evacuated to England 6/15/40, retaken by US forces 8/17/44

St. Nazaire (or **Saint**) (**sa(n)** na•**zair′**, nah-) French Atlantic port on the **Loire** estuary, site of a major German submarine base where concrete fortifications and anti-aircraft defenses resisted Allied air attacks. A bold British commando attack by sea 3/27-28/42 caused considerable damage.

Saint Pierre and Miquelon (US saynt **pyair** and **mik**•uh•**lahn′**, Fr sa(n) **pyair** ay meek•**law(n)**)) French islands off **Newfoundland**, taken from **Vichy** control 12/24/41 by **Free French** forces

Saint-Raphaël (**sa(n)** rah•fah•**el**) coastal town in S France overlooking the well-defended Golfe de Fréjus (**gohlf** duh **fray•zhoo**), taken in Operation **Anvil** 8/15/44

St. Valéry-en-Caux (sa(n) va•lay•**ree**-ah(n)- **koh**) French town on the Channel coast where 46,000 French and British troops surrendered to **Rommel** 6/12/40, retaken by Allied forces 9/2/44

St. Vith (sa(n) **veet**) Belgian town near the German border which played a key role in the Battle of the **Bulge** by delaying the German advance by a few days

Ste. Mère Église (sant **mair** ay•**gleez**) key town on the coast road behind **Utah Beach**, the first town taken by US forces in the **Normandy** Invasion

Saipan (sy•**pan**) one of the **Mariana Islands**, taken from the Japanese by US forces in a battle lasting from 6/15 to 7/9/44

Saito, Lt Gen Yoshitsugu (sah•ee•toh, **sy•**toh) the Japanese commander on **Saipan**, who committed suicide 7/6/44 rather than surrender

Saito, Sgt Maj (**sy•**toh, sah•ee•toh) director of the Japanese labor camp at Tamarkan in **Thailand**, in charge of building the bridge over the **Kwai** River

Sakai, Saburo (sah•**kah•**ee, **-ky**, sah•**boor•**oh) Japanese naval air ace from 1938 to 8/7/42, when he was seriously wounded, later flew missions at **Iwo Jima**

Sakhalin (**sak′•**uh•**leen, sahk′-**) a large island N of Japan. The S half, which had been ceded to Japan by Russia after their 1905 war, was returned to the Soviet Union after WWII and the entire Japanese population of the island was expelled.

Sakurai, Lt Gen Shozo (suh•**kur**•eye, **shoh**•zoh) led the
Japanese 55th Division against the **Admin Box** in Burma from
2/7/44 until withdrawing 2/24

Salamaua (**sal**•uh•**mow′**•uh) town on the N coast of E **New
Guinea (Papua)**, occupied by the Japanese 3/8/42, taken by
Australian forces 9/11/43

Salazar, Dr. António de Oliveira (**sal**•uh•**zahr′**, **sahl-**) ruler
of Portugal 1932-68, maintained a pro-British neutrality
throughout the war, permitting the US to build a base in the
Azores 10/43

Salerno (suh•**lair**•noh, -**luhr-**) Italian city 30 miles S of
Naples, site of a successful amphibious landing by **Mark
Clark**'s US 5th Army on 9/9/43

Salonica (or -**ika**) (suh•**lahn**•ih•kuh, sah- , **sal**•uh•**nee′**•kuh)
port city in N Greece, surrendered 4/9/40 to German forces,
which withdrew from Greece 8-10/44

Salo Republic (**sah**•loh, **sal**•oh) a government in name only,
founded by **Mussolini** in the Lake Garda (**gahr**•duh) area of N
Italy after the Italian surrender, lasted from 9/43 to 4/45

Salween River (**sal**•ween) the second largest river in Burma

Salzburg (US **sahlz**•buhrg, **sawlz-**) Austrian city, site of a
meeting between **Hitler** and **Mussolini** 4/7/43, surrendered to
US forces 5/4/45

Samar (**sah**•mahr) **Philippine** island between **Luzon** and
Mindanao, site of a naval engagement 10/25/44 during the
Battle of **Leyte Gulf**, taken by US forces early in 1945

Sammucro, Mount (sahm•**oo**•kroh) played a major role in the
battle for **San Pietro** in Italy 12/43, since the town is located on
its W slopes

Samos (**say•**mahs, **sam•**ohs) **Aegean** island, occupied by Britain 9/43 after the Italian surrender, taken by German forces 11/43

Samothrace (US **sam′•uh•thrays**) also **Samothráki** (Gr **sah•maw•thrah′•kee**) Greek island in the NE **Aegean**, occupied by German parachute troops in late April 1940

Samuel B. Roberts, USS -- destroyer escort in the Taffy 3 group, sunk off **Samar** 10/25/44 during the Battle of **Leyte Gulf**

San (**sahn**) river in S Poland

Sanatescu, Constantin (sahn•uh•**tes•**koo, **kawn•**stahn•**teen′**) Romanian general who served as Regent for the young **King Michael** 1940-44, then briefly as PM following an anti-German coup in 8/44

San Bernardino Strait (**san buhr•**nahr•**dee′•**noh) waterway between the S tip of **Luzon** and N tip of **Samar**, used by Japanese Admiral **Kurita**'s Center Force to advance to and retreat from the battle E of **Samar** 10/25/44

Sandys, Duncan Edwin (**sandz**) son-in-law of **Churchill**, Minister of Works 1944-45, chaired a War Cabinet committee to study defenses against **V-I** and **V-2** weapons

San Francisco Conference -- an international meeting convened 4/25/45 which produced the Charter of the United Nations, signed 6/26/45

Sangamon, USS (**sang•**guh•muhn) US escort carrier and class of four ships, commissioned 8/25/42

Sangro (**sang•**groh) a river in S Italy flowing E into the **Adriatic Sea** a little S of the **Gustav Line**, site of a battle 11/27-12/2/43 between **Montgomery**'s 8th Army and German defenders

San José (**san** oh•**zay′**, hoh-) a town in SW **Mindoro** in the **Philippines**, where an airfield was quickly built after a US landing 12/15/44

San Pietro (san pee•**ay**•troh) town and battle in C Italy, subject of an acclaimed documentary film directed by **John Huston** in 1944

Sansapor (**sahn**•sah•pawr) the last town to be captured (7/30/44) during the US campaign in **New Guinea**, became a staging base for the invasion of **Luzon** 1/45

Santa Cruz Islands (US **san**•tuh **krooz**) a British mandate in the SW Pacific, site of a US-Japanese naval battle 10/25-26/42 in which only carrier planes made contact with the enemy

Santo Tomás (**sahn**•toh toh•**mahs**, san-) university in **Manila**, used as a prison camp by the Japanese during their occupation

Sarajevo (**sar**•uh•**yay′**•voh) a city in Yugoslavia where an assassination led to WWI, held by German forces in WWII until 4/7/45

Saratoga, USS (**sar**•uh•**toh′**•guh) aircraft carrier active throughout the Pacific War, hit but not sunk by Japanese **kamikaze** planes and torpedo bombs off **Iwo Jima** 2/21/45, which ended her fighting career

Sarawak (suh•**rah**•wahk) a British colony on the N coast of **Borneo**, invaded by the Japanese 12/41 for its oil reserves

Sardinia (sahr•**din**•ee•uh, -**din**•yuh) a large Italian island in the W **Mediterranean**, taken by Allied forces 9/18/43 without opposition, the German garrison having withdrawn

Sarmi (**sahr**•mee) town in NW (Dutch) **New Guinea**, taken by Japanese forces 4/19/42, captured by US forces 5/44

SAS (Special Air Service) -- see **Stirling**

Sas, Colonel Jacobus (sahs, yah•koh•bus) Dutch Military Attaché in Berlin, who forwarded to the W powers information from high-ranking German officers 1939-40

Sato, Lt Gen Kotuku (sah•toh, koh•too•koo) led the Japanese 31st Division against **Kohima** from 4/5/44 until withdrawing 6/1

Sato, Naotake (sah•toh, nah•oh•tah'•keh) Japanese ambassador to the Soviet Union from 2/42 to the end of the war

Sauckel, Fritz (sow•kuhl) **Nazi** party functionary from 1927, became head of the German slave labor program 3/42, hanged at **Nuremberg** 10/46

Saudi Arabia (sow•dee, saw- , uh•ray•bee•uh) an independent kingdom from 1932, officially neutral during the war but aligned with the **Allies**, whom it supplied with oil

Savo Island (sav•oh) near **Guadalcanal**, site of a night naval battle 8/8-9/42 in which four Allied cruisers and a destroyer were sunk with no Japanese losses, the US Navy's greatest defeat

Savoy (suh•voy) Fr **Savoie** (sah•vwah) an area in SE France adjacent to the Swiss/Italian border, occupied by Italy after the fall of France 6/40

Savy, Jean (sah•vee, zhah(n)) a British agent in France, whose information led to the successful bombing of 2,000 **V-1** flying bombs stored N of Paris 7/44

Sayn-Wittgenstein, Major Heinrich Prinz zu (sayn vit'•guhn•styn, -shtyn, hyn•rikh) German fighter ace who died 1/21/44 in an air battle over **Magdeburg**

Sbeïtla (**z'bayt**•lah, -luh) key crossroads town and US divisional command post in C **Tunisia**, taken by German forces 2/17 on the way to **Kassarine Pass**

Sbiba (z'bee•**bah**) town in C **Tunisia** where US artillery turned back **Rommel**'s **Panzers** 2/19-20/43

Scapa Flow (**skah**•puh, **skap**•uh **floh**) British Home Fleet base in the Orkney Islands N of Scotland, penetrated 10/13-14/39 by a German submarine which sank the battleship **Royal Oak**

Schacht, Dr. Hjalmar (**shahkht**, **yahl**•mahr) the leading German economist of the 1920s and 30s, supported **Hitler** until 1939, when he resigned as President of the Reichsbank and gradually withdrew from public affairs, resuming his career after the war

Scharnhorst (**shahrn**•hawrst) German battlecruiser, largely ineffective during the war, finally sunk 12/26/43 N of Norway with the loss of 1,864 men

Scheer -- see **Admiral Scheer**

Scheldt (**skelt**) the major river of Belgium, flowing through **Antwerp** into the **Schelde** (**skel**•duh) estuary in Holland. Though the British captured **Antwerp**, the largest port in Europe, on 9/4/44, German forces occupying the estuary prevented its use until 11/29/44, a major flaw in Allied planning.

Schellenberg, SS Maj Gen Walter (Walther) (**shel'**•en•**bairg**, **vahl**•tuhr) head of German foreign intelligence from 6/41, increasingly urged his mentor **Himmler** to seek peace as the war progressed

Schepke, Captain Joachim (**shep**•kuh, **yoh**•ahkh•im) a leading German submarine ace, killed in action 3/41

Schindler, Oskar (**shin**•(d)luhr, US **ahs**•kuhr, Ger **aws'•kahr**) German war profiteer who ran a small armament company using Jewish slave labor, but increasingly used his position to save Jewish lives, as described in Steven Spielberg's 1993 Oscar-winning film *Schindler's List*

Schiphol (**skhip**•uhl) Dutch airport and town about 50 miles S of **Amsterdam**

Schirach, Baldur von (**sheer**•ahkh) leader of the Hitler Youth (Hitlerjugend) 1931-40, Governor (Gauleiter) of Vienna from 8/40 until the war's end, imprisoned for war crimes until 1966

Schlabrendorff, Dr. Fabian von (**shlah'•bren•dawrf**) high-ranking German army officer who conspired against **Hitler** before and during the war

Schlieben, General Karl Wilhelm von (**shlee**•buhn, -ben, **vil**•helm) German port commander of **Cherbourg** during the **Normandy** invasion, surrendered the city 6/26/40

Schlüsselburg (**shlu'•suhl•buhrg**) (also **Shlisselburg**) Russian town on the S end of Lake **Ladoga** where the **Neva** River joins it E of **Leningrad**, terminus of an ice road supplying the city

Schmidt, Maj Gen Harry (**shmit**) US Marine commander on **Iwo Jima**

Schmidt, Paul (**shmit**) the leading German interpreter (translator) 1935-45, often translated for **Hitler**'s meetings

Schmundt, General Rudolph (**shmunt, roo**•dawlf) **Hitler**'s **Wehrmacht** (Army) adjutant from 1938 until he was wounded by the bomb intended for Hitler 7/20/44 and died 10/1/44

Schnaufer, Heinz-Wolfgang (**shnow**•fuhr, **hyns-vawlf**•gahng) the **Luftwaffe**'s top night-fighter ace with 121 kills, mostly against RAF bombers, survived the war

Schnee Eifel (**shnay eye′•fuhl**) a fortified ridge, part of the German **West Wall** across the border from **St. Vith**, Belgium, where 8,000 Americans surrendered 12/19/44 during the Battle of the **Bulge**

Schnorchel (or **Schnorkel**) -- see **Snorkel**

Schörner, FM Ferdinand (**shur•nuhr**) German commander of the Army Group in the S **Ukraine** from 4/44, also commanded Army Group North from 7/44 and Army Group Center from 1/45, appointed by **Hitler** to succeed him as CiC German Army in his final testament 4/29/45

Schulenburg, Count Friedrich Werner von (**shoo′•len•burg, free•drikh vehr•nuhr**) German Ambassador to the Soviet Union 1935-6/41, opposed the German invasion, joined the **July Bomb Plot** group, executed 11/10/44

Schuschnigg, Kurt von (**shush•nig, -nik, kurt**) Chancellor of Austria from 1934 until forced out by **Hitler** 3/11/38, liberated from **Flossenbürg** by American forces 5/4/45

Schweinfurt (**shvyn•fuhrt**) German city in **Bavaria**, site of a ball-bearing factory complex bombed repeatedly by the **Allies** from 8/17/43

Schwerin von Krosigk, Count Lutz (**shfay•reen vahn kroh•sik**) German Minister of Finance 1932-45, opposed the invasion of the Soviet Union

Scobie, Gen Sir Robert MacKenzie (**skoh•bee**) British CiC in Greece after the German withdrawal 10/44, fought a communist-led civil war, achieved a peace treaty 1/11/45 and stayed until 1946 to enforce it

Scoglitti (**skuhl•yee•tee**) town on the S coast of **Sicily**, one of three landing sites for US forces (including Generals **Bradley** and **Middleton**) on 7/10/43 (Operation **Husky**)

Scoones, Lt Gen Sir Geoffrey (skoonz) British field commander at **Imphal** during the Japanese siege of 4-7/44 and the subsequent counterattack

Scott, Rear Adm Norman -- commander of a US cruiser group in the Battle of **Cape Esperance** (off NW **Guadalcanal**) 10/11-12/42, killed in action a month later

Scutari (skoot•uh•ree) city in NW **Albania**, on the S shore of Lake Scutari, one end of a German defense line abandoned 11/29/44. The city is now known by its Albanian name **Shkodër (shkoh•duhr)**.

Seabees (see'•beez) US Navy construction battalions (CBs) started 1/42, first employed at **Henderson Field** on **Guadalcanal**, grew to almost a quarter-million men by **V-J Day**

Seaborg, Glenn Theodore (see•bawrg) American chemist who isolated **plutonium** (element 94) while working on the **Manhattan Project**, winner of the Nobel Prize 1951, later chairman of the Atomic Energy Commission (AEC)

SEAC (Southeast Asia Command) (see•ak) the Burma-**Malaya-Sumatra-Thailand-French Indo-China** Theater, established 11/15/43 under **Mountbatten** and his deputy **Stilwell**, who outranked him

Seagrave, Dr. Gordon S. (see•grayv) US missionary surgeon in Burma 1922-65 and Lt Col in the US Medical Corps during the war

Sea Lion (or **Sealion**) Ger **Seelöwe (say'•lu•vuh)** the German plan to invade Britain after the conquest of France, postponed 9/17/40, abandoned 10/12/40

Sebou (suh•boo) river in **Morocco** flowing into the Atlantic, site of an Allied landing 11/42 (see **Dallas, USS**)

Second Front -- the land invasion of W Europe led by the US and Britain, eagerly sought by **Stalin**. After postponements, it finally occurred on **D-Day**, 6/6/44.

Sedan (US seh•**dan**, Fr sih•**dah(n)**) French town near the border with Belgium, a key defense point in both world wars, easily bypassed by the Germans 5/13/40

Seine (Fr **sen**, US **sayn**) a major French river that runs WNW through Paris to the **English Channel** near **Le Havre**

Sele Corridor (**say**•lay) a gap in the Allied beachhead SE of **Salerno** along the river of that name, 9/43

Selective Service System -- the first US peacetime draft, created by an act of Congress in 9/40, registered about 35 million men from 10/40 to the end of the war and actually inducted about 10 million

Sened Station (sen•**ed**) village in C **Tunisia** between **Gafsa** and **Maknassy**, taken by US forces 3/21/43 after lengthy fighting in the area

Senger und Etterlin, General Fridolin (Frido) von (sen•**guhr** unt et•**tuhr**•lin) commander of German forces in **Sicily,** conducted the successful German evacuation from **Messina** to mainland Italy, where he led the 14th **Panzer** Corps at **Cassino**

Seraph, HMS (**sair**•uhf) a British submarine that carried out several important secret missions in the **Mediterranean** between 9/42 and 4/43, involving as passengers **Mark Clark**, **Henri Giraud**, and a dead body carrying disinformation delivered to the Spanish coast

Serov, General Ivan A. (US **sair**•uhf, **eye**•vuhn, Rus seh•**ruhv**, ih•**vahn**) Soviet Deputy Commissar for State Security (under **Beria**) from 1941, after overseeing mass deportations and executions in the annexed **Baltic States** 1939-40, appointed Deputy Supreme Commander of Soviet Forces in Germany 1945

Servia Pass (**sair•vee•ah**) an access route into Greece held by Australia-**New Zealand** (Anzac) forces against the German 12th Army 4/41 until they were outflanked and withdrew 4/17

Sevastopol (or **Seb-**) (**suh•vas'•tuh•pohl**) the major city and naval base on the **Crimean** peninsula, occupied by German forces from 7/4/42 to 5/9/44

Seyss-Inquart, Artur (or **Arthur**) **von** (US **sys in•**qwahrt, Ger **sys ink•**vahrt, **ahr•**tur) Austrian **Nazi** who replaced **Schuschnigg** as Chancellor and then German Governor until 4/30/39, then served as Reich Commissioner of Holland from 5/40 to 1945, hanged at **Nuremberg** for war crimes 10/16/46

Sfax (**sfahks, sfaks**) port city in E **Tunisia**, taken from the retreating Germans by **Montgomery**'s 8th Army 4/10/43

Shaduzup (**shahd•uh•zuhp, shad-**) town in the **Mogaung** valley in Burma, site of a Japanese defeat by US and Chinese forces 3/44

SHAEF (**Supreme Headquarters, Allied Expeditionary Force**) (**shayf**) command center for Allied forces in NW Europe under **Eisenhower**'s command, in England before **D-Day** and France afterward

Shanghai (**shang•hy**) major Chinese port city, occupied by the Japanese in 1937 (Chinese section) and 12/41 (US and British sections)

Shaposhnikov, Marshal Boris M. (**shah•pahsh•nih•kuhv**) a leading Soviet military theorist and author between the wars, Chief of the Soviet General Staff 5/37-8/40, 7/41-6/42, when illness forced his resignation

Sheffield (**shef•**eeld) 1) British steel center bombed by Germany 12/12/40 2) **HMS** -- British cruiser in the Home Fleet which played a major role throughout the war

Sherman, Rear Admiral Forrest P. (**shuhr•**muhn) a leading US naval planner and mediator, CoS to **Nimitz** from 11/43, chief of war plans from 3/44

Sherman, Vice-Admiral Frederick (**shuhr•**muhn) led carrier task forces in the Pacific Theater 11/42-2/44, 8/44-9/45

Sherman Tank (M4 General Sherman) (**shuhr•**muhn) the standard US tank throughout the world from 1943, also used by British and **Free French** forces, first used operationally at **El Alamein** 10-11/42

Sherrod, Robert (**shair•**uhd) *TIME* magazine correspondent who reported most Pacific island campaigns from **Tarawa** to **Iwo Jima**, notably the three-week campaign on **Saipan** 6-7/44

Shibasaki, Rear Admiral Keiji (**shee•**buh•**sah•**kee, **shib•**uh- , **kay•**jee) commander of the 4,500 Japanese troops defending **Betio**

Shichina (shih•**chee•**nuh, shee-) town in **Okinawa**

Shigemitsu, Mamoru (**shig•**uh•**mit'•**soo, mam•**awr•**oo) Japanese Ambassador to the Soviet Union (1936-38), Great Britain (from late 1938), and **Vichy** France (1942-43), Foreign Minister 4/43-4/45, 8/45 until imprisoned for several years for war crimes, signed the Japanese surrender document 9/2/45

Shikoku (**shee'•**kaw•**koo**) the smallest of the four Japanese home islands

Shima, Vice-Admiral Kiyohide (**shee•**muh, -mah, **kee•**yoh•**hee'•**deh) Japanese naval force commander at the

Battles of the **Coral Sea** (5/42), **Leyte Gulf** (10/44), and elsewhere

Shimada, Shigetaro (shee•mah•duh, shig•uh•tah'•roh) a supporter of **Tojo** who served as Navy Minister from 10/41 to 7/44 and Chief of Naval Staff from 2/44 to 8/44, imprisoned after the war until 1955

Shinano (shih•nah•noh) a Japanese super-battleship converted into the world's largest aircraft carrier before completion, sunk by the US submarine Archerfish 11/29/44, less than one day into her first cruise, carrying 50 rocket-propelled mini-planes called **Ohkas**

Shindawaku (sheen•dah•wah•koo, shin•duh-) town in **Okinawa**

Shingbwiyang (shin•boo•ang) village and forward base on the **Ledo Road** in N Burma

Shirer, William L. (shy•ruhr) American journalist in Germany from 1934 to 12/40 who wrote *Berlin Diary* (1941) and *The Rise and Fall of the Third Reich* (1960)

Shkodër -- see **Scutari**

Sho-Go (Victory Plan) (shoh•goh) a group of Japanese plans for defense of its remaining empire after the loss of the **Marianas** in mid-1944. The **Philippines** were the next major US thrust, so that plan (**Sho-Ichi-Go**, or **Sho-1**) (-ee•chee-) was soon put into effect with the Battle of **Leyte Gulf**.

Shoho (shoh•hoh) Japanese light aircraft carrier sunk by air attack in the Battle of the **Coral Sea** 5/8/42

Shokaku (shoh•kah•koo) Japanese aircraft carrier, part of the **Pearl Harbor** task force, damaged 5/8/42 in the Battle of the

Coral Sea, sunk by a US submarine off **Saipan** 6/44 in the Battle of the **Philippine Sea**

Short, Lt Gen Walter C. -- Army CiC in Hawaii 2-12/41, held responsible for **Pearl Harbor**, retired 1942

Shostakovich, Dmitri (**shahs•tuh•koh′•**vich, dih•**mee•**tree) the most important composer produced by the Soviet Union, wrote war symphonies during and after the war

Shumilov, Col Gen Mikail S. (shoo•**mee•**lawv, shu- , mih•**kyl**) commanded the 64th Army at **Stalingrad** (later the 7th Guards Army) where he received **Paulus**'s surrender

Shuri Line (**shoor•**ee, **shur-**) Japanese defensive position across the S part of **Okinawa**, anchored at **Shuri Castle**

Shwebo (**shway•**boh) town and plain in Burma NW of **Mandalay**

Siauliai (**shyow•lee′eye, show-**) important railroad junction in N **Lithuania**, retaken by Soviet forces 7/27/44

Sibuyan Sea, Battle of the (**see•boo•yahn′**, see•**boo•**yahn) the first (10/24/44) of the four major engagements in the Battle of **Leyte Gulf**

Sicherheitsdienst (SD) (**zikh•**uhr•**hytz•deenst**) the intelligence branch of the **SS**

Sicily (**sis•**uh•lee) the S-most part of Italy, separated from the mainland by the Strait of **Messina**, invaded by Allied forces 7/10/43 (Operation **Husky**) who reached **Messina** 8/17/43

Sidi Barrani (**see•**dee buh•**rahn•**ee, bah-) Egyptian coastal town 60 miles from the Libyan border, a key defensive position throughout the N African campaign

Sidi bou Zid (**see**•dee boo **zeed**) town in C **Tunisia**, site of a major German victory over US forces 2/14-15/43

Sidi el Moudjad (**see**•dee el mood•**jahd**) coastal town in **Tunisia**, site of an abortive Allied commando landing 12/1/42

Sidi Rezegh (**see**•dee reh•**zehg**) town and airfield SE of **Tobruk**, scene of heavy fighting 11/41

Sidra (**sid**•rah, -ruh) large gulf off the coast of **Libya**

Siegfried Line -- see **West Wall**

Siena (see•**en**•uh, -ah) small city in Tuscany, in C Italy, **Alexander**'s HQ 8/44, where he was visited by **Churchill**

Sierra Leone (see•**air**•uh lee•**ohn**, -ohn•ee) small country on the W coast of Africa, British protectorate 1896-1961

Sikorsky, Igor I. (sih•**kawr**•skee, ee•**gawr**) Russian-born American aircraft designer who invented the helicopter in 1939. The **Sikorsky R-4** entered limited production in 1943.

Sikorsky, General Wladyslaw (or **Vladislav**) (sih•**kawr**•skee, vlahd'•is•**lahv**) set up a Polish government-in-exile in France 9/30/39, which moved to London after the fall of France 6/40, died in a suspicious plane crash 7/4/43

Silesia (sy•**lee**•zhuh, sih-) an industrial and mining area in E Germany, straddling the upper **Oder** river, now part of Poland and Czechoslovakia

Simi (see•mee, sim•ee) Greek island in the **Aegean Sea** N of **Rhodes**, occupied by German forces from 1940 until the end of the war

Simonds, Lt Gen Guy Grenville (sy•muhnz, **gy gren•**vil)
highly regarded Canadian commander who served in N Africa,
Sicily, Italy, and the Western Front

Simpson, Lt Gen William H. (simp•suhn) highly praised
commander of the US 9th Army, from **Brittany** 9/5/44 to final
victory in Germany

Sinclair, Sir Archibald -- British Minister of Air 5/40-5/45

Singapore (sing′•guh•pawr, -pohr, sing′•uh-) British island,
strait, colony, city, and fortress on the S tip of **Malaya**, taken by
the Japanese 2/15/42 from the N (land) side with the loss of
70,000 troops, the greatest defeat in British history; an
independent country since 1965

Singh, Major Mohan (sing, moh•hahn) a Sikh POW of the
Japanese in **Malaya** who volunteered to lead an Indian National
Army against the British 12/41

Sino-Japanese War (1937-41) (sy•noh) the name for the
Japanese invasion of China before it became part of WWII after
Pearl Harbor

Sinzweya (sin•zway•uh) HQ of the 7th Indian Division within
the **Admin Box** in Burma, a pivotal Japanese defeat 2/44

SIS (Secret Intelligence Service) -- British security
organization that included MI-6 (Foreign Intelligence), MI-5
(Domestic Counterintelligence), and the Government Code and
Cipher School (housed at **Bletchley Park** from early 1941 and
renamed Government Communications HQ). Headed by **Sir
Stewart Menzies** from 11/39 until 1952

Sittang (sit′•tahng, -tang) a major river in Burma, flowing S
into the **Andaman Sea** E of **Rangoon**, also a town on that river

Sittwe -- see **Akyab**

Sitzkrieg ("sit-down war") (**sits•**kreeg) humorous contrast to **Blitzkrieg** used to describe the inactivity on the Western Front from the declaration of war 9/39 until 5/40, called "the phony war" in Britain

Skagerrak (US **skag′•**uh•**rak,** Dan/Nor **skah′•**guh•**rahk**) a narrow waterway between Denmark and Norway

Skoda Works (US **skoh•**duh, Cz **shkoh•**dah) Czech producer of arms, especially tanks, under German control for most of the war

Skopje (or **Skoplje**) (**scawp•**yeh, -yay, -lyeh, -lyay) city in SE Yugoslavia, capital of **Macedonia**

Skorzeny, Lt Col Otto (skawr•**zen•**ee, -**zay•**nee, US **ah•**toh, Ger **aw-**) **SS** commando leader who rescued **Mussolini** 9/12/43, abducted the son of Hungarian ruler **Horthy** 10/15/44, and caused great disruption by infiltrating Allied lines in American uniforms during the Battle of the **Bulge** 12/44

Slapton Sands (**slap•**tuhn) a beach on the S coast of England where an amphibious exercise for **D-Day** on 4/28/44 was joined by seven German torpedo boats, which caused over 600 deaths

Slessor, Air Vice Marshal Sir John (**sles•**suhr) Though Slessor was a leading advocate of strategic bombing in the 1930s, he made his most important contribution during the war as head of RAF Coastal Command (1943) attacking **U-boats.**

Slim, General Sir William (later **FM Viscount**) -- from 10/43 Commander of the British 14th Army in SE Asia, which played the major role in driving the Japanese out of Burma. In 8/45 he became CiC Allied land forces SE Asia.

Slot, the -- US name for the vital internal waterway running the length of the **Solomon Islands**, heavily used by both sides during the battle for **Guadalcanal**

Slovakia (sloh•**vah**•kee•uh, -**vak**•ee•uh) remained intact as a puppet ally of Germany after **Hitler**'s annexation of W Czechoslovakia in 1938, again part of Czechoslovakia from the end of the war until becoming independent in 1993

Slovenia (sloh•**vee**•nee•uh, -**veen**•yuh) a constituent republic in the NW part of Yugoslavia 1918-91, an independent country since 1991

Smigly-Rydz, Marshal Edward (**smig**•lee **rij**, **ed**•vahrt) CiC Polish armed forces and de facto head of state when the Germans invaded 9/39, did little to help a hopeless situation

Smith, Lt Gen Holland M. ("Howlin' Mad") -- the leading Marine expert in amphibious warfare, directed landings throughout the Pacific 1943-45

Smith, Lt Gen Walter Bedell (bih•**del**) (aka "**Beetle**") **Eisenhower**'s CoS from N Africa until he signed the German surrender at **Rheims** on behalf of the Allied Expeditionary Force (AEF) 5/7/45

Smolensk (smoh•**lensk**) important Soviet rail junction about 250 miles WSW of **Moscow**, taken by German forces 8/6/41 and retaken by Soviet forces 9/25/43, in both cases after long and costly battles

Smuts, FM Jan C. (**smuhts**, **smuts**, **yahn**) pro-British PM of **South Africa** throughout the war

snorkel (Ger **Schnorchel** or **Schnorkel**) -- a device introduced in 1944 that enabled German **U-boats** to take in air and release exhaust without surfacing

Sobibor (**soh'**•bih•**bawr**) a German extermination camp in Poland from 3/42, closed late 1943 after a rebellion by prisoners

Sochi (**soh•**chee) a resort city on the NE shore of the **Black Sea**, successfully defended from the German advance of 1942-43

Socotra (also **Sok-**) (suh•**koh•**truh, **sahk•**uh•truh) an island in the **Indian Ocean** off the horn of Africa, site of an Allied monitoring station, part of Yemen since 1967

SOE (**Special Operations Executive**) -- established 11/40 in England with the mission of supporting resistance groups in German-occupied countries

Sofia (**soh•**fee•uh, soh•**fee•**uh) the capital of Bulgaria

Sokolovsky, Marshal Vasiliy (**-ily,-ili**) **D.** (US soh•kuhl•**ahv′•**skee, vah•**see•**lee, Rus suh•kuh•**lohv•**skee, **vuhs•yeel′•**yee) Soviet CoS Western Front under **Konev** 1941-43, **Zhukov**'s deputy front commander at Berlin

Sola (**soh•**lah) the largest airfield in Norway and the closest to **Scapa Flow**, captured by German forces 4/9/40

Solomon Islands (**sahl•**uh•muhn) Pacific island group E of **New Guinea** that includes **Guadalcanal** in the SE and **Bougainville** in the NW

Somaliland (soh•**mah′•**lee•land, suh-) an area on the horn of Africa consisting of a large Italian colony and a smaller British one, equivalent to the present country of Somalia, and a small French colony, now Djibouti (jih•**boot•**ee)

Somervell, General Brehon B. (**suhm′•**uhr•vel, **bree•**uhn, **bray-** , ahn) head of US Army Service Forces (supply and logistics) from 3/9/42 until the end of the war

Somerville, Admiral Sir James F. (**suhm′•**uhr•vil) assisted in the evacuation of **Dunkirk** (1940), commanded the naval force at **Gibraltar** from 6/27/40, personally (though reluctantly) led the action against the French Fleet at **Oran** 7/41, helped supply

Malta and sink the **Bismarck** (5/27/41), CiC Eastern Fleet in the **Indian Ocean** (1942-44)

Somme (US **sahm**, Fr **sawm**) river in N France flowing NW into the **English Channel**

sonar (**soh•nahr**) the US acronym for SOund NAvigation and Ranging, whose primary use was in submarine detection. The British acronym is **asdic**.

Songgram, FM Pibul (**sahng•gruhm**, **pee•buhl**) dictator of Siam, which he renamed **Thailand** ("free land") in 1939, became a Japanese puppet ruler during the war

Soong, T.V. (born **Tse-ven Sung**) (**soong**, **sung**) a member of China's most influential family, served **Chiang Kai-shek** as Finance Minister, Foreign Minister, and Chief Negotiator with the US until breaking with Chiang early in 1944

Sorge, Richard (**sawr•guh**, **rikh•ahrt**) a German journalist in Tokyo from 1933 and an important spy for the Soviet Union, gave **Stalin** advance notice of the German invasion and the Japanese decision to move S rather than against the Soviet Union. Arrested 10/18/41, executed 11/7/44

Soryu (**sawr•yoo**) Japanese aircraft carrier sunk in the Battle of **Midway**

Sousse (**soos**) coastal town in NE **Tunisia**, French naval base, taken from the retreating Germans by **Montgomery**'s 8th Army 4/12/43

South Africa -- a member of the British Commonwealth which actively supported Britain throughout the war

Southampton (**sowth•amp•tuhn, -hamp-**) the principal port city of the S coast of England, bombed 9/15/40 and 11/24/40

South Dakota, USS -- name ship of a class of four battleships that also included the Alabama, Indiana, and Massachusetts, fought throughout the Pacific from 1942 to the end of the war

Southern Rhodesia (roh•dee•zhuh) a member of the British Commonwealth in S Africa which provided pilots for the Battle of **Britain,** and Askaris (Black Africans) (az•**kahr**•eez), about 500 of whom died on other fronts

Soviet-Japanese Neutrality Pact -- signed 4/13/41 for a term of five years, committing each country to remain neutral in the event of an attack by a third country, broken 8/9/45 when the Soviet Union declared war on Japan and invaded **Manchuria**

Spaak, Paul-Henri (**spahk, pawl**-ahn•**ree**) Belgian PM before the war and Foreign Minister-in-exile in London during the war, headed Belgium's first delegation to the United Nations and became the first President of the General Assembly

Spaatz, USAAF General Carl A. (**spahts**) head of US bomber forces in Europe from 1/44, took over the same role in the Pacific 7/45

Spandau (US **span**•dow, Ger **shpahn**-) fortress prison in W Berlin used only for seven leading **Nazis** convicted at **Nuremberg**, beginning 7/18/47

Spanish Civil War -- After the socialist/communist Popular Front won elections held 2/36 and formed the Republican government, the regular army, led by **Franco**, revolted 7/36. Franco's Nationalist (fascist) regime was recognized 11/36 by **Hitler** and **Mussolini**, whose substantial military support led to a Nationalist victory 4/1/39 and helped the **Axis** leaders prepare for WWII.

Special Air Service -- see **Stirling, David**

Special Operations Executive -- see **SOE**

Speedy Valley -- a ravine nine miles SE of **Tébessa** in E **Algeria**, HQ of US General **Lloyd R. Freedendall** from late 1942 to 2/43

Speer, Albert (US **speer, al•buhrt**, Ger **shpair, ahl′•bairt**) the leading **Nazi** architect, who became Minister of Munitions following the death of **Fritz Todt** on 2/9/42, and on 9/2/43 was put in charge of all industrial production in Germany. Convicted at **Nuremberg**, he served a 20-year sentence at **Spandau** prison.

Speidel, Lt Gen Hans (US spy•del, Ger **shpy•duhl, hahns**) CoS to **Rommel** from 4/15/44, persuaded him to join the opposition to **Hitler**, arrested after the failure of the **July Bomb Plot** but acquitted by the Army Court of Honor, and though imprisoned by the **SS** survived the war

Sperrle, FM Hugo (**shpair•luh, hoo•goh**) German air commander in WWI, head of the **Condor Legion** in Spain 1936-37, commanded Air Fleet 3 in the Battle of **Britain**, air commander of the Western Front after 5/21/41, relieved by **Hitler** 8/18/44

Spezia -- see **La Spezia**

Spitfire -- the leading British fighter plane of the war, best known for its success in the Battle of **Britain**

Spitzbergen (now spelled **Spits-**) (**spits′•buhr•guhn, -bair•ghen**) large Norwegian island in the Svalbard (**svahl′•bahr**) archipelago between N Norway and N **Greenland**, target of Operation Gauntlet (8/41), a Canadian commando raid which destroyed oil and coal reserves to prevent the Germans from making use of them

Split (**split**) port city on the **Adriatic** in Yugoslavia, site of fighting between Germans and the partisans of **General Mihailovic** 9/43, now in **Croatia**

Sprauge, Rear Admiral Clifton (sprayg) On 11/25/44, in the battle off **Samar Island**, 6 escort carriers and 6 destroyers under his command attacked and drove away a much stronger force of Japanese ships, protecting the 6ᵗʰ Army's landing on **Leyte**.

Spruance, Admiral Raymond A. (sproo•uhns, -ahns) US commander of the victory at **Midway** (6/42), whose success continued across the Pacific to **Iwo Jima** and **Okinawa**

"Spruce Goose" -- the largest airplane ever built, a flying boat intended to avoid the **U-boats** in the Atlantic. When the US military contract with Hughes Aircraft lapsed, Howard Hughes completed one and flew it himself 11/2/47 for one minute at an elevation of 85 feet, as shown in the movie *Aviator* (2005).

Sri Lanka -- see **Ceylon**

SS (Schützstaffel -- "elite guard") **(shutz'•stah•fuhl, -shtah-)** the most loyal and ruthless **Nazis**, collectively judged war criminals at the **Nuremberg** trials

Stagg, Group Captain James M. -- The chief RAF meteorological adviser to **Eisenhower** 1943-45, his forecast of a break in bad weather persuaded Ike not to extend the one-day postponement of **D-Day**.

stalag (short for **Stammlager** "base camp") **(shtahm'•lah•guhr)** (US **sta•**lag, Ger **shtah•**lahg) German name for POW camps, best known in the US from the play (1951) and film (1953) *Stalag 17*

Stalin, Joseph (stah•lin, stal•in) (born **Iosif Vissarionovich Dzhugashvili**) ruler of the Soviet Union 1928-53

Stalingrad (stah'•lin•grad) (now called **Volgograd (vahl'•guh•grad))** long narrow city on the W bank of the **Volga River**, site of the decisive German defeat in the Soviet Union 8/42-1/31/43

Standley, William H. -- US Ambassador to the Soviet Union 2/42-9/43

Stangl, SS Captain Franz P. (**shtahn**•guhl, **frahns**) Commandant of the **Sobibor** (until 9/42) and **Treblinka** (until 8/43) death camps, arrested in **Brazil** 1967, extradited to Austria and sentenced to life imprisonment 1970, died 1971

Stark, Admiral Harold R. -- US Chief of Naval Operations (CNO) from 8/39 to 3/42, when he went to London to serve as Commander of US Naval Forces in Europe (a primarily diplomatic and administrative post) for the rest of the war

Starzyński, Stefan (stahr•**zhin**•skee, **stef**•ahn) highly regarded mayor of **Warsaw**, who inspired a heroic though hopeless defense of the city against the German invasion 9/39

Stauffenberg, Lt Col Count Claus (or **Klaus**) **von** (US **stowf**•uhn•buhrg, Ger **shtowf′**•en•**bairk**) placed the time bomb that failed to kill **Hitler** at **Rastenburg** 7/20/44 (the **July Bomb Plot**), shot that evening in Berlin

Stauning, Thorvald (**stow**•ning, **tawr**•vahld) PM of Denmark from 1935 until his death on 5/3/42, tried to preserve his country's autonomy under the German occupation that began 4/40

Stavanger (stah•**vahng**•uhr) port city in SW Norway, eight miles from **Sola** airfield, occupied by German forces 4/40

Stavropol (US stav•**roh**•puhl, Rus **stahv**•ruh•puhl) Soviet city in the **Caucasus**, reached by German forces 8/3/42

Steiner, SS General Felix (US **sty**•nuhr, Ger **shty-**) earned decorations and promotions fighting in Poland, France, and the Soviet Union, but ignored **Hitler**'s 4/21/45 order to confront **Zhukov**'s Soviet forces at Eberswalde (**eh**•buhrz•**vawld**•uh), NE of Berlin, and surrendered to the British 5/3

Steinhardt, Laurence A. (**styn**•hahrt) US Ambassador to the Soviet Union 1939-1941, Ambassador to **Turkey** from 1/42

Sten Gun (**sten**) British 9mm caliber submachine gun, used widely throughout the world from 1941

Stephenson, Sir William S. -- head of the British **SIS** (**Secret Intelligence Service**) station in New York 1940-45, where he helped **Bill Donovan** develop the **OSS**

Stettin (shteht•**teen**) German port city on the **Baltic Sea**, now **Szczecin** (shcheht•cheen) in NW Poland

Stettinius, Edward R., Jr. (steh•**tin**•ee•uhs) Administrator of **Lend-Lease** 8/41-9/43, Under Secretary of State from 10/43 (responsible for the 1944 **Dumbarton Oaks Conference**), Secretary of State 12/44-6/45

Stieff, Maj Gen Helmuth (**steef, shteef, hel**•moot) a conspirator in the **July Bomb Plot** who gave **Stauffenberg** the bomb he used on 7/20/44, tried and executed 8/8/44

Stilwell, General Joseph W. ("**Vinegar Joe**") (**stil'**•wel) led Chinese and American troops in the China-Burma-India (CBI) Theater from early 1942 until increasing disagreements with **Chiang Kai-shek** led to his recall 10/18/44

Stimson, Henry L. (**stim**•suhn) US Secretary of War from 6/40 to 9/18/45

Stirling -- British heavy bomber in use from 8/40 to 3/44

Stirling, Colonel David A. -- British commando who founded the **SAS** (**Special Air Service**) in **Egypt** 7/41, which carried out raids in N Africa on airfields behind enemy lines. Stirling was captured in **Tunisia** early in 1943 and imprisoned in Germany, but the SAS expanded and continued its sabotage missions for the rest of the war in Italy, France, and Germany.

Stopford, General Sir Montagu (stahp•fuhrd) As British commander of the 33rd Indian Corps from 1943, he broke the siege of **Kohima** 4/44 and opened the road to **Imphal**. After playing a major role in driving the Japanese out of Burma, he succeeded **Slim** as commander of 14th Army 5/7/45 and received the Japanese surrender.

Strasbourg (US **stras**•buhrg, **strahz**•burg, Fr strahs•**boor**) Ger **Strassburg** (**shtrahs**•burk) 1) city on the **Rhine** river in NE France near the German border, under German rule 1871-1919, 1940-44 2) French battle cruiser which escaped the British bombardment at **Oran** 7/3/40 and crossed the **Mediterranean** to **Toulon**, where it was scuttled by the French 11/27/42 when the Germans tried to seize it

Stratemeyer, Lt Gen George E. (strat•uh•my•uhr) commanded US Army Air Forces in the China-Burma-India (CBI) Theater 1943-45

Streicher, Julius (stry•kuhr, shtry-) **Nazi** editor of the anti-Semitic magazine *Der Stürmer* (dair shtur•muhr) 1923-45, hanged at **Nuremberg** 10/16/46

Strong, Maj Gen Kenneth W. -- British officer, **Eisenhower**'s head of intelligence from early 1943 to the end of the war

Stroop, SS Maj Gen Jürgen (shtrohp, yur•guhn, -ghen) directed the suppression of the **Warsaw Ghetto Uprising** and the destruction of the ghetto 4/18/43-5/16/43, executed on the site of the ghetto 9/8/51

Student, Col Gen Kurt (shtoo•dent, kurt) the leading German commander of airborne infantry forces (paratroops), best known for his successful but costly invasion of **Crete** 5/20/41, the last such major operation by Germany

Stuka (US **stoo•**kuh, Ger **shtoo•**kah) refers generally to any German dive-bomber (<u>Sturzk</u>ampfflugzeug) and specifically to the **Junkers Ju-87**, a ground-support plane used in **Blitzkrieg**

Stülpnagel, General Karl H., Graf von (shtulp′•nah•guhl) German military governor of France from 2/42 and a leader of the **July Bomb Plot**, hanged 8/30/44

Stülpnagel, Otto von (shtulp′•nah•guhl) German military governor of France 11/1/40-2/6/42, succeeded by his younger cousin **Karl** (above), committed suicide while awaiting trial in Paris 2/6/48

Stumme, General Georg (shtu•muh, gay•awrk) acting German commander at **El Alamein** while **Rommel** was on sick leave from 9/22/42, his death from a heart attack on the first full day of battle (10/24/42) hastened Rommel's return on 10/25/42

Stump, Rear Admiral Felix B. (stuhmp) -- commanded a group of six escort carriers (Taffy 2) in the Battle of **Leyte Gulf** (10/23-26/44), later supported landings at **Mindoro**, **Lingayen Gulf**, and **Okinawa**

Stumpff, General Hans Jürgen (shtumpf, hahns yur•guhn, -ghen) **Luftwaffe** CoS 1937-39, CiC Norway from 5/40, later commander of the home defense air force, signed the **Reims** surrender document in Berlin 5/8/45

Der Stürmer -- see **Streicher**

Stuttgart (**stuht•**gahrt, **stut-** , **shtut-**) city in SW Germany, site of a ball-bearing plant, bombed by the RAF frequently from 1940 to 1945

Stutthof (shtut′•hohf) German extermination camp E of **Danzig** (Gdansk) in Poland where over 60,000 Jews were killed

Subic Bay (soo•bik) site of a US naval base in the **Philippines**, separated from **Manila Bay** by the **Bataan Peninsula**

Süchow (soo•chow, su•joh) now **Xuzhow** (shu•joh) Chinese city brutalized by Japanese forces moving from **Shanghai** to **Nanking** 11/37

Suda Bay (soo•duh) the most important harbor in **Crete**, occupied by British forces 10/40, site of a successful Italian torpedo boat raid 3/25/41, captured by German airborne troops 5/26/41

Sudetenland (US soo•dayt'n•land, Ger -lahnt) a region in NW Czechoslovakia, transferred from Austria in 1919, which contained over three million ethnic Germans, annexed by **Hitler** in 10/38 as a result of the **Munich Pact** (9/30/38), soon followed by German control and dismemberment of the entire country

Suez Canal (soo•ez, soo•ez) vital link between the **Mediterranean Sea** and the **Indian Ocean**. Though threatened by **Rommel**'s advances in **Egypt**, it remained in British hands throughout the war.

Sugar Loaf -- a hill on **Okinawa**, site of a weeklong battle 5/45

Sugiyama, FM Hajime (soo•ghee•ah•muh, hah•jee•may) Japanese Army CoS 1938-2/44, War Minister in the **Koiso** government 7/44-4/45, commander of the 1st Imperial Army (responsible for the defense of N **Honshu** and **Hokkaido**) at the time of the surrender, committed suicide with his wife 9/12/45

Sukarno, Dr. Achmed (soo•kahr•noh, ahk•med) led the Indonesian Nationalist movement during the war and became President of Indonesia from 1945 to 1967

Sulfa Drugs (suhl•fuh) Developed in the late 1930s to kill bacteria, they were widely used throughout the war, contributing to a survival rate of American wounded more than double that of WWI.

Sullivan Brothers -- five US sailors who died in the battle off **Savo Island** 11/12-13/42 when the light cruiser **USS Juneau** was sunk, subject of the movie *The Fighting Sullivans* (1944)

Sullivan, Commodore William A. -- the US Navy's leading salvage expert, supervised the clearing of demolished harbors in **Casablanca, Palermo, Naples, Cherbourg**, and **Manila**

Sultan, Lt Gen Daniel I. (suhl•tuhn) Deputy CiC to **Stilwell** in the China-Burma-India (CBI) Theater from 1/44, became commander of the India-Burma Theater after **Stilwell**'s recall in 10/44, reopened the **Burma Road** early in 1945

Sulu Sea (soo•loo) body of water SW of the **Philippines**

Sumatra (su•mah•truh) a large island in the W **Dutch East Indies**, under Japanese control from 2/42 to the end of the war

Summersby, Kay (suhm•uhrz•bee) Irish-born member of the British Transport Service who served as **Eisenhower**'s chauffeur (7/42-10/44) and private secretary (from then until the end of the war). The two are thought to have had a romantic relationship.

Sumprabum (soom•prah•boom) ("the grassy hill") **Kachin** village on the **Irrawaddy** River in N Burma 80 miles N of **Myitkyina**

Sunda Straits (sun•duh) the passage between **Java** and **Sumatra**, where the US cruiser Houston and Australian cruiser Perth were sunk by a Japanese invasion force the night of 2/28-29/42

Sungshan (suhng•shan) mountain fortress overlooking the **Burma Road** at the **Salween** River, held by 2,000 Japanese, taken by Chinese forces 8/44

Sun Li-jen, Lt Gen **(sun lee-jen)** American-educated Chinese Army commander who fought with distinction in Burma, at one point commanding British troops

Suomussalmi **(soo′•oh•muhs•sahl•mee)** village in NC **Finland**, site of a major defeat for the invading Russians 12/40, with some 30,000 troops killed or captured

Surabaya **(sur•uh•bah′•yuh)** port in NE **Java**, principal base of the Allied Asiatic Fleet (**ABDA**) from 1/42 to 3/42, when the Japanese took control of the entire island

Surcouf **(sur•koof)** French cruiser submarine, the largest in the world in 1939, joined the **Free French** Navy 8/40, accidentally rammed and sunk by a US freighter 2/18-19/42 in the **Caribbean**

Suribachi, Mount **(sur•uh•bah′•chee)** key defense position on **Iwo Jima**, site of the famous **Joe Rosenthal** photo of Marines raising the American flag 2/23/45

Surigao Strait **(sur•uh•gow)** waterway on the SE end of **Leyte** where **Admiral Oldendorf**'s six battleships and destroyers repulsed Japanese Force Center 10/24-25/44

Susloparov, General Ivan **(soos•luh•pah•ruhv, ih•vahn)** signed the German surrender at **Reims** for the Soviet High Command 5/7/45

Sutherland, Lt Gen Richard K. -- **MacArthur**'s CoS throughout the war

Suzuki, Admiral Kantaro **(su•zoo•kee, kahn•tah•roh)** PM of Japan 4/7-8/15/45, a 78-year-old moderate statesman who was chosen to bring about an end to the war

Suzuki, Lt Gen Sosaku (su•**zoo**•kee) commander of the Japanese defense of **Leyte** from 8/44, killed 4/17/45 after the island was lost

Svalbard Archipelago -- see **Spitzbergen**

Sweeney, Major Charles W. -- flew a B-29 observation plane on the **Hiroshima** atomic bomb mission, and the bomb plane itself (**Bock's Car**) at **Nagasaki**

Sword -- the E-most of the five named **Normandy** beaches on **D-Day**, taken by the British 3rd Division

Sydney (**sid**•nee) city in SE Australia, whose harbor was raided by three Japanese midget submarines 5/31/42, an isolated night attack which caused little damage

Sydney, HMAS (**sid**•nee) Australian light cruiser which sank the Italian cruiser Bartolomeo Colleone off **Crete** 7/40 and was herself sunk by (and sank) the German commerce raider Kormoran off W Australia

Syracuse (**sir′**•uh•kyoos, **seer′**-) city in **Sicily**, the first Italian city taken by the **Allies**, 7/11/43

Szabo, Violette (zah•**boh**, vee•oh•**let**) SOE agent in France, captured by the **Gestapo** in 1944, executed in Germany 1/26/45, subject of the British book (1956) and film (1958) *Carve Her Name with Pride*

Szilard, Leo (**tsil**•ahrd, **zil**- , -uhrd, **lee**•oh) Hungarian-born nuclear physicist who played a key role in the US development of the atomic bomb (the **Manhattan Project**)

T

Tabarka (or -**qah**) (tah•bahr•**kah**) Tunisian coastal town near the Algerian border, taken by British forces 11/15/42

Tacloban (tah•**kloh**•bahn) seaport on NE **Leyte**, taken by US 6th Army troops 10/21/44 after an amphibious landing, site of an important airfield

Tafaroui (**tah**•fahr•ah•**wee′**) town and airfield S of **Oran**, taken by Allied forces 11/9/42 during the **Torch** landings

Tagalog (tuh•**gahl**•awg, -uhg) the primary language of the **Philippines**

Taganrog (**tag′**•uhn•**rahg**) port city on the Sea of **Azov** in S Russia, taken by German forces about 10/16/41, retaken by Soviet forces 8/30/43

Taiho (**ty**•hoh) when completed in 3/44 the largest Japanese aircraft carrier, sunk by the US submarine Albacore in the Battle of the **Philippine Sea** 6/19/44

Tai Li, General (**ty lee**) **Chiang Kai-shek**'s secret police and intelligence director, probably the second most powerful figure in the Nationalist Chinese government

Taiwan -- see **Formosa**

Takagi, Sokichi (tah•**kah**•ghee, soh•**kee**•chee) Japanese naval research specialist whose study of air and sea losses from 9/43 led him to support the peace movement

Takagi, Vice-Admiral Takeo (tah•**kah**•ghee, tahk•ay•oh) victorious Japanese naval commander in the Battle of the **Java Sea** (2/42), commander of the carrier force in the Battle of the **Coral Sea** (5/42), died at **Saipan** 7/44

Takahashi, Vice-Admiral Ibo (tah•kuh•**hah′**•shee, **ee**•boh) CiC Japanese 3rd Fleet 1941-42, CiC SW Area Fleet 4/42-11/42, retired from active duty 1944

Takao (tah•**kah**•oh, tah•**kow**) Japanese heavy cruiser and class (of four), permanently damaged by a US submarine during the Battle of **Leyte Gulf** (10/23/44), sunk in **Singapore** harbor by British submarines 7/31/45

Takoradi (tah•kawr•**ah′**•dee) Allied air supply route across Africa from the Gold Coast town of **Takoradi** to **Khartoum**, with a stop in **Fort Lamy** in **Chad**. Merged with the city of Sekondi (**sehk**•uhn•**dee′**) in 1946 to form the present-day city of Sekondi-Takoradi in W Ghana

Tallinn (or **Tallin**) (**tah**•lin, **tal**•in) capital of **Estonia** and important naval base, annexed by the Soviet Union in 1940, taken by Germany 8/41, retaken by the Soviets 9/22/44

Taman Peninsula (tah•**mahn**, tuh-) S of the Sea of **Azov**, held by German forces escaping from **Stalingrad** until 10/43

Tanaka, Rear Admiral Raizo (tuh•**nah**•kuh, tah- , rah•**eez**•oh, **ry**•zoh) outstanding Japanese naval commander during 1942, especially in the **Guadalcanal** campaign, relieved of command because of his criticism of that campaign

Tanaka, Lt Gen Shinichi (tuh•**nah**•kuh, tah- , shih•**nee**•chee) commanded the Japanese 18th Division in Burma

Tangier (tan•**jeer**) International Zone in Spanish Morocco, on the Strait of **Gibraltar**, including its capital city of **Tangier** (or **Tangiers**), a part of the country of **Morocco** since 1956

Tang, USS (tang) submarine completed in 1943, second in total tonnage sunk (under **Captain Richard O'Kane**), sunk by its own 24th and last torpedo after a bold and successful raid in the **Formosa** Channel in early October 1944

Tankan Bay (**tahn•kahn**) rendezvous and departure point in the **Kurile Islands** for the Japanese **Pearl Harbor** attack force

Tarakan (tah•**rah**•kahn, **ta•ra•kan**) oil-rich island off Dutch **Borneo**, taken by the Japanese 1/11/42

Taranto (**tahr′•uhn•toh, tar′-** , tuh•**ran•**toh) city in the arch of the Italian boot (on the **Gulf of Taranto**), main naval base of the Italian fleet, successfully attacked by British carrier planes 11/11-12/40, taken by the British 1st Airborne Division 9/9/43 as part of the Allied invasion of mainland Italy

Tarawa (**tar′•uh•wah**, tuh•**rah•**wuh) atoll in the C Pacific, occupied by Japan 12/9/41, taken by US Marines with heavy losses 11/20-23/43

Target for Tonight -- British documentary film focusing on a bombing raid over Germany, released 7/25/41

Tarnopol (tahr•**noh•**puhl) city in E Poland, now Ternopol (tuhr•**noh•**puhl) in W **Ukraine**

Tassafaronga Point (**tas•**uh•fuh•**rahn•**guh) on the NW coast of **Guadalcanal**, site of the final naval battle in the campaign for Guadalcanal 11/30-12/1/42, in which a US force prevented the Japanese from landing reinforcements, but suffered greater losses, with three heavy cruisers damaged and a fourth (Northampton) sunk

Tautog, USS (taw•**tahg, -tawg, taw**•tahg, taw•tawg) named for an Atlantic coast fish, completed in 1940, credited with sinking the greatest number of ships (26) of any US submarine, survived the war

Taylor, General Maxwell -- artillery commander of the 82nd Airborne Division in **Sicily** and commander of the 101st in N Europe, later Chairman of the Joint Chiefs of Staff (1962-64)

Taylor, Brig Gen Telford -- US chief prosecutor at **Nuremberg**, 6/45-10/46

Tbilisi -- see **Tiflis**

Tebaga Gap (teh•bah•gah) Tunisian valley W of the **Mareth Line**, breached by British forces 3/26/43 after stubborn German resistance

Tébessa (teh•bes•uh, -ah) Algerian town near the Tunisian border where part of **Rommel**'s forces were prevented from continuing a westward advance 2/21-22/43

Tébourbah (tay'•boor•bah) town E of **Tunis**, taken by the **Allies** in late 11/42, quickly retaken by the Germans

Tedder, Air Chief Marshal Sir Arthur (ted•uhr) Deputy Supreme Commander of the **Allied Expeditionary Force** (**AEF**) from 12/43 to **V-E Day** (5/45)

Tehran (or **Teheran**) (teh•ran, -rahn, tay•uh-) capital city of **Iran** (or **Persia**), where **Roosevelt**, **Churchill**, and **Stalin** met 11/28-12/1/43

Teller, Edward (tel•uhr) US physicist who was born in Hungary and a Jewish émigré from Germany, worked on the atomic bomb team at **Los Alamos** and campaigned for the development of the hydrogen bomb, which the US successfully tested in 1952

Templehof (US tem•puhl•hof, Ger -hohf) the major airfield in Berlin during the war

Tenaru (ten•uh•roo, teh•nah•roo) a river flowing a few miles E of **Henderson Field** on **Guadalcanal**, which gives its name to a battle fought 8/21/42 in which US Marines decisively defeated a Japanese force led by **Colonel Kiyono Ichiki**, the first Allied land victory against the Japanese

Tengchung (**teng•chung**) a Japanese stronghold on the **Burma Road** 40 miles N of **Lungling**

Tennant, Vice-Admiral Sir William (**ten**•uhnt) directed the naval evacuation at **Dunkirk** (1940), commanded the **Repulse** when she was sunk by Japanese bombers off **Malaya** (12/41), led the invasion of **Madagascar** (1943), and supervised the construction and placement of the two **Mulberries** at **Normandy** (1944)

Terauchi, FM Count Hisaichi (**teh**•rah•oo′•chee, **hee**•sah•ee•chee) CiC Japanese forces in N China from 1937, CiC SE Asia from 11/6/41 to the end of the war

Terboven, Josef (or **Joseph**) (**tair**•boh•ven) Reich Commissioner of Norway from 4/24/40 to 5/45, when he committed suicide in **Oslo**

Ter Poorten, General Hein (tuhr **poort**'n, **hyn**) CiC land forces in the **Dutch East Indies** from 10/41, surrendered 4/42 after destroying oilfields to deny them to the Japanese

Têtu, Marcel (**teh•too**, mahr•**sel**) Commander of French Air Forces on the German front from early 1940 until the fall of France in June

Thailand (Siam) ("free land") (**ty′•land**, -luhnd) officially on the side of Japan under puppet PM **Pibul Songgram** 1938-44, which resulted in a repressive Japanese occupation and widespread support for the **Allies**

Thala (**thah**•lah, **tah**•lah) Tunisian town N of **Kasserine** where **Rommel**'s brief westward advance was halted 2/22/43

Thames (**temz**) a river flowing E through London to the **North Sea**

Theobald, Rear Admiral Robert A. ("Fuzzy")
(**thee'•uh•bawld**, -oh-) Commander of US Naval Forces in the
Aleutians 5/27/41-1/4/43

Thermopylae (thuhr•**mahp'•uh•lee**) a pass in Greece where a
determined defense against invading German forces 4/19-25/41
enabled British and Commonwealth forces to evacuate from S
ports, mainly to **Crete**

Thoma, General Wilhelm Ritter von (toh•mah, vil•helm
rit•uhr vahn) commanded German tank units in the **Spanish
Civil War**, Poland, France, and the Soviet Union, assumed
command of the German **Afrika Korps** 9/17/42 under **Rommel**,
was captured 11/4/42 during the Battle of **El Alamein**

Tibbets, Colonel Paul W. -- pilot of the B-29 **Enola Gay** that
dropped the atomic bomb on **Hiroshima** 8/6/45

Tiber (ty•buhr) a river flowing SSW through Rome into the
Mediterranean

Tiddum Road (tid•um) British-built road running N from the
Burmese town of **Tiddum** to the Indian town of **Imphal**,
continuing N as the **Kohima** Road and then NE as the Dimapur
Road

Tientsin (tyen•tsin, tin-) (now called Tianjin (**tyahn•jin**))
coastal city in N China S of **Peking** (Beijing), whose American
garrison was seized by Japanese forces immediately after **Pearl
Harbor**

Tiflis (US **tif•lis**, Geor tyuh•**flees**) the capital of **Georgia** in the
SW Soviet Union, now called **Tbilisi** (tuh•buh•lee•see)

Tikhvin (teek•hvin, teekh•veen) key Soviet town on the
Moscow-Leningrad railway, held by German forces for just a
month, 11/9-12/9/41

Timor (tee•mawr, tee•**mawr**) island in the **Dutch East Indies**, held by Japan from 2/23/42 until the end of the war

Timoshenko, Marshal Semyon (tim•uh•**sheng**•koh, sim•**yawn**) led the Soviets to victory in the Soviet-Finnish War (ended 3/13/40), commanded the W front against the German invasion until 9/41, then the SW front, held less important positions after a defeat at **Kharkov** 5/42

Tinian (tin•ee•uhn) one of the **Mariana Islands** in the Pacific, taken by US Marines 7/24-8/1/44, base of the B-29s that dropped the atomic bombs on **Hiroshima** and **Nagasaki**

Tinnsjo (tin•shoo) Norwegian lake where the ferry boat Hydro (hy•droh) was sunk by Norwegian saboteurs 2/20/44 carrying Germany's entire heavy water supply, a major setback to **Hitler**'s hopes for an atomic bomb

Tirana (or **Tiranë**) (tih•rahn•uh) capital of **Albania**

Tirpitz (US **tuhr**•pits, Ger **teer**-) German battleship, sister ship of the **Bismarck**, stationed in Norwegian waters from 1/42 threatening Allied convoys to the Soviet Union. Damaged in port several times from 9/43, sunk at anchor near **Tromsö** by British bombers 11/12/44

Tiso, Monsignor Josef (or **Joseph**) (tee•soh, **yaw'•sef**) with **Hitler**'s backing, established the puppet republic of **Slovakia** and became PM in 10/38, then President in 10/39. Overthrown 8/44 and hanged for treason 4/18/47

Tisza (tis•aw) or **Tisa** (tee•suh) a river flowing S 600 miles through E Hungary and NE Yugoslavia into the **Danube**, crossed by Soviet forces at many points in 10/44

Tito, Marshal (Josip Broz (**brawz**, **brohz**, **yaw**•sip, -seep) or Brozovitch) (tee•toh) Yugoslav communist who led a resistance movement after the Germans defeated and occupied the country in 6/41, became ruler of Yugoslavia from 1945 until his death in 1980

Tobruk (toh•**bruk**, tuh- , **toh**′•**bruk**) a major fortress and harbor in **Libya**, taken from Italian control by British forces 1/22/41, then by **Rommel** 6/21/42, and finally by **Montgomery**'s 8ᵗʰ Army 11/13/42

Todt, Dr. Fritz (**toht**) outstanding **Nazi** construction administrator, whose projects in the 1930s included the Autobahn network and the **West Wall**. Appointed Minister of Armaments and Munitions 3/17/40, he was killed in a plane crash 2/9/42, possibly a victim of sabotage, and succeeded by **Albert Speer**

Togo, Shigenori (US **toh**•goh, Jap **toh(n)**•**goh**, shig•uh•**nawr**′•ee) Japanese ambassador to Germany 12/37-10/38 and the Soviet Union 10/38-8/40, Foreign Minister 10/16/41-9/1/42 and 4/7/45-8/45 (in the last wartime cabinet, under **Suzuki**). Though he consistently pursued peace, he was sentenced to 20 years in prison for war crimes in 1948, died 7/23/50.

Tojo, General Hideki (**toh**•joh, hih•**dek**•ee, **hee**•duh•kee) pro-war Japanese premier from 10/16/41 to 7/18/44, hanged for war crimes 12/23/48

Tokyo Rose -- a US citizen named Iva Ikuko Toguri d'Aquino who, with other women, broadcast American popular music and ineffective Japanese propaganda throughout the war. After the war she served six years in prison for treason and was later pardoned by President **Gerald Ford** on his last full day in office.

Tolbukhin, Marshal Fyodor (Feodor) (tuhl•**boo**•kin, -kyin, fyawd•**uhr**, -awr) commanded the Soviet 57ᵗʰ Army at **Stalingrad** from 7/42 and the 4ᵗʰ Ukrainian Front which liberated **Sevastopol** 5/9/44, then helped occupy Bulgaria, Hungary, Romania, and Austria

Tomuso (toh•moo•soh, tuh-) town in **Okinawa**

Tone (**toh**•nay) Japanese heavy cruiser and class (of two), active throughout the Pacific War, sunk 7/45

Torch, Operation -- code name for the Allied invasion of NW Africa, which began 11/8/42

Torgau (**tawr**•gow) German town on the **Elbe** river about 75 miles S of Berlin, official first meeting place of US and Soviet forces 4/25/45

Torokina (**tawr**•uh•**kee′**•nuh, -oh-) cape on **Empress Augusta Bay**, S **Bougainville**, site of a successful US landing 11/1/43

Toulon (too•**loh(n)**, -**law(n)**) port city and naval base in S France, home of most of the French Fleet after 6/40, under **Vichy** control until 11/27/42, when **Admiral Jean de Laborde** ordered all ships scuttled rather than turn them over to German control, surrendered to the **Allies** 8/28/44

Tournai (**-nay**) (tur•**nay**) small city in SW Belgium on the **Scheldt** River

Tours (**tur, toor**) a city in W France on the **Loire** river, briefly the seat of the French government during the fall of France in 6/40

Tovey, Admiral Sir John (**tuh**•vee) CiC British Home Fleet 12/40-5/43

Towers, Vice-Admiral John H. -- Commander, Air Force Pacific Fleet, **Nimitz**'s deputy in charge of staffing and training the carrier forces

Toyoda, Admiral Soemu (toy•**oh**•duh, -dah, soh•**ee**•moo, **soh**•uh-) replaced **Koga** as CiC Japanese Combined Fleet 3/44, became Chief of the Naval General Staff 5/45, favored

continuing the war but was acquitted of war crimes by the
International Military Tribunal in 1949

Toyoda, Admiral Teijiro (toy•oh•duh, -dah, tay(ee)•**jeer**•oh)
held ministerial posts in several Japanese cabinets, including
Foreign Minister under **Konoye** 7/18-10/16/41

Trapani (**trah**•puh•nee) port city in NW **Sicily** captured by US
forces 7/23/43

Treblinka (truh•**bling**•kuh, treh-) **Nazi** extermination camp in
Poland 1941-43

Tresckow, Maj Gen Henning von (**trez**•koh, **hen**•ing) CoS
German Army Group Center in Russia, active conspirator against
Hitler, committed suicide the day after the failure of the **July
Bomb Plot**

Trier (**treer**) Fr **Trèves** (**trev**) German city on the **Moselle**
river near the Luxemburg border

Trieste (US tree•**est**, It tree•**es**•tay) port city in NE Italy, object
of a power struggle at the end of the war between the **Allies** and
Yugoslavia

Trincomalee (**tring**•koh•muh•**lee**′, -mah-) port city and major
naval base in E **Ceylon** where the British aircraft carrier **Hermes**
and destroyer **Vampire** were sunk by Japanese carrier aircraft
4/42, along with 23 merchant ships in the Bay of **Bengal**

Trinidad (**trin**′•ih•dad) a large **Caribbean** island and British
colony off Venezuela which played a key role in Allied shipping,
under US control from 9/40 as part of an agreement with Britain

Tripartite Pact (try•**pahr**•tyt) the formal alliance of the **Axis**
powers – Germany, Italy, and Japan – signed in Berlin on
9/27/40

Tripoli (**trip•**uh•lee) 1) the capital of **Libya**, an important port city used by Italian and German forces in N Africa until it was taken by **Montgomery**'s 8th Army 1/23/43 2) a coastal city in N **Lebanon**

Tripolitania (**trip•**uh•lih•**tay′•**nee•uh, -**tayn′•**yuh, trih•**pahl•**ih-) the W portion of **Libya**

Trobriand Islands (**troh′•**bree•**and**, -**ahnd**) located about 100 miles N of the SE tip of **New Guinea** (**Papua**) and unoccupied by Japan. The single large island, **Kiriwina**, was taken by US forces 6/43 and used for air missions against **Rabaul** starting 8/43

Tromsö (now **Tromsø**) (US **trahm′•**soh, Nor **trum•**su) port in NW Norway that became the seat of government from late April to early June 1940, when **King Haakon** was evacuated to England

Trondheim (US **trahnd•**hym, Nor **trahn•**haym) the third largest city in Norway, taken by German forces 4/9/40

Trott zu Solz, Adam von (**trawt•**tsoo•**sohlts**, **traht-** , **ahd•**ahm) active German conspirator against **Hitler**, executed 8/26/44 after the failure of the **July Bomb Plot**

Trouville (troo•**veel**) French town on the **Normandy** coast E of the invasion beaches

Truk (**truhk**, **truk**) island group in the SC Pacific named for its chief town, which was the base for the Japanese Combined Fleet. Bypassed by US naval forces, it was neutralized by continual naval and air bombardment from 2/17/44

Truman, Harry S. (**troo•**muhn) A US senator from Missouri from 1934, he made his reputation successfully chairing a Senate special committee to investigate waste and corruption in the national defense program from 1941. Elected Vice-president in 1944, he became President upon **Roosevelt's** death 4/12/45.

Truscott, Lt Gen Lucian K., Jr. (truhs•kuht, loo•shuhn) fought in N Africa, **Sicily**, Italy, and the invasion of S France before returning to Italy in 11/44 to command the US 5th Army

Tsuji, Colonel Masanobu (tsoo•jee, **mah•**suh•**noh'•**boo) brutally effective, **Tsuji** was an influential Japanese staff officer during the attack on **Singapore** and the campaigns in **Bataan**, **Guadalcanal**, and Burma. He escaped post-war prosecution for war crimes by becoming an adviser to the Chinese Nationalists.

Tsukasan (tsoo•kuh•sahn) town in **Okinawa**

Tsushima (Jap tsoo'•shee•mah, US tsoo•shee•muh) two closely linked islands between **Korea** and **Kyushu**, which give their name to the strait between them and Kyushu

Tuapse (too•ahp•seh, tu•ahp•say') Russian port on the NE shore of the **Black Sea**, terminus of the oil pipeline from **Grozny**

Tube Alloys -- British code name for their atomic bomb research, which was incorporated into the US **Manhattan Project**

Tuker, Maj Gen Francis (too•kuhr) Commander of the 4th Indian Division in the British 8th Army in N Africa

Tula (too•luh) city S of **Moscow**, surrounded on three sides by German forces 11/41 but not captured

Tulagi (too•lah•ghee) island N of **Guadalcanal** with excellent anchorage for a fleet, occupied by Japan 5/3/42, taken by US Marines 8/7-8/42

Tunis (too•nis, tyoo-) the major city of **Tunisia** and an important supply port for **Axis** forces. Its capture by the **Allies** 5/43 marked the end of the N African campaign.

Tunisia (US too•nee•zhuh, Brit too•nis•ee•uh, -niz-) N African country between **Libya** and **Algeria** (see preceding entry)

Tupolev, Andrei N. (too•**poh**•luhf, **too**•puh•luhf, US **ahn′•dray**, Rus uhn•**dray**(ee)) Russian aircraft designer

Turin (tur•in, tur•in) a city in NW Italy, on the **Po** river

Turing, Alan M. (tur•ing) British mathematician and computer pioneer who helped decipher the German **Enigma** codes

Turkey -- Though generally favoring the **Allies**, **Turkey** remained officially neutral, supplying Germany with valuable chrome, but finally declared war on Germany 2/45 to get a seat in the newly forming United Nations

Turku (tur•koo) a port city in S **Finland** which repulsed a Soviet naval attack 12/39

Turner, Admiral Richmond Kelly -- planned and executed US amphibious invasions across the Pacific from **Guadalcanal** to **Okinawa**

Tuscaloosa, USS (tuhs•kuh•loo′•suh) heavy cruiser which supported landings in NW Africa, **Normandy**, and S France

Tuskegee Airmen (tuhs•**kee**•ghee) black US Army Air Force officers who trained at the Tuskegee Institute in Alabama from 1941 in the segregated environment normal at that time, eventually producing a few squadrons that saw action in Europe, still segregated

Twining, Lt Gen Nathan F. (twy•ning, nay•thuhn) commanded US Army Air Forces in the Pacific and the

Mediterranean 1943-45, later CoS Air Force (1953-57) and Chairman of the Joint Chiefs of Staff (1957-60)

Tynemouth (**tyn•**muhth) port city in NE England at the mouth of the **Tyne** river

Tyre (**tyr**) port city in **Lebanon**, taken from **Vichy** control 7/9/41 by British forces

Tyulenev, General Ivan (**too•**leh•nev, **tyoo-** , ih•**vahn**) led the Soviet defense of the **Caucasus** against the Germans 7/42 to 1/43, preventing them from reaching the oil fields of the **Caspian Sea** and driving them out in 2/43

U

U-boat (Unterseeboot) (**yoo**•boht) (**un'**•tuhr•**zay**•**boht**)
German submarine

Udet, Lt Gen Ernst (oo•**det, airnst**) German fighter ace in
WWI, head of **Luftwaffe** construction and supplies from 2/39.
Unsuited for administrative responsibility, he committed suicide
11/17/41 and was replaced by **Erhard Milch**.

Ugaki, Vice-Admiral Matome (oo•**gah**•kee, mah•**toh**•mee,
-may) Japanese CoS to **Yamamoto** until the latter's death
4/18/43, commander of battleships under **Kurita**, commander of
5th Air Fleet (on **Kyushu**) at the end of the war

U-Go (**oo**•**goh**) the Japanese invasion of India from Burma 3-
6/44

Ukraine (yoo•**krayn**) one of the Soviet Socialist Republics
1922-91, located in E Europe, an independent country since
12/91

Ulithi (oo•**lee**•thee) an atoll in the W **Carolines** with an ideal
fleet anchorage, which became the base of US naval activity in
the W Pacific after its unopposed capture 9/23/44

Ultra -- British name for its intercepts of the German **Enigma**
codes, which continued throughout the war

Uman (oo•**mahn**) town in C **Ukraine** where a German pincer
movement in 7/41 resulted in the capture of over 100,000 Soviet
troops by the end of resistance on 8/8/41

Umberto, Crown Prince of Italy (oom•**bair**•toh) the only son
of **King Victor Emmanuel III**, led Italian forces against France
6/40, named regent by his father 6/44, officially succeeded him
5/9/46, but in June the monarchy was replaced by a republic

Umezu, General Yoshijiro (oo•**meh**•zoo, yoh•shih•**jeer′**•oh, -shee-) commander of Japanese forces in **Manchuria** and China 1939-1944, succeeded **Tojo** as Army CoS 7/44 and served until the end of the war, when he signed the document of surrender; died 1/8/49 while serving a life sentence for war crimes

Urakami (oor•uh•**kah**•mee) suburb of **Nagasaki** where the second atomic bomb actually detonated, missing the designated target by a few miles due to cloud cover

Ural Mountains (or **Urals**) (**yur**•uhl) a range in the Soviet Union running mostly NS from the Arctic Sea almost to the **Caspian Sea**, the boundary between Europe and Asia

Urey, Harold Clayton (**yur**•ee) A chemist and Nobel laureate (1934) at Columbia University, his contributions to the development of the atomic bomb included the discovery of heavy water and work on the isotope U-235.

Urquhart, Maj Gen Robert E. (**ur**•kahrt) Commander of the British 1ˢᵗ Airborne Division at **Arnhem** 9/44 (the "bridge too far")

Ushijima, Lt Gen Mitsuru (oo•shee•**jee′**•muh, mit•**sur**•oo) Commander of Japanese forces on **Okinawa**, committed suicide by hara-kiri at the end of the campaign 6/22/45

Ustashi (oo•**stah**•shih, -shee) Croatian nationalists allied with Germany, controlled **Croatia** 1941-45 under **Ante Pavelich**, whose regime was notable for its brutality

Utah Beach -- US assault area on the right (W) flank in the **Normandy Invasion** (**D-Day**) 6/6/44

Uyu (oo•yoo) river in NW Burma

V

V-1, V-2 (for Vergeltung – retaliation) -- The German **V-1**, a jet-powered flying bomb, used from 6/13/44 to 3/30/45 against England and then **Antwerp**, could be launched from land or a modified bomber. The **V-2** rocket bomb was used from 9/44 to 3/27/45, primarily against London, **Liège**, and especially Antwerp.

Vaerst, General Gustav von (**fairst, gus•**tahf) succeeded **von Arnim** as Commander of the German 5th **Panzer** (Tank) Army in **Tunisia** 3/43, surrendered 5/7/43 to **Omar Bradley**

Valiant, HMS -- British battleship that served in the Norwegian campaign, the **Mediterranean**, and the **Indian Ocean**

Valletta (vuh•**let•**uh, val-) chief town and harbor of **Malta**

Valmontone (**val•**mohn•**toh'•**nay) key town in a mountain gap along Route 6 SE of Rome

Vandegrift, Lt Gen Alexander A. (**van'•**duh•**grift**) commanded the US 1st Marine Division in the successful landing on **Guadalcanal** 8/7/42 and the defense of **Henderson Field** against the Japanese, for which he was awarded the **Medal of Honor**, became Commandant of the Marine Corps 1/1/44 and the first four-star general among active Marines

Vandenberg, Arthur H. (**van'•**duhn•**buhrg**) Republican senator from Michigan, first elected 1928. An isolationist before the war, he became a strong supporter of **Roosevelt**'s foreign policy, was appointed by him a US delegate to the **San Francisco Conference** that drafted the UN Charter (4-6/45), and helped persuade the Senate to ratify it and support the **Marshall Plan**.

Vandenberg, Lt Gen Hoyt S. (**van′•**duhn•**buhrg**) nephew of **Arthur** (above), Deputy Air CiC for the **Normandy** invasion, commanded the US 9th Air Force 8/2/44-5/23/45, CoS US Air Force 4/48-6/53

Vargas, Getulio (**vahr•**guhs, jay•**too•**lee•oh, jeh•**too•**lyoh) President of **Brazil** 1930-45, declared war on Germany and Italy 8/22/42 and sent 25,000 troops to Italy, as well as fully supporting operations against **U-boats** by the US 4th Fleet in the S Atlantic

Vasilevsky, Marshal Alexander (or -**dr**) **M.** (US **vah•**sih•**lev′•**skee, **al•**ig•**zan′•**duhr, Rus vah•see•**lyev•**skee, uhl•yik•**sahn•**duhr) Soviet Chief of the General Staff from 6/26/42 to 1948, with leaves of absence to command the 3rd Belorussian Front 2-5/45 and the campaign against Japan 8/45

Vatutin, General Nicholai (or **Nikolai**) **F.** (US vah•**toot**'n, **nik•**uh•ly, Rus vah•**too•**teen, nyik•uh•**ly**) fought successfully in the defense of **Moscow** and at **Stalingrad** as CiC from 10/22/42, fatally wounded 2/29/44 by Ukrainian nationalists while commanding the 1st Ukrainian Front, died 4/15-16/44 in **Kiev**

V-E Day (vee•ee) Victory-in-Europe Day, 5/8/45

Vella Gulf, Battle of (veh•lah) On the night of 8/6-7/43, in the C **Solomon Islands**, a US destroyer group commanded by Frederick Moosbrugger sank three out of four Japanese destroyers attempting to reinforce **Kolombangara** with no losses

Vella Lavella (veh•lah lah•veh•lah) one of the **Solomon Islands**, the site of two naval engagements in 1943, the first (8/17-18) involving a Japanese landing, the second (10/6-7) a Japanese evacuation

Vemork (veh•mawrk) town in S Norway, site of the **Rjukan** heavy water plant put out of commission by Norwegian resistance groups 2/43 and a US bombing raid 11/16/43

Venlo (ven•loh) Dutch town near the German border where two British agents were kidnapped 11/9/39 after being lured across the border by **SS** agents masquerading as informants

Vercors (vair•kawr) a mountainous plateau in SE France where 3,500 French partisans were attacked by German forces shortly after **D-Day** with severe losses

Verona (vuh•roh•nuh) city in N Italy, site of the trial and execution (1/11/44) of five former Fascists by **Mussolini**'s puppet **Salo Republic**, including his son-in-law **Count Ciano**

Versailles (vair•sy, vuhr-) 1) small city WSW of Paris, location of **SHAEF** (Allied HQ in Europe) from 9/20/44 to the end of the war 2) palace built by Louis XIV in the city above, site of the signing of the **Treaty of Versailles**, including the **League of Nations**, 6/28/19, a flawed resolution of WWI that some historians consider the beginning of WWII

Vian, Rear Admiral Sir Philip (vee•ahn) Captain of the destroyer **HMS Cossack**, which rescued 299 British seamen from the German tanker **Altmark** in Norwegian waters 2/40 and participated in the sinking of the **Bismarck** 5/26-27/41. On 3/22/42 his group of destroyers and cruisers enabled a convoy from **Alexandria** to reach **Malta** by defeating a force of larger Italian ships. He commanded the carrier force covering the Allied landing at **Salerno** (9/43) and the Eastern Task Force covering the **D-Day** landings in **Normandy**.

Vichy (vee•shee, **vish**•ee) a spa in S France, HQ and namesake of the government of unoccupied France from 7/40 until the Germans occupied the entire country in 11/42, officially dissolved after the **Normandy** invasion

Victor Emmanuel III (vik•tuhr ih•man•yoo•uhl) King of Italy from 1900 to 1946. With limited constitutional power, he yielded control of the government to **Mussolini**'s Fascists in 1922, finally replacing and arresting Mussolini 7/25/43 after the

Fascist Grand Council forced his resignation. Abdicated 5/8/46 in favor of his son **Umberto** (oom•**bair**•toh), who abdicated in turn 6/16/46 after a referendum on 6/2 demanded a republic

Victoria Cross -- the highest British military award, a bronze Maltese cross created in 1856, awarded solely for bravery

Victorious, HMS -- British aircraft carrier which entered service early in 1941, active in various theaters throughout the war

Victory Gardens -- some 20 million individual and community gardens created in the US to help the war effort

Victory Ships -- mass-produced US cargo ships which succeeded the **Liberty Ships** in late 1943

Vierville (or **Vierville-sur-Mer**) (vehr•**veel** sur **mair**) village behind **Omaha Beach**

Vietinghoff-Gennant-Scheel, Col Gen Heinrich-Gottfried von (**veet'**•ing•**hahf, feet'**- , ghen•**nahnt shayl, hyn**•rikh **gaht**•freed, -freet) After commands in Poland, France, the **Balkans**, and the Eastern Front, he took command of the German 10th Army in S Italy 8/43 and succeeded **Kesselring** as CiC Italy 10/44-1/45 (acting) and 3/45 (official). Surrendered German forces 5/2/45

Viet Minh (or **Vietminh**) (vee•et min', vyet, **vee**•it) anti-Japanese resistance group in **Indochina** from 1941, increasingly led by **Ho Chi Minh**, who overthrew the Japanese puppet regime of Bao Dai (**bow dy**) in 8/45 and proclaimed the Democratic Republic of Vietnam 9/2/45, then fought against the French

Viipuri (vee•pur•ih, -ee) a city on the Gulf of **Finland** NW of **Leningrad**, taken by the Soviet Union in the **Russo-Finnish War** and retained by it after WWII. Now called Vyborg (**vee**•bawrg)

Vilna (**vil•**nuh) a city in NE Poland, transferred to **Lithuania** after the fall of Poland, then absorbed by the Soviet Union in 1940, now Vilnius (**vil•**nee•us), the capital of Lithuania

Vincennes, USS (vin•**senz**) heavy cruiser sunk in the Battle of **Savo Island** 8/8-9/42, named for a city in Indiana

Vinnitsa (vin•it•suh) Ukrainian city, site of **Hitler**'s "Werewolf" Field HQ 7-10/42

Vinson, Carl (vin•suhn) Democratic member of the US House of Representatives from 11/14 to 1/65, a leading advocate of naval expansion, especially the construction programs of 1940-41

Vinson, Frederick Moore (vin•suhn) a US federal judge who was appointed Director of the Office of Economic Stabilization (5/43) by **Roosevelt**, and Secretary of the Treasury (7/45) and Chief Justice of the Supreme Court (1946) by **Truman**

Vis (**vees**) island off Yugoslavia in the **Adriatic Sea**, **Tito**'s HQ 5-10/44

Visayan Islands (vih•**sy•**uhn) the C **Philippine** islands, between **Luzon** and **Mindanao**, including **Leyte**, **Cebu**, **Negros**, **Panay**, and **Samar**. The water separating them is called the **Visayan Sea**.

Vistula (vis•chu•luh) a river in Poland flowing N from the **Carpathian Mountains** through **Warsaw** and into the **Baltic Sea** at **Gdansk (Danzig)**

Vitebsk (vee•tepsk) Belorussian city NW of **Smolensk** taken by German forces 7/9/41 with almost 300,000 Soviet prisoners, retaken by the Soviets 6/26/44 with 80,000 German prisoners; now **Vitsyebsk** (veet•syipsk) in NE Belarus

Vittorio Veneto (veet•**tawr**•yoh **ven'**•eh•**toh, vay'**•nih•**toh**)
Italian battleship completed in the spring of 1940, damaged in
the Battle of **Cape Matapan** 1941, seriously damaged by a
British submarine 12/41, surrendered at **Malta** 9/43, interned at
Alexandria for the rest of the war

V-J Day -- Victory-over-Japan Day, usually 8/15/45, the day
after Japan announced its surrender; sometimes 9/2/45, when the
surrender document was signed on the **USS Missouri**

Vladivostok (vlad•uh•**vahs'**•tahk, -vuh•**stahk'**) coastal city in
the SE Soviet Union through which considerable US aid passed
without interference from Japan, much to the dismay of Germany

Vlasov, Lt Gen Andrei A. (**vlas**•awf, **vlah**•sawf, -suhv, US
ahn•dray, Rus **uhn**•**dray'**(ee)) Soviet army commander
captured by the Germans 7/42, from 11/44 nominal commander
of the Russian Army of Liberation (ROA), Russian POWs
opposed to **Stalin** and the Soviet system. Exploited but never
given meaningful support by the Germans, he fell into Soviet
hands 5/45 and was hanged in **Moscow** 8/1/46.

Vogelkop (**voh**•guhl•**kahp**) (Bird's Head) a peninsula in NW
New Guinea, occupied by US forces beginning 7/30/44

Volga (**vohl**•guh, **vahl-** , **vawl-**) the longest river in Europe,
flowing 2,300 miles from NW Russia E and then S past
Stalingrad to the **Caspian Sea**

Volturno River (vohl•**tur**•noh, vahl-) German defense line N
of **Naples**, crossed by the US 5th Army 10/43 as the Germans
made an orderly withdrawal to another defensive line on the
Garigliano River

Vorobyev, Mikhail P. (vohr•uh•**byev**, mih•**kyl**) the leading
Soviet military engineer during the war, promoted to the rank of
Marshal 2/21/44

Voronezh (vuh•**raw**•nish, -**roh**-) a city in S Russia on the E bank of the **Don** River, taken by German forces 7/6/42, retaken by Soviet forces 1/25/43

Voronov, Marshal Nikolai N. (US vawr•**ahn**•awv, **nik**•uh•ly, Rus **vawr**•uh•**nawv'**, nyik•uh•**ly**) Soviet chief of artillery and advisor to the Soviet High Command from 6/41 until the end of the war, played a prominent and effective role in the planning of almost every major campaign, notably **Stalingrad**

Voroshilov, Marshal Kliment E. (**vawr**•uh•**shee'**•luhf, -lahf, -lawf, **klee**•myent) one of the five members (including **Stalin**) of the State Defense Committee (GKO), formed in response to the German invasion, Chairman of the Presidium of the Supreme Soviet 1953-60. Throughout his career, his political reliability outweighed his incompetence.

Vosges (**vohzh**) mountain range in NE France

Vyazma (vee•**ahz**•muh, -mah, **vyahz**-) a Russian town E of **Smolensk** on the invasion route to **Moscow**, taken by the Germans 10/41 and held until 3/43. The German encirclement of the **Vyazma-Bryansk** NS defense line captured over 600,000 prisoners.

Vyshinsky, Andrei Y. (vih•**shin**•skee, vee- , US **ahn**•dray, Rus **uhn**•dray'(ee)) Chief Prosecutor of the Soviet Union 1935-40 (the period of **Stalin**'s Great Purges), Deputy Foreign Minister to **Molotov** throughout the war, organizing Soviet puppet governments in **Latvia** (1940) and Romania (1945)

W

Wadi Akarit (**wah•**dee ah•kah•**reet**) German defense line in **Tunisia** N of **Gabès**

Wadi Zigzaou (**wah•**dee zig•**zow**) German defense position N of **Mareth** in **Tunisia**, where **Montgomery**'s attack was repulsed 3/20-22/43

Waffen ("Armed") **SS** (**vah•**fuhn) a German military force consisting of **SS** volunteers under **Hitler**'s personal control, which grew to about 600,000 men by the end of 1944

Wagner, General Eduard (**vahg•**nuhr, **ay•**doo•ahrt) Deputy CoS of the German Army in 1944 and an active member of the **July Bomb Plot**, committed suicide a few days after its failure

Wainwright, Lt Gen Jonathan M. (**wayn•**ryt) assumed command of US and Philippine forces on **Bataan** and **Corregidor** after **MacArthur**'s withdrawal to Australia 3/11/42, became a Japanese POW from the surrender of Corregidor 5/6/42 until 1945, was present at the Japanese surrender ceremony on the **USS Missouri** 9/2/45

Wakde (**wahk•**day) an island off NW **New Guinea**, near the mainland town of **Sarmi**, with a strategically important airfield, taken from the Japanese by US forces 5/18-20/44

Wake Island (**wayk**) US naval base about 2,000 miles W of Hawaii, attacked by the Japanese immediately after **Pearl Harbor**, but not taken until 12/23/41 by a larger second assault

Walawbum (**wah•**luh•**boom**) village in Burma SE of **Maingkwan** where **Merrill's Marauders** defeated Japanese forces 3/4-9/44

Walcheren Island (**vahl•**khuh**•**ruhn) part of the N bank of the **Scheldt** estuary, its occupation by German forces prevented the **Allies** from using **Antwerp** as a supply port until 11/44, almost three months after its capture

Waldheim, Lt Kurt (**wahld•**hym, Ger **vahlt-** , **kurt**) German interpreter and intelligence officer decorated for service in Yugoslavia and Greece, later Secretary-General of the UN (1972-81) and President of Austria (1986-92). His suppression of his war record damaged his reputation when it became known during his presidency.

Walke, USS (**walk**) the name of two US destroyers, the first sunk in battle near **Savo Island** 11/14-15/42, its successor hit by a **kamikaze** off **Lingayen** on 1/6/44, killing its captain but failing to sink the ship

Walker, Captain F. J. -- the leading British commander of anti-submarine escort groups until his death from a stroke 7/9/44

Walker, Maj Gen Fred L. -- commander of the US 36th Infantry Division in Italy from **Salerno** (9/9/43) until 6/44

Wallace, Henry A. -- US Secretary of Agriculture 1933-40, **Roosevelt**'s Vice-President during his third term (1941-45), then Secretary of Commerce under **Truman** 1945-46

Wallenberg, Raoul (**wahl•**uhn**•**buhrg, rah**•ool**) Swedish diplomat best known for saving at least 20,000 Hungarian Jews between 7/44 and 1/45

Wallis, Barnes N. (**wahl•**uhs, -is) British engineer who developed several innovative bombs, including the "bouncing bomb" used on the **Möhne** and **Eder** dams, and the "Tall Boy" which sank the **Tirpitz** 11/44

Walloon Legion (wahl•**loon**) Belgian **SS** volunteer fighting unit

Wana Draw and **Ridge** (or **Hill**) **(wah•nuh)** a particularly difficult portion of the **Shuri Line** on **Okinawa**, two miles NE of **Sugar Loaf**, which took the 1st Marine Division ten days of fighting to capture 5/18/45

Wang Ching-wei **(wang ching•way)** head of a Japanese puppet government based in **Nanking** from 3/30/40 until his death 11/10/44 in a Japanese hospital

Wannsee Conference **(vahn•say, -zay)** a meeting of 15 **Nazi** leaders in the Berlin suburb of that name (aka Grossen-Wannsee) on 1/20/42, which dealt with the logistics of the **Final Solution** – the extermination of European Jews

Warburton-Lee, Captain Bernard **(wawr′•buhrt'n-lee**, US buhr•nahrd, Brit buhr•nuhrd) received a posthumous **Victoria Cross** for leading his flotilla of five destroyers in a successful engagement against German ships in **Narvik** fjord and harbor 4/10/40

Ward, Maj Gen Orlando -- commanded the US 1st Armored Division in **Algeria** and **Tunisia** 1942-43, and the 20th Armored Division in Germany 1945

Warlimont, Maj Gen Walter **(vawr•lih•mahnt, vahl•tuhr)** Deputy Chief of Operations Staff at **OKW** from 9/39 until he suffered a concussion from the bomb intended to kill **Hitler** on 7/20/44 and was placed on sick leave 9/44. His postwar writings provide important description of the operation of Hitler's HQ.

Warsaw **(wawr•saw)** the capital of Poland and the site of two uprisings against the German occupation that began 9/39, the first in the Jewish ghetto from 4/19/43 to 5/16/43, the second led by the underground Home Army from 8/1/44 to 10/2/44

Warspite, HMS -- British battleship active in many areas throughout the war, including the N Atlantic, Norway, the **Mediterranean**, the **Indian Ocean**, and **Normandy**

Wasatch, USS (**waw**•sach, **wah**•sahch) a converted merchant ship named for a range in the Rocky Mountains, **Kincaid**'s flagship in the Battle of **Leyte Gulf** (10/44) and the **Luzon** landings (1/45)

Washington, USS -- see **Kirishima**

Wasp, USS -- aircraft carrier fatally hit by Japanese submarine torpedoes S of **Guadalcanal** 9/15/42, best known for making two trips to **Malta** with loads of 47 British planes 4/20 and 5/9/42, succeeded by an **Essex**-class fleet carrier 11/43

Watson, Maj Gen Edwin M. ("Pa") -- an aide to **Roosevelt** from 1933 to 1939 and his secretary from 1939 until his death at sea 2/20/45 returning from the **Yalta** Conference

Watson-Watt, Sir Robert A. -- British inventor of radar in the mid-1930s who devoted the war years to finding new applications for the device

Wau (**wow**) site of an airfield on **New Guinea** about 30 miles inland from **Salamaua**, successfully defended by Australian forces against a Japanese assault in late January 1943

Wavell, FM Sir Archibald P. (**way**•vuhl) British CiC Middle East (including N and E Africa) from 7/39 until relieved by **Auchinleck** 7/41, then CiC India until again relieved by Auchinleck 6/43, during which time he also served as supreme commander of **ABDA** for the six weeks of its existence (1-2/42). Viceroy of India from 6/43 until succeeded by **Mountbatten** 2/47

We Island -- see **Sabang**

Wedemeyer, Maj Gen Albert C. (**wed'**•uh•**my**•uhr, **weed'**-) Deputy CoS of SE Asia Command (**SEAC**) under **Mountbatten** from 10/43, became Commander of US Forces in China and CoS to **Chiang Kai-shek** 10/44 after **Stilwell**'s recall and served until 9/46

Wehrmacht (**vair•**mahkt) literally "defense force," the German Armed Forces

Weichs, FM Maximilian von (**vykhs**) German CiC SE Europe (**Balkans**) from 1943 until dismissed by **Hitler** 3/45

Weimar Republic (US **wy•**mahr, Ger **vy-**) the German government from 1919 to 1933, named for the small city in C Germany where it was founded

Weizmann, Dr. Chaim (US **wyts•**muhn, Ger **vyts′•mahn**, **khy•**(y)im) the leading diplomat of the Zionist movement, lobbied in the US and Britain throughout the war for a Jewish state in **Palestine**, became the first President of Israel 1948-52

Welles, Sumner (**welz**) US Under Secretary of State from 1937 to 9/30/43

Wellington (**wel•**ing•tuhn) British bomber adapted for various uses throughout the war

Wenck, General Walter (**vaynk**, **vahl•**tuhr) A German staff officer for most of the war, he led the 12th Army during the last few months in a futile attempt to break the Soviet encirclement of Berlin.

Werth, Alexander (**wuhrth**) Russian-born British war correspondent who spent the years 1941-48 in Russia and in 1964 published the acclaimed ***Russia at War 1941-45***

Wesel (**vay•**zuhl) German town on the E bank of the **Rhine**, taken by British forces 3/24/45

Weser (**vay•**zuhr) river in N Germany flowing N into the **North Sea**

West Virginia, USS -- battleship sunk in **Pearl Harbor** that returned to see action in 1944-45 from **Leyte** to **Okinawa**

West Wall (Ger **Westwall**) -- a line of fortifications several miles deep along Germany's W frontier from **Luxemburg** (N) to Switzerland (S), which the **Allies** called the **Siegfried Line** (**sig•**freed, **seeg-**), overrun 3/45

Wewak (**wee•**wak) Japanese stronghold on the NE coast of **New Guinea**, bombed 8/17-18/43, then leapfrogged in the US advance, captured by Australian forces 5/10/45

Weygand, General Maxime (US **way•**ghend, mak•**seem**, Fr vay•**gahn(d)**, mahk•**seem**) replaced **Gamelin** as CiC of Allied ground forces in France 5/19/40, but was unable to stem the German advance and joined with **Petain** in calling for an armistice. Served as Defense Minister in the **Vichy** government 6/16-9/9/40, then CiC in N Africa until removed 11/18/41 under pressure from Germany

Weymouth (**way•**muhth) town and naval base in SW England

Wheeler Field (**hwee•**luhr, **wee-**) US army air base in the center of **Oahu**

Wheeler, Lt Gen Raymond A. (**hwee•**luhr, **wee-**) A US engineering specialist, he replaced **Stilwell** as Deputy Supreme Commander to **Mountbatten** in the SE Asia Command (**SEAC**) 11/12/44 and became Commanding General of the India-Burma Theater 6/23-9/29/45

Whitehead, Lt Gen Ennis C. -- became Deputy Commander of the US 5th Air Force, SW Pacific, under **Kenney** in 1942, then Commander in 6/44

White Sea -- an enclosed body of water in NW Russia, S of the **Barents Sea**, includes the major convoy port of **Archangel**

Why We Fight -- the official US propaganda film series during the war, released in seven one-hour episodes beginning in 1943 (see List of Sources)

Wigner, Eugene (wig•nuhr) Hungarian-born US physicist who played a major role in developing the atomic bomb

Wilhelm Gustloff (vil•helm **gust**•lawf) German cruise liner transporting at least 6,500 soldiers and civilians fleeing **East Prussia** 1/30/45, when it was sunk by a Soviet submarine with the loss of 6,000 lives, the largest death toll in a maritime disaster in history

Wilhelmina, Queen of the Netherlands (US **wil**•uh•**mee′**•nuh, -hel- , Dutch **vil**•hel•**mee′**•nah, **veel-**) led a government-in-exile in London during the German occupation and returned at the end of the war, abdicating to her daughter Juliana 9/48

Wilhelmshaven (**vil′**•helms•**hah**•fuhn) small port city in NW Germany on the **North Sea**

Wilkinson, Vice-Admiral Theodore S. (**wil**•kuhn•suhn, -kin-) US amphibious force commander in the Pacific 7/15/43-1/18/45

Willkie, Wendell L. (**wil**•kee, **wen**•duhl) Republican presidential candidate in 1940 who nevertheless supported **Roosevelt**'s foreign policy, served as a special envoy in 1941-42, and published the influential *One World* in 1943

Wilson, FM Sir Henry Maitland (**"Jumbo"**) (**mayt**•luhnd) after holding several high commands in the **Mediterranean** and Middle East, became British CiC Middle East 2/43 and SAC Mediterranean Theater 1/44

Winant, John G. (**wy**•nuhnt) US Ambassador to Britain 1941-45

Wingate, Maj Gen Orde C. (**win•**gayt, **awrd**) British specialist in guerrilla warfare whose **Gideon Force** helped the Ethiopians overthrow their Italian occupiers and take **Addis Ababa** 5/5/41. Led the **Chindits** in Burma from 2/43 until his death in a plane crash 3/24/44

Witzig, Major Rudolph (**vit•**sikh, **veet•**zeek) led a German parachute engineer battalion of 78 men which captured the key Belgian fort **Eben Emael** 5/10-11/40

Witzleben, FM Erwin von (**vits′•lay•**buhn, -ben, US **uhr•**wuhn, Ger **air•**veen) A conspirator against **Hitler**, he was to have become CiC of the German armed forces if the **July Bomb Plot** had succeeded; instead, he was executed 8/8/44.

Wolff, SS Gen Karl (**vawlf**) German Military Governor of N Italy who met secretly with **Allen Dulles** several times from 3/8/45 to arrange an early surrender of his forces on 5/2/45

Wolf's Lair (Wolfsschanze) (**vawlfs′•shahn•**suh) **Hitler**'s HQ near **Rastenberg** in **East Prussia**, site of the **July Bomb Plot** assassination attempt 7/20/44

Wood, Sir Kingsley -- British Secretary of State for Air 5/38-4/40, Chancellor of the Exchequer from 5/40 until his sudden death 9/21/43

Woodlark Island -- part of the **Trobriand** group in the SW Pacific, occupied by US Marines 6/22/44

Woolton, Sir Frederick J. (**wul•**tuhn) highly regarded British Minister of Food 4/40-1943 and Minister of Reconstruction 1943-45

Wotje (**wawt•**jay) an atoll in the **Marshall Islands** used as an air base by the Japanese, bypassed by advancing US forces 2/44

Y

Yagachi Shima (yah•gah•chee shee•muh, -mah) island off NW **Okinawa**, taken by US forces 4/45

Yahagi (yah•hah•ghee) Japanese light cruiser sunk with the **Yamato** on its suicide mission to **Okinawa** 4/7/45

Yakovlev (**Yak 1, 3, 7, 9**) (**yahk**•uhv•lev, **yah**•kawf•lehf) a series of Soviet fighter planes, named for their designer **Alexander**, which entered service beginning 7/41 and performed successfully throughout the war

Yalta (**yawl**•tuh) Crimean resort city in SE **Ukraine**, site of the second and final meeting of **Roosevelt, Churchill**, and **Stalin** 2/4-11/45

Yamaguchi, Rear Admiral Tamon (ya•muh•goo′chee, **yah-** , **tam**•ohn, **ta**•mohn) commanding officer of the Japanese 2nd Carrier Division, which he led at **Pearl Harbor** and **Midway**, where he refused to leave his sinking flagship **Hiryu**

Yamamoto, Admiral Isoroku (ya•muh•moh′toh, **yah-ee**•suh•roh′•koo, -soh-) CiC Japanese Combined Fleet from 8/39 until his death on 4/18/43, when his plane was ambushed by 18 US P-38 Lightnings acting on information gained from breaking the Japanese naval code. Though he opposed war with the US, having spent time there including study at Harvard, he masterminded the **Pearl Harbor** attack and the victories of the following six months.

Yamashiro (ya•muh•sheer′•oh, **yah-**) Japanese battleship and flagship of **Admiral Nishimura** in the Battle of **Surigao Strait** (10/25/44), where it went down along with the admiral and almost all of his crew

Yamashita, Lt Gen Tomoyuki (yahm•uh•shee′•tuh, ya•muh- , yah•**mah**•shih•tuh, toh•moh•**yuk**•ee, -**yook**-) As commanding general of the Japanese 25ᵗʰ Army, he led the victorious campaign that began 12/8/41 with landings in S **Thailand** and N **Malaya** and concluded with the fall of **Singapore** 2/15/42, which earned him the nickname "Tiger of Malaya." He later led the defense of the **Philippines** from 10/5/44 until the end of the war. Hanged for war crimes 2/23/46 after a trial that remains controversial.

Yamato (yah•**mah**•toh, ya-) Japanese battleship, whose name refers to the Japanese race, with her sister ship **Musashi** the largest and most powerful ever built. Sunk by US carrier planes while on a suicide mission to **Okinawa** 4/7/45 with the loss of about 2,500 (90%) of her crew

Yamauchi, Lt Gen Masafumi (yah•mah•oo′•chee, ya -, **mah•sah•foo′•mee)** commander of the Japanese 15ᵗʰ Division in Burma

Yanagida, Lt Gen Motozo (yah•nuh•ghee•duh, moh•toh•zoh) commander of the Japanese 33ʳᵈ Division in Burma

Yangtze (yang•see) now Chang Jiang (**chahng jyahng**) the longest river in Asia, flowing about 3,200 miles E through China to the East China Sea near **Shanghai**

Yap (yap) a major Japanese naval base in the C Pacific, located between **Ulithi** and **Peleliu**, bypassed by advancing US forces following **Halsey**'s recommendation 9/44

Yenan (yen•ahn) now Yan'an (**yan•an**) small city on the Yan River in NW China that served as HQ for the Chinese Communists from 1935 to 1946

Yenangyaung (yay•nahn•jowng) town in C Burma on the **Irrawaddy** River about 250 miles N of **Rangoon**, a center of oil production

Yeo-Thomas, Forest Frederick ("White Rabbit") (**yoh-**)
British secret agent (**SOE**) in France until captured on his third
mission, during or shortly after 2/44, survived the war

Yeremenko, Marshal Andrei I. (US **yair**•uh•**menk'**•oh,
ahn•dray, Rus yeh•reh•**myen**•kuh, uhn•**dray**(ee)) Soviet
commander on several fronts during the war, including **Bryansk**
(from 8/16/41 until wounded 10/13/41), **Stalingrad** (from 8/42),
and **Kalinin** (from 4/43). Led the 2nd **Baltic** Army from 4/44
and the 4th Ukrainian from 3/45

Yokohama (**yoh**•kuh•**hah'**•muh) a city on W Tokyo Bay

Yonai, Admiral Mitsumasa (**yoh**•ny, yu•**ny**(ee),
mit•soo•**mah'**•sah, -suh) CiC Japanese Combined Fleet 1936-
37, Navy Minister 2/2/37-8/30/39, PM 1/16-7/22/40, Navy
Minister 1944-45 after helping to force out **Tojo** 7/44

Yontan (**yahn**•tan) Japanese airfield on C **Okinawa**

Yorck von Wartenburg, Count Peter (**yawrk** vahn
vahrt'n•**boork**) with **Moltke**, a co-founder of the anti-**Hitler**
Kreisau Circle, executed 8/8/44

Yorktown, USS -- aircraft carrier sunk 6/7/42 in the Battle of
Midway, succeeded by an **Essex**-class carrier that served during
and beyond the war

Yoshikawa, Takeo (**yoh**•shee•**kah'**•wuh, -**kow'**- , -wah,
tah•**kay**•oh) Japanese spy in the **Oahu** consulate 3/27/41-
12/7/41, provided Tokyo with detailed information and maps for
Pearl Harbor

Yunnan (or **Yunan**) (**yoo**•nahn, -nan) a province in SW China
connecting with Burma via the **Burma Road**, India via the
Himalayan **Hump** air route, and **Indochina** via the Yunnan-
Indochina railway

Z

Zaghouan (now **Zaghwan**) (zah•**gwahn**) Tunisian town 25 miles S of **Tunis**, site of a costly attack by **Montgomery**'s 56th Division 5/10/43, near the site of **Arnim**'s surrender 5/12

Zagreb (**zah**•greb) city which became the capital of **Croatia** (as it still is today) after the German dismantling of Yugoslavia 4/41

Zakarov, General Georgi F. (zah•**kahr**•uhv, ghee•**awr**•ghee) served under **Yeremenko** in the **Bryansk** and SE Fronts (1941-42), then commanded the 51st Army (2-7/43), the 2nd Guards Army (from 7/43), and the 2nd Belorussian Front (6-11/44) before rejoining Yeremenko as Deputy Commander of the 4th Ukrainian Front (3/45)

Zamboanga (zam•boh•**ahng'**•guh, -buh•**wahng'**-) city and peninsula in SW **Mindanao**, occupied by Japanese forces 3/2/42, invaded by US forces 3/10/45 but not finally secured until the Japanese surrender 8/15/45

Zaporozhe (zah•puh•**raw'**•zhuh, -**roh'**-) city in SE **Ukraine** on the **Dnieper** river, site of a visit by **Hitler** to **Manstein** at the HQ of Army Group South 9/8/43

Zeebrugge (**zee'**•brug•uh, **zay'**-) port in Belgium near the border with Holland

Zeitzler, General Kurt (**tsyts**•luhr, **kurt**) succeeded **Halder** as German Army CoS 9/42, was himself succeeded by **Guderian** 7/44 when **Hitler** finally granted his repeated requests to resign

Zero (**zeer**•oh) the outstanding Japanese fighter plane of the war, in combat from 9/40 as a carrier plane, but also designed for land-based use

Zhavoronkov, Marshal Semyon F. (**zhahv′•**ah•ruhn•**kuhv,** -**kahv,** syim•**yawn**) Commander of the Soviet Naval Air Force from 1939 to the end of the war, promoted to Marshal of Aviation in 1944

Zhdanov, Andrei (or **Andrey) A.** (US **zhdah•**nawf, **ahn•**dray, Rus -nuhf, uhn•**dray**(ee)) Communist party leader of **Leningrad** from 1935 and an influential member of the Politburo from 1939, actively supported the pact with Germany, the annexation of the **Baltic States**, and the invasion of **Finland**

Zhitomir (zhih•**toh•**meer, -taw-) Ukrainian city and rail center W of **Kiev**, which changed hands four times before finally returning to Soviet control 12/31/43

Zhukov, Marshal of the Soviet Union Georgi K. (zhoo•kawf, -kahf, ghee•**awr•**ghee) gained fame defeating Japanese forces at **Khalkhin Gol** on the Mongolian border 8/39, as Soviet CoS directed the defenses of **Leningrad** and **Moscow** (1941), and as Deputy Supreme Commander of the Army (under **Stalin**) from 8/42 to the end of the war directed major battles from **Stalingrad** (1942-43) and **Kursk** (7/43) to the final assault on Berlin (1945)

Ziegler, General Heinz (tzeeg•luhr, **hynts**) **Arnim**'s deputy commander in **Tunisia**, directed the successful German counterattack at **Kassarine Pass** which began 2/15/43, rose to command of the 14th Army in Italy in 1945

Zog, Ahmed, King of Albania (**zahg**, ahkh•**med**) An increasingly unpopular dictator since 1925, he was driven into exile when Italy occupied the country 4/39.

Zossen (tsaw•suhn, **tsah-**) a town about 20 miles SSE of Berlin, site of German Army HQ from 8/39 until overrun by Soviet forces 4/21/45

Zuckerman, Solly (**zuhk•**uhr•muhn, **sahl•**lee) influential British scientific advisor who used insights from his study of primates to analyze the effects of bombing, which led him to support strategic (i.e. civilian) bombing and destruction of railroad centers before the **Normandy** invasion

Zuikaku (**zoo•ee•kah′•**koo) Japanese aircraft carrier active throughout the war until sunk in the Battle of **Leyte Gulf** 10/25/44

Zyklon B (**zy•**klahn **bee**) a chemical compound (prussic acid) in crystalline form used to produce a cyanide gas responsible for millions of deaths in **Nazi** extermination camps

Print Sources

I. General Histories of World War II

Arnold-Forster, Mark. *The World at War*. New York: Stein and Day, 1973.

Churchill, Winston S. *Memoirs of the Second World War* (an abridgement of the six volumes of *The Second World War* (1948-1953) with an epilog by the author). Boston: Houghton Mifflin, 1959.

Gilbert, Martin. *The Second World War*. New York: Henry Holt, 1989.

Keegan, John. *The Second World War*. New York: Viking Penguin, 1990.

Morison, Samuel Eliot. *The Two-Ocean War* (an abridgement of the fifteen-volume *History of United States Naval Operations in World War II. 1947-1962)*. Boston: Little, Brown, 1963.

Weinberg, Gerhard L. *A World at Arms*. Cambridge: Cambridge University Press, 1994.

II. Dictionaries and Encyclopedias of World War II

Barnett, Correlli, ed. *Hitler's Generals*. New York: Weidenfeld and Nicolson, 1989.

Baudot, Marcel, Henri Bernard, Hendrik Brugmans, Michael R. D. Foot, and Hans-Adolf Jacobsen, eds. *The Historical Encyclopedia of World War II*. Translated by Jesse Dilson. New York: Facts on File, 1980, 1989. Originally published as *Encyclopedie de la Guerre*, 1939-1945. Paris: Editions Casterman, 1977.

Boatner, Mark M. III. *The Biographical Dictionary of World War II*. Novato, Calif.: Presidio Press, 1996.

Dear, I. C. B., and M. R. D. Foot, eds. *The Oxford Companion to World War II*. Oxford: Oxford University Press, 1995.

Hogg, Ian V. *Dictionary of World War II*. Chicago: NTC Pocket References, 1997.

Howarth, Stephen, ed. *Men of War: Great Naval Leaders of World War II*. New York: St. Martin's Press, 1993. London: George Weidenfeld and Nicolson, 1992.

Keegan, John, ed. *Churchill's Generals*. New York: Weidenfeld and Nicolson, 1991.

————. *Who's Who in World War II*. New York: Oxford University Press, 1995. London: Weidenfeld and Nicolson, 1978.

Parrish, Thomas, ed. *The Simon and Schuster Encyclopedia of World War II*. New York: Simon and Schuster, 1978.

Perrett, Bryan, and Ian V. Hogg. *Encyclopedia of the Second World War*. Novato, Calif.: Presidio Press, 1989.

Polmar, Norman, and Thomas B. Allen. *World War II: America at War, 1941-1945*. New York: Random House, 1991.

Shukman, Harold, ed. *Stalin's Generals*. New York: Grove Press, 1993. London: Weidenfeld and Nicolson, 1993.

Snyder, Dr. Louis L. *Encyclopedia of the Third Reich*. New York: McGraw-Hill, 1976.

Wheal, Elizabeth-Anne, Stephen Pope, and James Taylor, eds. *A Dictionary of the Second World War*. New York: Peter Bedrick Books, 1989.

III. General Dictionaries

The American Heritage College Dictionary. 4th ed. Boston: Houghton Mifflin, 2002.

Bollard, John K., ed. *Pronouncing Dictionary of Proper Names*. 2nd ed. Detroit: Omnigraphics, 1998.

Random House Webster's College Dictionary. New York:
Random House, 1991, 2001.

IV. Atlases

The Columbia Gazetteer of the World Online. New York:
Columbia University Press, 2005.
http://www.columbiagazetteer.org

Essential World Atlas. New York: Oxford University Press,
1996.

Keegan, John, ed. *The Times Atlas of the Second World War.*
London: Times Books, 1989, 1994.

New Concise World Atlas. New York: Oxford University Press,
2005.

Swanston, Alexander and Malcolm. *The Historical Atlas of
World War II.* Edison, New Jersey: Chartwell Books, 2007.

V. Others

Ambrose, Stephen E. *D-Day, June 6, 1944: The Climactic Battle
of World War II.* New York: Simon and Schuster, 1994.

Behr, Edward. *Hirohito: Behind the Myth.* New York: Random
House, Villard Books, 1989.

Connaughton, Richard, John Pimlott, and Duncan Anderson. *The
Battle for Manila.* London: Bloomsbury, 1995.

Conot, Robert E. *Justice at Nuremberg.* New York: Harper &
Row, 1983

D'Este, Carlo. *Anzio and the Battle for Rome.* New York:
HarperCollins, 1991.

————. *Bitter Victory: The Battle for Sicily, 1943.* New York: E.
P. Dutton, n.d. London: William Collins and Sons, 1988.

Friedman, Kenneth I. *Afternoon of the Rising Sun: The Battle of Leyte Gulf.* Novato, Calif.: Presidio Press, 2001.

Kersaudy, Francois. *Norway, 1940.* Translated by the author. New York: St. Martin's Press, 1991.

Morison, Samuel Eliot. *History of United States Naval Operations in World War II, Volume XV: Supplement and General Index.* Boston: Little, Brown, 1962. Reprint, Edison: N.J.: Castle Books, 2001.

Morris, Eric. *Circles of Hell: The War in Italy 1943-1945.* London: Random House, 1993. New York: Crown, n.d.

Porch, Douglas. *The Path to Victory: The Mediterranean Theater in World War II.* New York: Farrar, Straus and Giroux, 2004.

Prange, Gordon W. *At Dawn We Slept: The Untold Story of Pearl Harbor.* New York: McGraw-Hill, 1981. Reprint, with a new afterward by Donald M. Goldstein and Katherine V. Dillon, New York: Viking Penguin, 1991.

———, with Donald M. Goldstein and Katherine V. Dillon. *Miracle at Midway.* New York: McGraw-Hill, 1982. New York: Viking Penguin, 1983.

Rhodes, Richard. *The Making of the Atomic Bomb.* New York: Simon & Schuster, 1986.

Shirer, William L. *The Rise and Fall of the Third Reich.* New York: Simon & Schuster, 1960. Reprint, with an afterword by the author, New York: MJF Books, 1990.

Spector, Ronald H. *Eagle Against the Sun: The American War with Japan.* New York: The Free Press, 1985.

Trotter, William R. *A Frozen Hell: The Russo-Finnish Winter War of 1939-40.* Chapel Hill, N.C.: Algonquin Books of Chapel Hill, 1991.

Tuchman, Barbara W. *Stilwell and the American Experience in China, 1911-1945.* New York: Macmillan, 1970. Reprint, with an introduction by John K. Fairbank, New York: Grove Press, 1985.

Werth, Alexander. *Russia at War 1941-1945*. New York: E. P. Dutton, 1964. Reprint, New York: Carroll & Graf, 1984.

Audio Sources

I. Audio Books

Ambrose, Hugh. *The Pacific: The Official Companion Audiobook to the HBO (TV) Miniseries*. Prince Frederick, MD: Recorded Books, 2010. Narrated by Mike Chamberlain.

Ambrose, Stephen E. *World War II Audio Collection: D-Day*, 1994; *Citizen Soldiers*, 1997; and *Band of Brothers*, 1998. New York: Simon and Schuster Audio, n.d. Abridged, 15 CDs, read by the author (1) and Cotter Smith (2,3).

————. *The Wild Blue: The Men and Boys Who Flew the B-24s over Germany*. New York: Simon and Schuster, 2001, print and audio versions. Abridged, 4 cassettes, read by Jeffrey DeMunn.

Atkinson, Rick. *An Army at Dawn: The War in North Africa, 1942-1943*. New York: Henry Holt, 2002, print version. Prince Frederick, Md.: Recorded Books, 2004. Complete, 19 cassettes, read by George Guidall.

————. *The Day of Battle: The War in Sicily and Italy, 1943-1944*. New York: Simon and Schuster, print and audio versions, 2007. Abridged, 8 CDs, read by the author.

Beschloss, Michael. *The Conquerors: Roosevelt, Truman, and the Destruction of Hitler's Germany, 1941-1945*. New York: Simon and Schuster, print and audio versions, 2002. Abridged, 4 cassettes, read by the author.

Brinkley, Douglas. *The Boys of Pointe du Hoc: Ronald Reagan, D-Day, and the U.S. Army 2nd Ranger Battalion*. HarperCollins (print version) and Harper Audio, 2005. Complete, 5 CDs, read by the author.

Chang, Iris. *The Rape of Nanking*. New York: Basic Books, 1997. New York, Penguin Books, 1998, print versions. Ashland, Ore.: Blackstone Audiobooks, 2005. Complete, 7 CDs, read by Anna Fields.

Cooke, Alistair. *The American Home Front, 1941-1942*. New York: Grove Atlantic, 2006, print version. Grand Haven, Mich.: Brilliance Audio, 2006. Complete, 11 CDs, read by John Byrne Cooke.

Cowley, Robert, ed. *No End Save Victory: Perspectives on World War II* (essays originally published in *MHQ: The Quarterly Journal of Military History*). St. Paul, Minn.: Highbridge, 2001. Complete, 5 CDs, read by Leo Burmester.

    1) Caleb Carr, "Poland 1939," 1989
    2) John Gabay, "Diary of a Tail Gunner," 1996
    3) John Keegan, "Berlin," 1990
    4) Stephen E. Ambrose, "The Last Barrier," 1997
    5) Thaddeus Holt, "King of Bataan," 1994
    6) Kanji Suzuki, "A Kamikaze's Story," 1992
    7) Thomas B. Allen and Norman Polmar, "The Voice of the Crane," 1995

Cowley, Robert, ed. *No End Save Victory, Vol. 2*. See above. Complete, 4 cassettes.

    1) William Manchester, "Undaunted by Odds"
    2) Joseph H. Alexander, "The Turning Points of Tarawa"
    3) Alvin Kernan, "The Day the Hornet Sank"
    4) W. A. B. Douglas, "Beachhead Labrador"
    5) Ferenc M. Szasz, "Peppermint and Alsos"
    6) David Balme (as told to John McCormick), "Gott mit Whom?"
    7) William H. White, "Patrolling Guadalcanal"
    8) George Feifer, "The Last Picture Show"
    9) Haruko Taya Cook, "The Myth of the Saipan Suicides"

Davies, Norman. *No Simple Victory: World War II in Europe, 1939-1945*. New York: Viking, 2007, print version. Tantor Media, 2007. Complete, 17 CDs, read by Simon Vance.

Hastings, Max. *Inferno: The World at War, 1939-1945*. New York: Alfred A. Knopf, 2011, print version. Blackstone Audio, 2011. Complete, 26 CDs, read by Ralph Cosham.

————. *Retribution: The Battle for Japan, 1944-45*. New York: Random House, 2007, print version. Westminster, MD: Books on Tape, 2008. Complete, 22 CDs, read by Simon Vance.

Haynes, Major General Fred (USMC ret.) and James A. Warren. *The Lions of Iwo Jima*. New York: Henry Holt and Company, 2008, print version. Tantor Media, 2008. Complete, 8 CDs, read by Michael Prichard.

Hornfischer, James D. *Neptune's Inferno: The U.S. Navy at Guadalcanal*. New York: Bantam Books, 2011, print version. Random House Audio, 2011. Complete, 15 CDs, read by Robertson Dean.

Jordan, Jonathan W. *American Warlords: How Roosevelt's High Command Led America to Victory in World War II*. New York: NAL Caliber, 2015, print version. Blackstone Audio, 2015. Complete, 16 CDs, read by Malcolm Hillgartner.

Kershaw, Alex. *The Few* (U.S. pilots in the Battle of Britain). New York: Da Capo Press, 2006, print version. Grand Haven, Mich.: Brilliance Audio, 2006. Complete, 8 CDs, read by Scott Brick.

Pellegrino, Charles. *The Last Train from Hiroshima*. New York: Henry Holt and Company, 2010, print version. Tantor Media, 2010. Complete, 10 CDs, read by Arthur Morey.

Prange, Gordon W., with Donald M. Goldstein and Katherine V. Dillon. *The Pearl Harbor Collection (At Dawn We Slept, Pearl Harbor: The Verdict of History*, and *December 7, 1941*). St. Paul, Minn.: Highbridge, 2001. Abridged, 9 CDs, read by Tony Roberts.

Smith, Jean Edward. *FDR*. New York: Random House, 2007, print and audio versions. Abridged, 8 CDs, read by Richard McGonagle.

Snyder, Timothy. *Bloodlands: Europe Between Hitler and Stalin.* New York: Basic Books, 2010, print version. Blackstone Audio, 2010. Complete, 15CDs, read by Ralph Cosham.

Stafford, David. *Roosevelt and Churchill: Men of Secrets.* New York: The Overlook Press, 2000, print version. Auburn, Calif.: Audio Partners, 2001. Complete, 8 cassettes, read by Richard McGonagle.

Thomas, Evan. *Sea of Thunder: Four Commanders and the Last Great Naval Campaign 1941-45* (the Battle of Leyte Gulf, October 23-26, 1944). Simon and Schuster, 2006, print and audio versions. Complete, 13 CDs, read by George K. Wilson.

Ward, Geoffrey C. and Ken Burns. *The War: An Intimate History 1941-1945.* New York: Random House, 2007, print and audio versions, based on the 7-part PBS series. Abridged, 8 CDs, read by Ken Burns, with Tom Hanks, Josh Lucas, and Rebecca Holtz.

Webster, Donovan. *The Burma Road: The Epic Story of the China-Burma-India Theater in World War II.* New York: Farrar, Straus and Giroux, 2003, print version. New York: HarperAudio, 2003. Abridged, 5 CDs, read by the author.

II. Documentary Videos

America's Unsung Heroes of World War II. The History Channel (AAE-42809-12), 2000. 4 VHS tapes, each about 50 minutes. Distributed by New Video.

    1) "Red Mike Edson: Marine Raider"
       "Roy Geiger: Flying Leatherneck"
    2) "Rangers in Korea" (Korean War)
       "Colonel David Pergrin: Panzer Stopper"
    3) "Dateline Tarawa: Correspondents from Hell"
       "The Flag Raisers of Iwo Jima"
    4) "Swede Momsen: Submarine Savior"
       "Peter Tomkins: The Spy Who Sparred With Hitler"

The Cold War. Produced by Jeremy Isaacs for BBC (Britain) and TBS (U.S.), 1998. 24 50-minute episodes on 8 VHS cassettes, narrated by Kenneth Branagh. I used episodes 1-4 and 7.

From Normandy to Berlin. Portland, Ore.: Columbia River Entertainment Group, 2007. 2 DVDs, total 200 minutes.

Disc One: 1) "D-Day: The Normandy Landings"
            2) "Operation Cobra: Breakout and Pursuit"
            3) "The Liberation of Paris"

Disc Two: 1) "The Siegfried Line"
            2) "The Battle of the Bulge"
            3) "The Battle of Remagen"

Heroes of Iwo Jima. A&E Television Networks, AAE-43214, 2001. VHS cassette, 100 minutes, hosted by Gene Hackman. Distributed by New Video.

The Road to Stalingrad and *The Road to Berlin*. Portland, Ore:, Columbia River Entertainment Group, 2001. 2 DVDs, 110 minutes each, "based on previously classified secret film archives."

The Road to Victory: Rattling the Saber, 1931-1941. MBI/Ulanoff, 1990. VHS cassette, 60 minutes.

Uncommon Valor (the story of the U.S. Marines in WW II). First aired in the U.S. 1955, 230 minutes. Reissued on 2 DVDs, Eugene,Ore.: Timeless Media Group, 2006. Hosted by General Holland M. Smith, in ten segments (Guam, Midway, Guadalcanal, Bougainville, Rabaul, Saipan, Tinian, Peleliu, Iwo Jima, Okinawa).

Untold Stories of World War II: Three Secrets That Changed the War. National Geographic Video, 1998. VHS tape, 60 min.

1) "Battle of Heavy Water," produced in Norway, 1948
2) "Midget Subs at Pearl Harbor"
3) "Kamikazis"

Victory at Sea (the story of the U.S. Navy in WW II). First aired in the U.S. 1952-53 in 26 half-hour episodes. Reissued by The History Channel, A&E Home Video, on 4 DVDs, 2003.

The War. Produced and directed by Ken Burns and Lynn Novick for PBS Home Video, 2006. Issued as a 15-hour boxed set on 6 DVDs, 2007. Narrated by Keith David et al.

The War in the Pacific. The History Channel, AAE 95172-5, 2001. 4 VHS cassettes, each about 45 minutes. Distributed by New Video. Volumes 1-3 originally aired in 1993 as *WW II: The War Chronicles*, volume 4 in 1994 as *Biography: Admiral William "Bull" Halsey*.

      1) "Island Hopping: The Road Back"
        "Jungle Warfare: New Guinea to Burma"
      2) "Air War in the Pacific"
        "The Bloody Ridges of Peleliu"
      3) "The Return to the Philippines"
        "Okinawa . . . The Last Battle"
      4) "Admiral William 'Bull" Halsey: Naval Warrior"

The World at War. Produced by Jeremy Isaacs for BBC-TV, 1973. Reissued as a boxed set by HBO Home Video. 26 50-minute episodes on 9 VHS cassettes, narrated by Laurence Olivier.

World War II with Walter Cronkite. CBS News, 1982, 22 hours. Reissued on 8 DVDs by Timeless Media Group, 2003, 2005.

III. Documentary Films

Note: Most of the titles below can be found in the following video collections. Running times should be considered approximate. Additional credits come from *Films and the Second World War* by Roger Manvell, London: J. M. Dent & Sons, 1974, reprinted New York: Dell, 1976. Unless otherwise noted, the films were produced by branches of the U.S. military, consist of combat footage, and were completed by the end of the war.

World War II: The Great War. St.-Laurent, Que., Canada: Madacy Music Group, 1994. 10 VHS Cassettes. Noted as MM.

World War II. St.-Laurent, Que., Canada: Madacy Video, n.d. 12 VHS Cassettes. Noted as MV.

World War II Collection: Volumes I & II. New York: GoodTimes, 2004. 2 DVDs totaling 8 hours. Noted as GT-04.

GoodTimes Collector Series. New York: GoodTimes, 2001. 3 separately packaged DVDs totaling 4 ½ hours. Noted as GT-01.

(Individual titles)

America: The War Years, 1941. About 35 minutes of newsreels. GT-04.

America: The War Years, 1942. About 35 minutes of newsreels. GT-04.

Appointment in Tokyo (55 minutes). Warners Production, 1944. GT-01.

Attack in the Pacific. (60 minutes), n.d. "Armed forces information film." MV.

Attack! The Battle for New Britain (52 minutes), 1944. Supervised by Frank Capra. MM, GT-01.

The Battle of Midway (20 minutes), 1942. Directed by John Ford. GT-04.

The Battle of San Pietro (40 minutes), 1944. Directed by John Huston 1944. MM.

D-Day: The Normandy Invasion (51 minutes), n.d. MV

December 7 (37 minutes), 1943. Directed by John Ford. GT-01.

Desert Victory (60 minutes). Britain: 1943. Directed by Roy Boulting.

The Fleet That Came to Stay (Okinawa) 15 minutes, n.d. GT-01.

Global War (35 minutes), 1942. GT-04

The Last Chapter (Polish Jewry), 90 minutes, 1966. Produced and directed by Benjamin and Lawrence Rothman, written by S. L. Shneiderman, narrated by Theodore Bikel.

The Nuremberg Trials (76 minutes), 1946. MM.

Payoff in the Pacific (58 minutes), n.d. MV.

Pearl Harbor Payback (23 minutes), n.d. GT-01.

Report from the Aleutians (45 minutes), 1943. Directed by John Huston. MM.

Return to Guam (20 minutes), n.d. MM.

The Stilwell Road (53 minutes), 1945. MM.

Submarine Warfare (53 minutes), n.d. MM.

Target Tokyo (21 minutes), 1945. Narrated by Ronald Reagan. GT-01.

This Is Guadalcanal (20 minutes), n.d. MM.

Thunderbolt (aerial warfare in Italy), 46 minutes, 1945. MM.

To the Shores of Iwo Jima (30 minutes), 1945. MM, GT-04.

Tunisian Victory (a.k.a. *Victory in Tunisia*), 77 minutes. U.S./British co-production, 1944. Directed by Frank Capra and Roy Boulting. MM.

The Wannsee Conference (85 minutes), Germany, 1984. Directed by Heinz Schirk. English subtitles. Reissued on VHS cassette by Homevision, with English subtitles, 2000.

We Take New Guinea (35 minutes), 1944. DVD also includes *The Pacific War* (20 minutes), *Battles of Tarawa and Makin* (15 minutes), and *Fury in the Pacific* (Peleliu) (15 minutes), 1945. New York: GoodTimes, 2001.

Why We Fight (1942-1945), a series of seven information films, each about one hour, sponsored by the U.S. government and produced under the supervision of Frank Capra.

　　　1) *Prelude to War,* 1942. Directed by Frank Capra. MV.

2) *The Nazis Strike,* 1942. Dir. Capra and Anatole Litvak. MV.

3) *Divide and Conquer,* 1943. Dir. Capra and Litvak. MV, GT-04.

4) *The Battle of Britain,* 1943. Dir. Anthony Veiller. MV, GT-04.

5. *The Battle of Russia* 1943. Dir. Litvak. MV.

6. *The Battle of China* 1944. Dir. Capra and Litvak. MV, GT-04.

7. *War Comes to America* 1945. Dir. Litvak. MV, GT-04.

With the Marines at Tarawa (20 minutes), n.d. GT-04.

The World at War (1931-1941), 70 minutes, 1943. Produced by Samuel Spewack. MV, GT-04.

IV. Radio

War on Radio: The Pacific and European Theaters. Renton, Wash.: Topics Entertainment, 2002. 38 broadcasts from WWII on 8 cassettes totaling 6 hours.

World War II on the Air. Naperville, Ill.: Sourcebooks, Inc., mediaFusion, 2003. About 50 broadcasts on one CD, 66 minutes, narrated by Dan Rather, accompanying book by Mark Bernstein and Alex Lubertozzi.

V. Online Sources

There are numerous sites, accessible without charge, that provide spoken pronunciation. None are World War II specific, so most entries in this book are not included . In order of preference, the sites I have found most useful are Howjsay.com, Forvo.com, and HowToPronounce.com. The best approach is to type a name into a search engine, like Google, follow it with "pronunciation," and check whatever sources come up.

VI. Consultants

The following people generously took the time to discuss with me all the entries for the languages indicated.

Elizabeth Chamberlin (German)

Oksana Hirniak (Ukrainian and Russian)

Cindy Kaag (Norwegian and Danish)

Judy Neave (French)

www.ingramcontent.com/pod-product-compliance
Lightning Source LLC
Chambersburg PA
CBHW062126280526
45788CB00001B/71